D0132619

Introducing
Research Methodology

SAGE has been part of the global academic community since 1965, supporting high quality research and learning that transforms society and our understanding of individuals, groups, and cultures. SAGE is the independent, innovative, natural home for authors, editors and societies who share our commitment and passion for the social sciences.

Find out more at: **www.sagepublications.com**

Introducing
Research Methodology

A Beginner's Guide to Doing a Research Project

UWE FLICK

Los Angeles | London | New Delhi
Singapore | Washington DC

Originally published under the title SOZIALFORSCHUNG
Copyright © 2009 by Rowohlt Verlag GmbH, Reinbek bei Hamburg

First published 2011
Reprinted 2011

SAGE Publications Ltd
1 Oliver's Yard
55 City Road
London EC1Y 1SP

SAGE Publications Inc.
2455 Teller Road
Thousand Oaks, California 91320

SAGE Publications India Pvt Ltd
B 1/I 1 Mohan Cooperative Industrial Area
Mathura Road, New Delhi 110 044
India

SAGE Publications Asia-Pacific Pte Ltd
33 Pekin Street #02–01
Far East Square
Singapore 048763

Library of Congress Control Number: 2010936663

British Library Cataloguing in Publication data

A catalogue record for this book is available from the British Library
Library of Congress

ISBN 978-1-84920-780-5
ISBN 978-1-84920-781-2 (hbk)

Typeset by C&M Digitals (P) Ltd, Chennai, India
Printed and bound in Great Britain by the MPG Books Group
Printed on paper from sustainable resources

Contents

Table of Contents

List of Boxes

List of Figures

List of Tables

About the Author

Uwe Flick is trained as a psychologist and sociologist. He is Professor of Qualitative Research at Alice Salomon University of Applied Sciences in Berlin, Germany. Previously, he was Adjunct Professor at the Memorial University of Newfoundland at St. John's, Canada and has been a Lecturer at the Free University of Berlin in Research Methodology, a Reader and Assistant Professor at the Technical University of Berlin in Qualitative Methods and Evaluation, and Associate Professor and Head of the Department of Medical Sociology at the Hannover Medical School. He has held visiting appointments at the London School of Economics, the Ecole des Hautes Etudes en Sciences Sociales in Paris, at Cambridge University (UK), Memorial University of St. John's (Canada), University of Lisbon (Portugal), University of Vienna (Austria), in Italy and Sweden, and at the School of Psychology at Massey University, Auckland (NZ). His main research interests are qualitative methods, health and homelessness, sleep problems in nursing homes and social representations in the fields of individual and public health. He is author of *An Introduction to Qualitative Research – Fourth Edition* (London: Sage 2009), *Designing Qualitative Research* (London: Sage 2008) and *Managing Quality in Qualitative Research* (London: Sage 2008) and editor of *The SAGE Qualitative Research Kit* (London: Sage 2007), *A Companion to Qualitative Research* (London: Sage 2004), and of *Psychology of the Social* (Cambridge: Cambridge University Press, 1998).

Preface

Two main developments have shaped the context of this book. First, the political and practical relevance of social research has grown. Empirically based knowledge on such issues as the gap between the poor and the rich, changes in the incidence of diseases and the effects of social disadvantage provide the basis for decision-making, both in policy and in professional practice.

Second, an increasing number of university programs include either introductory or advanced training in the principles and methods of social research. In most cases this covers questions not only of how to understand existing research, but also of how to conduct research projects (of whatever scale). Sometimes this training is embedded in a course or research-based teaching. Often, however, the research project forms a basis for the final (masters, bachelor, doctoral) thesis and the students may be more or less working on their own whilst planning and running their research projects.

Background to the Book

Two background experiences have informed the writing of this book. First, there is my own experience of conducting social research in several fields (including health, youth studies, technological change, ageing and sleep): this experience has taught me a good deal about the problems that arise in research and how to deal with them. Second, there is my experience of teaching social research methods to students and doing social research projects with them. This experience has taken several forms, including research-based teaching, seminar projects, and supervising numerous bachelor, master's and PhD theses. This work has helped me to discover which examples of other researchers' work most serve to inform what research is about.

Aims of the Book

This book is designed to help readers who are embarking on social research projects. There are, of course, numerous resources on social research already available, including some comprehensive textbooks. For introducing social research, however, comprehensiveness is not necessarily a virtue. Comprehensive treatments tend to be bulky and unwieldy and they can be overwhelming in the detail they present.

In contrast, this book aims to provide the reader with a concise overview. It outlines the most important approaches likely to be used in social research projects. And it provides a good deal of practical information on how to proceed with a project. It also includes guidance on, and reference to, further sources on the subject.

Overview of the Book

The first part of the book will give you an *orientation* to the field of social research. It focuses on issues that come into play as one begins to approach a research project. Chapter 1 provides an introductory overview of what social research is, what you can do with it – and what you can't. Chapter 2 shows how research questions originate and how they can be developed and refined. It considers research questions in the context of both qualitative and quantitative research. This chapter also outlines the role of hypotheses. Chapter 3 shows how to find existing research literature and how to use it in your own project.

The second part of the book deals with *planning and designing* a research project. The fourth chapter provides a short overview of the major steps involved in the research process (for both quantitative and qualitative research). Chapter 5 focuses on the design of quantitative and of qualitative research. First, it provides guidance on how to develop a research proposal and a timescale for your project. In the next step, it discusses key research designs in quantitative and qualitative research. The last part deals with sampling – the selection of participants. Some of the major strategies of sampling are described. The sixth chapter outlines the selection of methods and approaches to be used for pursuing your own research question. A central focus is on the decisions you will need to make at various stages of the research process.

In the third part of the book we turn to the business of *working with data*. Methods of data collection are the focus of Chapter 7. Surveys, interviews, observation and the use of existing datasets and documents are all discussed here and issues concerning measurement and documentation are outlined. The analysis of quantitative and qualitative data is the topic of Chapter 8. This chapter introduces content analysis, descriptive statistics and qualitative analysis, as well as case studies and the development of typologies. Chapter 9 focuses on the options for and limitations of doing social research on the Internet (e-research) in the era of Web 2.0. Chapter 10 discusses the limitations of the various methods in quantitative and qualitative research and of each approach in general. Furthermore it considers ways of combining approaches through triangulation, mixed methods and integrated research, which are presented as alternatives.

The fourth and final part of the book addresses issues of *reflection* about your project as a whole and *writing* about its results. Chapter 11 focuses on evaluation of empirical studies in quantitative and qualitative research. Criteria for evaluation in both areas, as well as questions of generalization, are discussed. Chapter 12 outlines issues of research ethics in quantitative and qualitative research, including data protection, codes of ethics and the role of ethics committees. The final chapter discusses issues of writing about research. It describes how results in qualitative and quantitative research can be presented and, in particular, how to provide feedback to participants and how to use results in practical contexts and in wider debates.

Features of the Book

Every chapter begins with a *list of objectives*. These specify what I hope you will learn from each chapter. A *navigator* through a research project is also provided so that you can see at a glance how each chapter fits into the whole. To illustrate, the navigator for Chapter 1 is shown here.

Table   The navigator

You are here in your project	Orientation	• What is social research? • Research question • Literature review
	Planning and design	• Planning research • Designing research • Deciding methods
	Working with data	• Gathering data • Analyzing data • E-research • Integrated research
	Reflection and writing	• Evaluating research • Ethics • Writing and using research

Case studies and other material are provided throughout in boxes to illustrate methodological issues. At the end of each chapter you will find a *checklist* of what you should keep in mind whilst planning and conducting a research project. These checklists provide readily accessible guidance that can be referred to over and over again as your project progresses. *Key points* and suggestions for *further reading* conclude every chapter. A *glossary* explaining the most important terms and concepts used in the text is included at the end of the book.

I hope this book will stimulate your curiosity about doing a social research project and, by guiding you through such a project, show you that doing a research project can be an enjoyable and exciting experience.

PART I
ORIENTATION

Part I of this book has two aims. First, it seeks to introduce social research in general. It considers what social research is, what distinguishes it, what forms it takes, and how it can (and cannot) be used. These are the topics of Chapter 1.

Second, it seeks to lay a foundation for your own research project. In particular, it introduces the issues of research questions, hypotheses and research literature. Chapter 2 focuses on research questions. It considers what a research question is and how such questions may be developed. This chapter also considers hypotheses – what they are and how and when they are useful.

Chapter 3 considers research literature. It outlines the nature of research literature and how it can – and should – inform the planning of your own research project.

These three chapters together also introduce a theme that runs throughout the book, namely the distinction and the relationship between qualitative and quantitative research.

CHAPTER 1
WHY SOCIAL RESEARCH?

Chapter Overview

Chapter Objectives

This chapter is designed to help you:

- gain an introductory understanding of social research
- begin to see the similarities and differences between qualitative and quantitative research
- appreciate (a) the tasks social research has, (b) what social research can achieve, and (c) what aims you can achieve through it.

Table 1.1   Navigator for Chapter 1

You are here in your project →	Orientation	• What is social research? • Research question • Literature review
	Planning and design	• Planning research • Designing research • Deciding methods
	Working with data	• Gathering data • Analyzing data • E-research • Integrated research
	Reflection and writing	• Evaluating research • Ethics • Writing and using research

What Is Social Research?

Increasingly, science and research – their approaches and results – inform public life. They help to provide a basis for political and practical decision-making. This applies across the range of sciences – not only to natural science and medicine, but to social science too. Our first task here is to clarify what is distinctive about social research.

Everyday Life and Science

Many of the issues and phenomena with which social research engages also play a role in everyday life. Consider, for example, one issue that is obviously highly relevant to everyday life, namely health. For the most part, health becomes an explicit issue in everyday life only when health-related problems occur or are threatening individuals. Symptoms produce an urge to react and we start to look for solutions, causes and explanations. If necessary, we may go to see a doctor and maybe end up changing our habits and behaviors – for example, by taking more exercise.

This search for causes and explanations, and people's own experiences, often lead to the development of everyday theories (for example: 'An apple a day keeps the doctor away'). Such theories are not necessarily spelled out explicitly: they often remain implicit. The question of whether everyday explanations and theories are correct or not is usually tested pragmatically: do they contribute to solving problems and reducing symptoms or not? If such knowledge allows the problem at hand to be solved, it has fulfilled its purpose. Then it is not relevant whether such explanations apply to other people or in general. In this context, scientific knowledge (for example, that smoking increases the risk of cancer) is often picked up from the media.

Health, health problems, and how people deal with them constitute issues for social research too. But in social science we take a different approach. Analysis of problems is foregrounded and study becomes more systematic. This aims at breaking up routines in order to prevent harmful behaviors – for example the relation between specific behaviors (like smoking) and specific health problems (such as the likelihood of falling ill with cancer). To achieve such an aim, we need to create a situation free of pressure to act. For example, you will plan a longer period for analyzing the problem, without the pressure of immediately finding a solution for it. Here, knowledge results not from intuition, but from examination of scientific theories. The development of such theories involves a process of explicitly spelling out and testing relations, which is based on using research methods (like a systematic review of the literature or a survey). For both aims – the developing and testing of theories – the methods of social research are used. The resulting knowledge is abstracted from the concrete example and further developed in the direction of general relations. Unlike in everyday life, here the generalization of knowledge is more important than solving a concrete problem in the single case.

Everyday knowledge and problem-solving can of course become the starting points for theory development and empirical research. We may ask, for example, which types of everyday explanations for a specific disease can be identified in interviews with patients.

Table 1.2 presents the differences between everyday knowledge and practices on the one hand, and science and research on the other. It does so on three levels, namely (1) the context of knowledge development, (2) the ways of developing knowledge and the state of the knowledge which is produced, and (3) the mutual relations between everyday knowledge and science.

What, then, characterizes social research in dealing with such issues? Here we may itemize a number of characteristics, each of which is explored further in this book. They are:

- Social research approaches issues in a systematic and above all empirical way.

- For this purpose, you will develop research questions (see Chapter 2).

- For answering these questions, you will collect and analyze data.

- You will collect and analyze these data by using research methods (see Chapters 7 and 8).

- The results are intended to be generalized beyond the examples (cases, samples etc.) that were studied (see Chapter 11).

Table 1.2   Everyday knowledge and science

	Everyday knowledge and practices	Science and research
Context of knowledge (production)	Pressure to act Solving of problems is the priority: • routines are not put to question • reflection in case of practical problems	Relief from a pressure to act Analyzing of problems is the priority: • systematic analysis • routines are put to question and broken down
Ways of knowledge (production)	Intuition Implicit development of theories Experience-driven development of theories Pragmatic testing of theories Check of solutions for problems	Use of scientific theories Explicit development of theories Methods-driven development of theories Methods-based testing of theories Use of research methods
State of knowledge	Concrete, referring to the particular situations	Abstract and generalizing
Relation of everyday knowledge and science	Everyday knowledge can be used as starting points for theory development and empirical research	Everyday knowledge is increasingly influenced by scientific theories and results of research

- From the systematic use of research methods and their results, you will derive descriptions or explanations of the phenomena you study.

- For a systematic approach, time, freedom and (other) resources are necessary (see Chapter 5).

As we shall see, there are different ways of doing social research. First, though, we can develop a preliminary general definition of social research derived from our discussion so far (see Box 1.1).

BOX 1.1

Definition of social research

Social research is the systematic analysis of research questions by using empirical methods (e.g. of asking, observing, analyzing data etc.). Its aim is to make empirically grounded statements that can be generalized or to test such statements. Various approaches can be distinguished and also a number of fields of application (health, education, poverty etc.). Various aims can be pursued, ranging from an exact description of a phenomenon to its explanation or to the evaluation of an intervention or institution.

The Tasks of Social Research

We can distinguish three main tasks for social research. To do so, we use the criterion of how the results of social research may be used.

Knowledge: Description, Understanding and Explanation of Phenomena

A central task of social research originates from scientific interests, which means that the production of knowledge is prioritized. Once a new phenomenon, e.g. a new disease, arises, a detailed description of its features (symptoms, progression, frequency etc.) on the basis of data and their analysis becomes necessary. The first step can be a detailed description of the circumstances under which it occurs or an analysis of the subjective experiences of the patients. This will help us to understand the contexts, effects and meanings of the disease. Later, we can look for concrete explanations and test which factors trigger the symptoms or the disease, which circumstances or medications have specific influences on its course, etc. For these three steps – (a) description, (b) understanding, and (c) explanation – the scientific interest in new knowledge is dominant. Such research contributes to basic research in that area. Here science and scientists remain the target group for the research and its results.

Practice-Oriented Research: Applied and Participative Research

Increasingly, social research is being conducted in practical contexts such as hospitals or schools. Here, research questions focus on practices – those of teachers, nurses or physicians – in institutions. Or they focus on the specific conditions of work in these institutions – routines in the hospital or teacher–student relations, for example. The results of applied research of this kind are also produced according to rules of scientific analysis. However, they should become relevant for the practice field and for the solution of problems in practice.

A special case here is participatory action research. Here the changes initiated by the researcher in the field of study do not come only after the end of the study and the communication of its results. The intention is rather to initiate change *during* the process of research and by the very fact that the study is being done. Take, for example, a study of nursing with migrants. A participatory action research study would not set out merely to describe the everyday routines of nursing with migrants. Rather it would initiate the process of research immediately in those everyday routines. It would then feed back to participants the information gathered in the research process.

This changes the relationship between researcher and participant. A relation which is usually monologic in traditional research (e.g. the interviewees unfold their views, the researchers listen) becomes dialogic (the interviewees unfold their views, the researchers listen and make suggestions for how to change the situation). A subject–object relation turns into a relation between two subjects – the researcher and the participant. The evaluation of the research and its results is no longer focused solely on the usual scientific criteria (as will be discussed in Chapter 11). Rather, the question of the usefulness of the research and its results for the participant becomes a main criterion. Research is no longer just a knowledge process for the researchers, but rather a process of knowledge, learning and change on both sides.

Basis for Political and Practical Decisions

Since the middle of the twentieth century, social research has become more important as a basis for decisions in practical and political contexts. In most countries, regular surveys in various areas are common practice; reports on health, on poverty, and on the situation of the elderly and of youth and children are produced, often commissioned by government. In many cases, such monitoring does not involve extra research, but rather summarizes existing research and results in the field. But as the PISA studies or the HBSC study (Hurrelmann et al. 2003) show, in areas like health, education and youth, additional studies do sometimes contribute to the basis of these reports. In the HBSC study, representative data about 11 to 15-year-old adolescents in the population are collected. At the same time, case studies with purposefully selected cases are included. Where data from representative studies are not available or cannot be expected, sometimes only case studies provide the data basis.

In many areas, decisions about establishing, prolonging or continuing services, programs or institutions are based on evaluations of existing examples or experimental programs (for evaluation see Chapter 5 and Flick 2006). Here, social research not only provides data and results as a basis for decisions, but also makes assessments and evaluations – by, for example, examining whether one type of school is more successful in reaching its goals than a different type.

Table 1.3 summarizes the tasks and research areas of social research outlined above, using the context of health as an example.

What Can You Achieve with Social Research?

In the areas just mentioned, we can use social research to:

- explore issues, fields and phenomena and provide first descriptions
- discover new relations by collecting and analyzing data
- provide empirical data and analyses as a basis for developing theories
- test existing theories and stocks of knowledge empirically
- document the effects of interventions, treatments, programs etc. in an empirically based way
- provide knowledge (i.e. data, analyses and results) as an empirically grounded basis for political, administrative and practical decision-making.

Table 1.3 Tasks and research areas of social research

Research area	Features	Aims	Example	Studies refer to:
Basic research	Development or testing of theories	General statements without a specific link to practices	Trust in social relationships	Random sample of students or unspecific groups
Applied research	Development or testing of theories in practical fields	Statements referring the particular field	Trust in doctor–patient relations	Doctors and patients in a specific field
Participatory action research	Analyzing fields and changing them at the same time	Intervention in the field under study	Analysis and improvement of nursing for migrants	Patients with a specific ethnic background, for example, who are (not sufficiently) supported by existing home care services
Evaluation	Collection and analysis of data as a basis for assessing the success and failure of an intervention	Assessment of institutional services and changes	Improvement of the trust relations between doctors and patients in a specific field with better information	Patients in a specific field
Health monitoring	Documentation of health-related data	Stocktaking of developments and changes in the health status of the population	Frequencies of occupational diseases	Routine data of health insurance

What Is Social Research Unable To Do and What Can You Do with It?

Social research has its limits. For example, the aim of developing a single grand theory to explain society and the phenomena within it, which also withstands empirical testing, could not be achieved. And there is no one method for studying all relevant phenomena. Moreover, social research cannot be relied upon to provide immediate solutions for current, urgent problems. On all three levels, we have to rein in our expectations of social research and pursue more realistic aims.

What we can aim to do is develop, and even test empirically, a number of theories. They can be used to explain certain social phenomena. We can also continue to develop a range of social science methods. Researchers can then select the appropriate methods and apply them to the problems they wish to study. Finally, social research provides knowledge about details and relations, which can be employed for developing solutions for societal problems.

Quantitative and Qualitative Research

We need now to turn to the distinction between qualitative and quantitative research. This distinction will feature frequently throughout this book. The notions of 'qualitative research' and 'quantitative research' are umbrella terms for a number of approaches, methods and theoretical backgrounds on each side. That is, each of these two terms in fact covers a wide range of procedures, methods and approaches. Nevertheless, they are useful. Here, therefore, we develop an outline of the two approaches (for more details see Flick 2009 and Bryman 2008) and consider what characterizes each.

Quantitative Research

Quantitative research can be characterized as follows. In studying a phenomenon (e.g. stress of students), you will start from a concept (e.g. a concept of stress), which you spell out theoretically beforehand (e.g. in a model of stress, which you set up or take from the literature). For the empirical study, you will formulate a hypothesis (or several hypotheses), which you will test (e.g. that for students in humanities, university is more stressful than for students in the natural sciences). In the empirical project, the procedure of measurement has high relevance for finding out differences among persons concerning the characteristics you study (e.g. there are students with more and less stress).

In most cases, we cannot expose a theoretical concept immediately to measurement. Rather, we have to find indicators that permit a measurement in place of the concept. We may say that the concept has to be *operationalized* in these indicators. In our example, you could operationalize stress before an exam by using physiological indicators (e.g. higher blood pressure) and then apply blood pressure measurements. More often researchers operationalize research through using specific questions (e.g. 'Before exams, I feel often under pressure') with specific alternatives of answering (like in the example in Figure 1.1).

Data collection is designed in a standardized way (e.g. all participants in a study may be interviewed under the same circumstances and in the same way). The methodological ideal is the kind of scientific measurement achieved in the

Figure 1.1 Alternatives for answering on Likert scale

natural sciences. By standardization of the data collection and of the research situation, the criteria of reliability, validity and objectivity (see Chapter 11) can be met.

Quantitative research is interested in causalities – for example, in showing that stress before an exam is caused by the exam and not by other circumstances. Therefore, you will create a situation for your research in which the influences of other circumstances can be excluded as far as possible. For this purpose, instruments are tested for the consistency of their measurement, for example in repeated applications. The aim of the study is to achieve generalizable results: that is, your results should be valid beyond the situation in which they were measured (the students also feel the stress or have the higher blood pressure before exams when they are not studied for research purposes). The results from the group of students that participated need to be transferable to students in general. Therefore, you will draw a sample, which you select according to criteria of representativity – the ideal case is a random sample (see Chapter 5 for this) – from the population of all students. This will mean that you can generalize from the sample to the population. Thus the single participants are relevant not as individuals (how does the student Joe Bauer experience stress before exams?) but rather as typical examples. It is not so much the students' entire situation, but rather their specific (e.g. physiological) reactions to a certain condition (a coming exam), that are relevant.

The emphasis on measurement, as in the natural sciences, relates to an important research aim, namely replicability – i.e. the measurement has principally to be able to be repeated, and then, provided the object under examination has not itself changed, to produce the same results. In our example: if you measure blood pressure for the same student before the exam repeatedly, the measured values must be the same – except if there are good reasons for a difference, for example if blood pressure rises as the exam gets closer.

Quantitative research works with numbers. To return to our example: because measurement produces a specific figure for blood pressure, the alternatives for answering in Figure 1.1 can be transformed into numbers from 1 to 5. These numbers make possible a statistical analysis of the data (see Bryman 2008 for a more detailed presentation of these features of quantitative research). Kromrey (2006, p. 34) defines the 'strategy of the so-called quantitative research' as 'a strictly goal-oriented procedure, which aims for the "objectivity" of its results by a standardization of all steps as far as possible and which postulates intersubjective verifiability as the central norm for quality assurance'.

The participants may experience the research situation as follows. They are relevant as members of a specific group, from which they were selected randomly. They are confronted with a number of predefined questions, for which they have a number of also predefined answers, of which they are expected to choose only one. Information beyond these answers, as well as their own assumptions, subjective states or queries and comments on the questions or the issue, are not part of the research situation.

Qualitative Research

Qualitative research sets itself other priorities. Here you normally do not necessarily start from a theoretical model of the issue you study and refrain from hypotheses and operationalization. Also, qualitative research is not modeled on measurement as found in the natural sciences. Finally, you will be interested neither in standardizing the research situation as far as possible nor in guaranteeing representativity by random sampling of participants.

Instead, qualitative researchers select participants purposively and integrate small numbers of cases according to their relevance. Data collection is designed much more openly and aims at a comprehensive picture made possible by reconstructing the case under study. Thus fewer questions and answers are defined in advanced; there is greater use of open questions. The participants are expected to answer these questions spontaneously and in their own words. Often, researchers work with narratives of personal life histories.

Qualitative research addresses issues by using one of the following three approaches. It aims (a) at grasping the subjective meaning of issues from the perspectives of the participants (for example, what does it mean for interviewees to experience their university studies as a burden?). Often, (b) latent meanings of a situation are in focus (for example, which are the unconscious aspects or the underlying conflicts that influence the experience of stress for the student?). It is less relevant to study a cause and its effect than to describe or reconstruct the complexity of situations. In many cases, (c) social practices and the life world of the participants are described. The aim is less to test what is known (e.g. an existing theory or hypothesis) than to discover new aspects in the situation under study and to develop hypotheses or a theory from these discoveries. Therefore, the research situation is not standardized; rather it is designed to be as open as possible. A few cases are studied, but these are analyzed extensively in their complexity. Generalization is an aim not so much on a statistical level (generalization to the level of the population for example) as on a theoretical level (for a more detailed presentation of these features see Flick 2009).

The participants in a study may experience the research situation as follows. They are involved in the study as individuals, who are expected to contribute their experiences and views from their particular life situations. There is scope for what they see as essential, for approaching questions differently and for providing different kinds of answers with different levels of detail. The research situation is designed more as a dialogue, in which probing, new aspects and their own estimations find their place.

Table 1.4   Differences between quantitative and qualitative research

	Quantitative research	Qualitative research
Theory	As a starting point to be tested	As an end point to be developed
Case selection	Oriented on (statistical) representativity, ideally random sampling	Purposive according to the theoretical fruitfulness of the case
Data collection	Standardized	Open
Analysis of data	Statistical	Interpretative
Generalization	In a statistical sense to the population	In a theoretical sense

Differences between Quantitative and Qualitative Research

From the above outlines of features of both approaches, some of the main differences in assessing what is under study (issue, field and persons) have become evident. These are summarized in Table 1.4.

Common Aspects of Quantitative and Qualitative Research

Despite the differences, the two approaches have some points in common. In both approaches, you:

- work systematically by using empirical methods (see Chapters 7 and 8)
- aim at generalizing your findings – to situations other than the research situation and to persons other than the participants in the study (see Chapter 11)
- pursue certain research questions, for which the selected methods should be appropriate (see Chapter 2)
- should answer these questions using a planned and systematic procedure (see Chapter 5)
- have to check your process of research for ethical acceptability and appropriateness (see Chapter 12)
- have to make your process of research transparent (i.e. understandable for the reader) in presenting the results and the ways that lead to them (see Chapter 13).

Advantages and Disadvantages

An advantage of quantitative research is that it allows the study of a large number of cases for certain aspects in a relatively short time and its results have a high degree of generalizability. The disadvantage is that the aspects that are studied are not necessarily the relevant aspects for the participants and that the context of the meanings linked to what is studied cannot be sufficiently taken into account.

An advantage of qualitative research is that detailed and exact analyses of a few cases can be produced, in which the participants have much more freedom to determine what is relevant for them and to present it in its contexts. The disadvantage is that these analyses often require a lot of time and you can generalize results to the broad masses in only a very limited way.

Synergies and Combinations

The strengths and weaknesses just mentioned can provide the basis for deciding which methodological alternative you should select for your specific research question (see Chapter 6). At the same time, we should remember that it is possible to combine qualitative and quantitative research (as is explored in more detail in Chapter 10) with the aim of compensating for the limitations and weaknesses of each approach and producing synergies between them.

Doing Research On-site and Doing it Online: New Opportunities and Challenges for Social Research

In the last decade or so a new trend has arisen which has considerably extended the reach of social research. With the development of the Internet, both qualitative and quantitative approaches can now be used in new contexts.

Traditionally, interviews, surveys and observations have mostly been done on-site. You make appointments with your participants, meet them at a specific time and location, and interact with them face to face or send them your questionnaire by mail and they return it in the same way. This kind of research has its limitations. Sometimes, practical reasons will make these encounters difficult: participants live far away, are not ready to meet researchers, or are relevant for your study as members of a virtual community.

These limitations can sometimes be overcome if you decide to do your study online. Quantitative and qualitative methods have been adapted to online research. E-mail or online interviews, online surveys and virtual ethnography are now part of the methodological toolkit of social researchers. This means not so much (or, at least, not only) that you apply social science methods to study (the use of) the Internet, but rather that you use the Internet to apply your methods for answering your research questions. In particular the new forms of communication in the context of Web 2.0 provide new options for communicating in and about social research. They also facilitate doing research collaboratively (see Chapter 9 for details).

Social Research between Frustration and Challenge: Why and How Research Can Be Fun

For many students, completing courses in research methods and statistics seems to be nothing more than an unpleasant duty; it seems you have to go through this, even if you do not know why and for what purpose. To learn methods can be exhausting and painful. If the whole enterprise leads to a difficult written test at the end, sometimes any excitement is submerged by the stress of the exam. To apply methods can be time consuming and challenging.

However, the systematic nature of the procedures and the concrete access to practical issues in empirical research in the studies and the later professional work (as a sociologist, social worker and the like) may provide new insights. You may discover new insights in the analysis of your data. Interviews, life histories or participant observation can provide insights into concrete life situations or into how institutions function. Sometimes these insights come as surprises, which may give you the chance to overcome your prejudices and limited perspectives on how people live and work. And you will learn a lot about how life histories develop or about what happens in practical work in institutions or in the field.

In most research processes you will learn a lot not only about the participants, but also about yourself – especially if you work with issues like health, stress in the university, existential problems in cases of social discrimination etc. in concrete life situations. In particular in the context of theoretically ambitious studies and their contents, working with empirical data can form not only an instructive alternative or complement to theory, but also a concrete link between the theory and everyday problems and life situations.

Working with other people can be an enriching experience, and if you have the chance to do your research among a group of people – a research team or a group of students – that will be a good way out of the isolation students sometimes experience. For many students, work with technical devices, computers, programs and data can be satisfying and a lot of fun. For example, using the communication forms in Web 2.0 for your research purposes will provide new experiences of social networking and practical experiences with what is up to date in the context of using new media in a professional way. And in the end you will have concrete products at hand: examples, results, what they have in common and how they are different for a variety of people, and so on.

Finally, to work on an empirical project requires working on one issue in a sustained way. This is good experience, given that many students' experiences today are characterized more by 'bits and pieces' work. Empirical research in your fields of study can also be a test of how much you like those fields. If this test ends positively, that can reassure you in your decision to become, for example, a social worker or a psychologist.

Landmarks in the Field of Social Research

Knowledge about social research helps in two ways. It can provide the starting point and basis for doing your own empirical study, for example in the context of a thesis or of later professional work in sociology, education, social work etc. And it is also necessary for understanding and assessing existing research and perhaps for being able to build an argument on such research. For both, we can formulate a number of guideline questions, which allow a basic assessment of research (in the planning of your own or in reading other researchers' studies). These are shown in Box 1.2.

BOX 1.2

Guideline questions for an orientation in the field of social research

1. What is studied exactly?

   - What is the issue and what is the research question of the study?

2. How is it assured that the research really investigates what is supposed to be studied?

   - How is the study planned, which design is applied or constructed, how are biases prevented?

3. What is represented in what is studied?

   - Which claims of generalization are made and how are they fulfilled?

4. Is the execution of the study ethically sound and theoretically grounded?

   - How are the participants protected from any misuse of the data referring to them?
   - What is the theoretical perspective of the study?

5. Which methodological claims are made and fulfilled?

   - Which criteria are applied?

6. Does the presentation of results and of the ways they were produced make transparent for the reader how the results came about and how the researchers proceeded?

   - Is the study transparent and consistent in its presentation?

7. Is the chosen procedure convincing?

   - Are the design and methods appropriate for the issue under study?

8. Does the study achieve the degree of generalization that was expected?

These guideline questions can be asked regardless of the specific methodology that has been chosen and can be applied to the various methodological alternatives.

They are relevant for both qualitative and quantitative studies and can be used for assessing a case study as well as for a representative survey of the population of a country. They offer a framework for observations as well as for interviewing or for the use of existing data and documents (see Chapter 7 for this in more detail).

Key Points

- Social research is more systematic in its approach than everyday knowledge.
- Social research can have various tasks: research may be focused on knowledge, practice and consulting.
- Quantitative research and qualitative research offer different approaches. Each has strengths and limitations in what can be studied.
- Quantitative research and qualitative research can mutually complement each other.
- Both can be applied on-site and online.
- We can identify common features across the various approaches.

▉ ▇ Further Reading ▇

The first and fourth texts listed below provide more details of quantitative research and include some chapters on qualitative methods, too. The second and the third books give more insights into the variety of qualitative research methods.

Bryman, A. (2008) *Social Research Methods*, 3rd edn. Oxford: Oxford University Press.

Flick, U. (2009) *An Introduction to Qualitative Research*, 4th edn. London: Sage.

Flick, U., Kardorff, E. v. and Steinke, I. (eds) (2004) *A Companion to Qualitative Research*. London: Sage.

Neuman, W.L. (2000) *Social Research Methods: Qualitative and Quantitative Approaches*, 4th edn. Boston: Allyn and Bacon.

CHAPTER 2
FROM RESEARCH IDEA TO RESEARCH QUESTION

Chapter Overview

Chapter Objectives

This chapter is designed to help you:

- recognize the starting points for social research
- appreciate where research questions come from
- understand how research questions differ between qualitative and quantitative research
- understand the use of hypotheses.

Table 2.1   Navigator for Chapter 2

You are here in your project →	Orientation	• What is social research? • Research question • Literature review
	Planning and design	• Planning research • Designing research • Deciding methods
	Working with data	• Gathering data • Analyzing data • E-research • Integrated research
	Reflection and writing	• Evaluating research • Ethics • Writing and using research

This chapter seeks to show how research questions for empirical studies emerge from general interests and from the personal and social backgrounds of the researcher. For this purpose, let's look first at some examples.

Starting Points for Research

The literature of the history of social research recounts many examples of how ideas for research have emerged and been developed into research questions. For example, Marie Jahoda (1995; see also Fleck 2004, p. 59) has described the origins of her study with Paul Lazarsfeld and Hans Zeisel on *Marienthal: The Sociology of an Unemployed Community* (Jahoda et al. 1933/1971). The impulse for the study came in the late 1920s from Otto Bauer, leader of the Austrian Social Democratic Party. The background to the study included the Great Depression of 1929 and also the political interests and orientation of the researchers. As a result, the researchers developed the idea of studying how a community changes in response to mass unemployment. From this general idea they formulated research questions concerning the attitude of the population towards unemployment and the social consequences of unemployment.

Another example, this time from the 1950s, is provided by Hollingshead and Redlich's (1958) study of social class and mental illness. Their study stemmed from the general observation that 'Americans prefer to avoid the two facts studied in this book: social class and mental illness' (1958, p. 3). From this starting point they proceeded to explore possible relationships between social class and mental illness (and its treatment). For example, people with a lower social status might be more at risk of becoming mentally ill and their chance of receiving good treatment for their illness might be lower compared to people with a higher social status. From their general interest, the authors developed two research questions: '(1) Is mental illness related to class in our society? (2) Does a psychiatric patient's position in the status system affect how he [*sic*] is treated for his illness?' (1958, p. 10).

They then elaborated these two questions into five working hypotheses (1958, p. 11):

1. The prevalence of treated mental illness is related significantly to an individual's position in the class structure.

2. The types of diagnosed psychiatric disorders are connected significantly to the class structure.

3. The kind of psychiatric treatment administered by psychiatrists is associated with the patient's position in the class structure.

4. Social and psychodynamic factors in the development of psychiatric disorders correlate with an individual's position in the class structure.

5. Mobility in the class structure is associated with the development of psychiatric difficulties.

To test these hypotheses, Hollingshead and Redlich conducted a community study in a city of 24,000 people. They included all psychiatric patients diagnosed within a certain period, using a questionnaire about their illness and their social status. They also interviewed health professionals.

A contrasting example, also from the mid-twentieth century, is provided by a study by Glaser and Strauss (1965). Following their own experience of their mothers dying in hospital, they developed the idea of studying 'awareness of dying'. The authors (1965, pp. 286–7) described in some detail how these experiences stimulated their interest in the processes of communicating with and about dying persons and what they later described as 'awareness contexts'. Here the background for developing the research idea, interest and question was very much a personal one – the recent autobiographical experiences of the researchers.

And – to give one more example – Hochschild (1983, p. ix) has described how early experiences as a child of her family's home and social life became the source of her later 'interest in how people manage emotions'. Her parents worked for the US Foreign Service. This provided Hochschild with opportunities to see and interpret the different forms of smiles – and their meanings – produced by diplomats from different cultural backgrounds. Hochschild learned from these experiences that emotional expressions, such as smiles and handshakes, conveyed messages on several levels – from person to person and also between the countries the people represented. This led, much later, to her specific research interest:

> **I wanted to discover what it is that we act upon. And so I decided to explore the idea that emotion functions as a messenger from the self, an agent that gives us an instant report on the connection between what we are seeing and what we had expected to see and tells us what we feel ready to do about it. (1983, p. x)**

From that interest she developed a study (*The Managed Heart*) of two types of public-contact workers (flight attendants and bill collectors), showing how work functioned to induce or suppress emotions when the workers were in contact with their clients.

If we compare the examples above, we can see that they show diverse sources for developing research interests, ideas and subsequently research questions. They range from very personal experiences (Glaser and Strauss) to social experiences and circumstances (Hochschild), through social observations (Hollingshead and Redlich), to societal problems and political commissioning (Jahoda et al.). In each case, a general curiosity arose, which the researchers pursued and subsequently formulated in concrete terms.

Research, then, can take various starting points. In particular:

- Research problems are often discovered in everyday life. For example, in the everyday life of an institution someone may discover that, say, waiting times emerge in specific situations. In order to find out what determines waiting times and, perhaps, how they might be reduced, systematic research may be undertaken.

- Second, there may be a lack of data and empirical insights about a specific problem – for example, the health situation of young people in Germany – or about a specific subgroup – for example, adolescents living on the street.

- A third source for identifying a research problem may be the literature. For example, a theory might have been developed which requires testing empirically. Or analysis of the existing literature may reveal that gaps exist in the knowledge about a problem. Empirical research may be designed to close such gaps.

- Fourth, research problems may grow out of previous studies producing new questions or leaving some questions unanswered.

Origins of Research Questions

We can illustrate the development of research questions by using two recent examples. They concern health behavior and the health of adolescents living on the street.

The 'Health Behavior in Social Context' Study of the World Health Organization (WHO)

In the 'Health Behavior in Social Context' (HBSC) study, children and adolescents from 36 countries were interviewed, using a standardized questionnaire, concerning their health status and behavior. This research was conducted in order to produce a health report for the young generation and thus to contribute to an improvement in illness prevention and health promotion for this age group. In Germany, for example, this survey has been repeatedly run since 1993 – most recently in 2006 (see Hurrelmann et al. 2003; Richter et al. 2008). Hurrelmann et al. have described the aims of this study as follows:

> **In this youth health survey, several questions shall be answered: descriptive questions about physical, mental and social health and about the health behavior; in the focus is the question, how far health relevant life styles are linked to subjective health; and how far personal and social risk and protective factors can be identified for the prevention of health problems together with their subjective representation in physical and in mental respects. (2003, p. 2)**

For this study in Germany, adolescents aged 11, 13 and 15 years were interviewed in schools. For the international study, a representative sample was drawn (see Chapter 5), comprising about 23,000 adolescents in different areas of Germany. For the German study, a subsample of 5650 adolescents was drawn randomly from this sample. This subsample was asked to answer a questionnaire about their subjective health, risks of accidents and violence, the use of substances (tobacco, drugs and alcohol), eating, physical activity, peer and family and school. The research question for this study resulted from the interest in developing a representative overview of the health situation and the health relevant behavior of adolescents in Germany and in comparison with other countries.

Health on the Street: Homeless Adolescents

A different approach to a similar topic is provided by our second example. The study just discussed has provided a good overview of the health situation of the average young person in Germany and other countries. However, such a broad study cannot focus on particular (mainly very small) subgroups. The reasons for this are the use of random sampling and also the fact that the access to the participants was via schools. Adolescents living on the street, who attend school rarely if at all, were not represented in such a sample. For analyzing the specific situation and the health behavior and knowledge of this group, a different approach was required. Accordingly, in our second example (see Flick and Röhnsch 2007; 2008), adolescents were selected purposefully at the specific meeting points and hangouts of homeless adolescents and asked for interviews. Participants were aged between 14 and 20 and had no (regular) housing. To gain a more comprehensive understanding of their health knowledge and behavior under the conditions of 'the street', we not only interviewed them but also followed them through phases of their everyday lives, using participant observation. The topics of the interviews were similar to our first example above, with additional questions about the specific situation of living on the street and about how the participants entered street life.

In the first part of the study, the sampling and the interviews did not focus on illness. The second part of the study focused on the situation of chronically ill homeless adolescents. In addition to interviewing adolescents with various chronic diseases (from asthma to skin diseases and hepatitis), we conducted expert interviews with physicians and social workers in order to obtain their views of the service situation for this target group.

In both the above examples, the health and social situations of adolescents were studied – either of youth in Germany in general, or of a specific subgroup with particularly stressful conditions of living. In both cases, the results should be useful for helping to prevent health problems in the target groups and to improve the design of services for them.

Characteristics of Research Questions

Research questions may be regarded from different angles. From an external point of view, they should address a socially relevant issue. In our examples, the issues are the health situation of and the support for youth – and in particular the deficits in both. Are there particularly strong or frequent health problems, and are there service gaps for particular subgroups or for adolescents in general?

Answering the research questions should lead to some kind of progress – through, for example, providing new insights or new suggestions for how to solve the problem under study. Thus documentation of the changes in the health situation across repeated studies can progress the development of knowledge (as in the youth health survey). If you are studying an issue that to date has been analyzed only generally, progress may result from studying this issue with a specific subgroup (as in our second example).

Seen more from the internal point of view, i.e. of science itself, research questions should be theoretically based, i.e. embedded in a specific research perspective. In the youth health survey, for example, the basis was provided by a model of the links between social structures, the social position of the individuals in those structures, the social and material environments they live in, and behavioral and physiological factors. These links influence the likelihood of suffering from illness and harm, with their respective social consequences (see Richter et al. 2008, p. 14). From this theoretical model, the concrete research questions in the project and then the items in the questionnaire were derived. In the example of the homeless adolescents, the theoretical background was provided by the approach of social representations (see Flick 1998a; 1998b). The core assumption of this approach is that, depending on social context conditions in different social groups, specific forms and contents of knowledge are developed which occur alongside group specific practices. A further assumption is that topics have specific contents and meanings for each group and its members. These assumptions formed the background for developing the general research questions, which focused on the lived experience of homelessness and the meaning of health in it, and also the specific questions in the interviews.

Research questions should also be suitable for study through the methods of social research. A research question should be formulated in such a way that you can apply one or more of the available methods for answering them – if necessary after adapting or modifying one of them. (We will examine this point further in Chapters 7 and 8.) For example, the research questions of the youth health survey could be investigated by using the questionnaire method. In the second example, the research questions are studied by using two methods, namely (episodic and expert) interviews and participant observation. (These methods will be discussed in detail in Chapter 7.)

Important qualities of research questions are their specificity and their focus. That is, you should formulate your research questions so that they are (a) clear and (b) goal directed, so as to facilitate the exact decisions to be made concerning who or what should be investigated. Note that research questions define not only exactly what to study and how, but also which aspects of an issue may remain excluded. This does not mean that a study cannot pursue several subquestions; it means only that you should ensure that your research questions are not fuzzy and that your study is not overloaded with too many research questions.

Overall, a number of possible basic research questions in social research can be distinguished, notably:

1. What type is it?

2. What is its structure?

3. How frequent is it?

4. What are the causes?

5. What are its processes?

6. What are its consequences?

7. What are people's strategies?

These research questions can be studied at various levels (such as knowledge, practices, situations or institutions) and for different units (for example, persons, groups or communities). Generally speaking, we can differentiate between research questions oriented towards describing states and those describing processes. In the first case, you should describe a certain given state: what types of knowledge about an issue exist in a population? How often can each type of knowledge be identified? In the second case, the aim is to describe how something develops or changes: how has this state come about? Which causes or strategies have led to this state? How is this state maintained – by which structure? What are the causes of such a change? Which processes of development can be observed? What are the consequences of such a change? Which strategies are applied in promoting change?

We can apply these two major types of research questions, i.e. those concerning states and those concerning processes, to a variety of study units (see Flick 2009, pp. 101–2; Lofland and Lofland 1984). For example:

8. Meanings

9. Practices

10. Episodes

11. Encounters

12. Roles

13. Relationships

14. Groups

15. Organizations

16. Lifestyles

We can now begin to differentiate between quantitative and qualitative research in relation to the above lists. The former is more interested in frequencies (and distributions) of phenomena and the reasons for them, whereas qualitative research focuses more on the meanings linked to certain phenomena or on the processes that reveal how people deal with them. In the case of the research projects discussed above, the youth health survey asks for frequencies (item 3 in the first list) and structures (2) in dealing with health in a specific group (14 – here adolescents). The second example focuses on meanings (8) and practices (9) at the level of the participants' strategies (7) with a focus on the types (1) of meanings and the adolescents' practices.

Good Research Questions, Bad Research Questions

Obviously you need not only to have a research question, but also to have a good one. Here we will consider what tends to distinguish good research questions from bad ones.

Good Questions

What characterizes a good research question? First of all, it should be an actual question. For example, 'The living situation of immigrants from Eastern Europe' is not a research question but an area of interest. 'What characterizes the living situation of immigrants from Eastern Europe?' is a question, but it is too broad and unspecific for orienting a research project. It addresses a variety of subgroups implicitly – and supposes that immigrants from say Poland and Russia are in the same situation. Also the term 'living situation' is too broad; it would be better to focus on a specific aspect of the living situation, for example health problems and the use of professional services. An example might then be: 'What characterizes the health problems and the use of professional services of immigrants from Russia?'

There are three main types of research question. (1) Exploratory questions focus on a given situation or a change, for example: 'Has the health situation of homeless adolescents changed in the last 10 years?' (2) Descriptive questions aim at a description of a certain situation, state or process, for example: 'Do homeless adolescents come from broken families?' or 'How do adolescents find themselves homeless?' (3) Explanatory questions focus on a relation. This means that more than just a state of affairs is investigated (so one goes further than asking a question such as 'What characterizes … ?'); rather, a factor or an influence is examined in relation to that situation. For example: 'Is a lack of sufficient specialized health services a major cause of more serious medical problems among homeless adolescents?'

Bad Research Questions

Neuman (2000, p. 144) has characterized what he calls 'bad research questions'. He identifies five types of such questions: (1) questions that cannot be empirically tested or are non-scientific questions, for example, 'Should adolescents live on the streets'; (2) statements that include general topics but not a research question, for example, 'Treatment of drug and alcohol abuse of homeless adolescents'; (3) statements that include a set of variables but no questions, for example, 'Homelessness and health'; (4) questions that are too vague or ambitious, for example, 'How can we prevent homelessness among adolescents?'; (5) questions that still need to be more specific, for example, 'Has the health situation of homeless adolescents become worse?'

As these examples may show, it is important to have a research question that really is a question (not a statement) that can be answered. It should be as focused and specific as possible instead of being vague and unspecific. All the elements of a research question should be clearly spelled out instead of remaining broad and full of implicit assumptions. To test your research question before you do your study, reflect on what possible answers to that question would look like.

The Use of Hypotheses

The more explicit and focused your research question is, the easier it is to develop a hypothesis from it. A hypothesis formulates a relation, which then will be tested empirically. (We saw examples of hypotheses in the case study above of Hollingshead and Redlich's study of social class and mental illness.)

Such relations may, for example, be statements taking the form of 'if, then' or 'the more of one, the more of the other'. The first type of relation is found in a hypothesis like: 'If adolescents come from a lower social class, their risk of certain diseases is much higher.' The second form of relation is illustrated by the following hypothesis: 'The lower the social class adolescents come from, the more often they will fall victim to specific diseases.'

Hypotheses should clarify:

- for which area they are valid (are they assumed to be valid always and everywhere or only under some specific local and temporal conditions?)
- to which area of objects or individuals they apply (e.g. humanity as a whole, or just men, or just women younger than 30 years etc.)
- whether they apply to all objects or individuals in this area
- to which issues they apply, i.e. features of the individuals in the object area.

The example of Hollingshead and Redlich's (1958, p. 10) first hypothesis helps to illustrate these features. Their hypothesis was: 'The prevalence of treated mental illness is related significantly to an individual's position in the class structure.' The two issues are 'social class' and 'illness risk'. They have not delimited their hypothesis to specific local or temporal conditions, but assumed that it should be valid for all the people in a specific social situation (social class).

Furthermore, hypotheses should be clearly formulated in terms of the concepts they use. In our example, it has to be specified what is counted as 'mental illness' (e.g. which diagnoses are used to identify this feature). It should also be defined what 'treated' means (for example, only people who are in treatment with medications, or also those who receive consultations?). Finally, the phrase 'position in the class structure' should be defined.

Hypotheses should also be embedded in a theoretical framework. The authors in our example refer to a number of other studies and theoretical works in which the class structure of America in the 1950s was defined, and do the same for 'mental illness'.

Hypotheses should be specific, i.e. all predictions included should be made explicit. In our example, the authors did not look at a general relation between illness and social situation; instead they had a specific focus on mental illness and on the position in a hierarchy of five social classes, which they had carefully identified and defined beforehand.

Hypotheses should be formulated in relation to the available methods and have empirical links (how and with which methods can they be tested?). In our example, the hypothesis was formulated such that diagnostic instruments could be used for identifying the illness situation of the participants and that household surveys could be used for identifying their position in the social class structure.

Just as the research questions that characterize quantitative research may be distinguished from those that characterize qualitative research, so a distinction between the two types of research may be made in terms of the role of hypotheses. Quantitative research should always start from a hypothesis. The procedures in quantitative research are normally oriented towards testing the hypotheses formulated in advance. This means that you should look for empirical pieces of evidence, which allow hypotheses to be either confirmed or contradicted.

Whereas quantitative research starts from hypotheses, they play a minor role in qualitative research. In qualitative research, the aim is not to test a hypothesis that was formulated in advance. In some cases, in the process of research, working hypotheses may be formulated. For example, first observations of differences in reacting to a symptom of skin diseases by male and female adolescents living on the street may lead to a working hypothesis that reactions to illness in this context are gendered. Such a working hypothesis will provide an orientation, for which you will search for evidence or counter-examples. But the aim will not be to test this hypothesis in the way you test a hypothesis in a quantitative study. In qualitative research, the use of the word 'hypothesis' has more in common with how you would use this term in everyday life than with the principles of testing hypotheses in quantitative research mentioned above.

Each form of social research should start from a clear research question. Different types of research questions suggest one or the other methodological procedure or may only be answered with specific methods. Hypotheses play various roles: in quantitative research they form an indispensable starting point, in qualitative research sometimes a heuristic tool.

Checklist for Formulating Research Questions

Box 2.1 lists points that you should consider when formulating your research question(s). You can use these guideline questions both for planning your own study and for assessing existing studies by other researchers.

BOX 2.1

Checklist for formulating research questions

1. Does your study have a research question, which is spelled out clearly?
2. You should be aware of where your research questions come from and what you want to achieve with them.

- Is your interest in the contents of the research question the main motivation?
- Or is answering the research question more a means to an end, like achieving an academic degree?

3. How many research questions has your study?

  - Are there too many?
  - Which is the main question?

4. Can your research question be answered?

  - What could an answer look like?

5. Can your research question be answered empirically?

  - Who can provide insights for that?
  - Can you reach these people?
  - Where can you find such people?
  - Which situations can give you insights for answering your research questions, and are these situations accessible?

6. How clearly is your research question formulated?
7. What are the methodological consequences of the research question?

  - What resources are needed (e.g. how much time is needed)?

8. If necessary for the type of study you chose, did you formulate hypotheses?

  - Are they formulated clearly, in a well-defined and testable way?

9. Can they be tested? By which methods?

Key Points

- Research questions may be developed from practical problems, they may be rooted in the researcher's personal background, or they may arise from social problems.
- Research questions can aim at representative results or at specific subgroups of society.
- Research questions should be embedded theoretically and be ready to be empirically studied. Above all, they should be specific and focused.
- Quantitative research is based on hypotheses, which are empirically tested. When qualitative research uses hypotheses, it will be based on a different conception of hypotheses, i.e. as working hypotheses.

■ ■ Further Reading ■

The first and the last texts listed below go into more detail about research questions in standardized research; the other three references discuss this more for qualitative studies.

Bryman, A. (2008) *Social Research Methods*, 3rd edn. Oxford: Oxford University Press.

Flick, U. (2008) *Designing Qualitative Research*. London: Sage. Chapter 1.

Flick, U. (2009) *An Introduction to Qualitative Research*, 4th edn. London: Sage. Chapter 9.

Lofland, J. and Lofland, L.H. (1984) *Analyzing Social Settings*, 2nd edn. Belmont: Wadsworth.

Neuman, W.L. (2000) *Social Research Methods: Qualitative and Quantitative Approaches*, 4th edn. Boston: Allyn and Bacon.

CHAPTER 3
READING AND REVIEWING THE LITERATURE

Chapter Overview

Chapter Objectives

This chapter is designed to help you:

- appreciate the relevance of existing literature for planning your own research project
- recognize that you should be familiar with methodological literature as well as research findings in your area of social research
- understand how to find the relevant literature for your research project.

Table 3.1 Navigator for Chapter 3

You are here in your project →		
Orientation	• What is social research? • Research question • Literature review	
Planning and design	• Planning research • Designing research • Deciding methods	
Working with data	• Gathering data • Analyzing data • E-research • Integrated research	
Reflection and writing	• Evaluating research • Ethics • Writing and using research	

The Scope of a Literature Review

In general, you should begin your research by reading. You should search, find and read what has been published so far about your issue, about the field of your research, and about the methods you wish to apply in your study. (Research methods will be discussed in detail in Chapters 6–10.)

It is also helpful to read to understand the basics of social research (discussed in Chapter 1) and the overall process in which it is applied (discussed in Chapter 4).

Of course, you cannot read everything that has been said about social research. Fortunately, that is not necessary! However, you should find out what is necessary and helpful for doing a research project on your chosen issue and research question.

Sometimes, you may come across the notion that a qualitative study need not be based on knowledge of the existing theoretical or empirical literature. This notion is, however, based on an outdated conception of what it means to develop a theory from empirical data. Today, there is a consensus amongst qualitative, as well as quantitative, researchers that you should be familiar with the ground on which you move and wish to make progress; finding new insights needs to be based on knowing what is known already.

What Do We Mean by 'Literature'?

Types of Literature

When you start researching the issue you have selected, you can search for and find different types of literature and evidence. First, you may find articles in the press. Newspapers and magazines may from time to time take up that issue, perhaps in order to sensationalize it. This kind of literature will help to show what kind of attention the public pays to your issue and perhaps its relevance in public discourse. However, you should be careful not to treat such publications as if they were scientific literature.

Primary and Secondary Sources

You should take care to distinguish between different types of sources. There are primary sources and secondary sources. An example here may explain this distinction. Autobiographies are written by the persons themselves. Biographies are written by an author about a person, sometimes without knowing him or her personally (e.g. if it is a historical person). If we transfer this distinction to scientific literature, a monograph about a theory is a primary source. The same is the case for an article or a book describing the empirical results of a study, when it was written by the researchers who did the study. A textbook summarizing the various theories in a field or giving an overview of the research in a field is a secondary source. Consider too a third example for clarifying this distinction: original documents like death certificates are primary sources, whereas official statistics summarizing causes of death in their frequencies and distribution in groups are secondary sources. The difference rests on how immediate is the access to the reported fact: primary sources are more immediate, whereas in secondary sources usually several primary sources have been summarized, condensed, elaborated or reworked by others.

Original Works and Reviews

Amongst scientific articles, we can distinguish between articles reporting research results for the first time (e.g. Flick and Röhnsch 2007, which reports findings from our interviews with homeless adolescents) and review articles (e.g. Kelly and Caputo 2007, which reviews several studies and gives an overview of health and homeless youth in Canada). Similarly, we can distinguish between original publications about a theory and textbooks that summarize theories across a field.

Amongst review articles, we can further distinguish between narrative and systematic reviews. A narrative review gives an account of the literature in the sense of a general overview (as in Kelly and Caputo 2007) including different types of literature (research, government reports etc.). A systematic review has a stronger focus on research papers, which have been selected according to specific criteria, and has a narrower focus on one aspect of a general issue. An example of a systematic review is the work by Burra et al. (2009) in which a defined range of databases was searched for articles that met a number of criteria predefined in order to assess studies of homeless adults and cognitive functioning. The method of searching (and the choice of databases, criteria, periods of publication etc.) is specified in order to make the review systematic, replicable, and assessable in itself.

An alternative form of summarizing studies is meta-analysis. Again existing research is reviewed, but here the focus is on the effect of a specific variable and how this can be identified in the studies under analysis. For example, Coldwell and Bender (2007) conducted a meta-analysis of studies about the effectiveness of a specific treatment for homeless people with severe mental illness.

Gray Literature

In addition to what is published about your specific issue in books and scientific journals, for example, you should look for 'gray' literature, such as practice reports or reflections of practitioners about their work with this target group. These may be reflections in essay form, and sometimes also empirical reports based on numbers of clients, diagnoses, treatment outcomes and the like. Gray literature is defined as 'literature (often of a scientific or technical nature) that is not available through the usual bibliographic sources such as databases or indexes. It can be both in print and, increasingly, electronic formats' (University Library 2009). Examples are technical reports, preprints, working papers, government documents or conference proceedings. This type of literature will often give you more immediate access to ongoing research or debates as well as institutional ways of documenting and treating social problems. Thus, gray literature can be a valuable first hand source for your study.

Finding Literature

In general, it depends on your topic where you should search for and will find relevant literature. If you want to find out whether your usual library holds the literature you are looking for, you can simply go to the library and check the catalogue. This can be time-consuming and frustrating if the book is not in stock. If you want to find out which library holds the book (or journal) you are looking for, you can access the library's OPAC via the Internet. Therefore, you should go to the homepage of one or more libraries. Alternatively you can use a link to several libraries at the same time. Examples are copac.ac.uk for 24 of the major university libraries and the British Library, or www.ubka. uni-karlsruhe.de/hylib/en/kvk.html for most of the German university libraries and also many in the UK and US. There you can find an exhaustive overview of the existing books or the information for completing your reference lists. Many books are now available as e-books, which you can obtain via your library even from home or from your office.

For journal articles, you can use search engines like wok.mimas.ac.uk. This will lead you to Thomson Reuters' *Social Sciences Citation Index* (also accessible through http://thomsonreuters.com) which you can search by authors, titles, keywords and so on. Other electronic databases that you can use if they fit your issue include for example PubMed and MEDLINE. PubMed comprises more than 20 million citations for biomedical literature from MEDLINE, life science journals and online books. Citations may include links to full-text content from PubMed Central and publisher websites (http://www.ncbi.nlm.nih.gov/pubmed). These are databases that document the publications in journals in the field of health and medicine. 'Athens' is an access management system developed by Eduserv that simplifies access to the electronic resources that your organization has subscribed to. Eduserv is a not-for-profit professional IT services group (www. athensams.net/myathen). If you want to read the whole article, you may need to buy the right to download it from the publisher of the journal or book. More and more articles are available online and for free in open access repositories (e.g. the Social Science Open Access Repository at http://www.ssoar.info/); 'open access' means that everybody can use this literature without paying for access.

You may also use online publication services organized by publishing houses such as Sage (the publisher of this book). At online.sagepub.com you can search all the journals published by this publisher, read abstracts, and get the exact reference dates for free. If you want to read the whole article, you will need to subscribe to the service or the journal, or to buy the article from the homepage (or see whether your library has subscribed to the journal in question).

Of course, a first step in finding your way into the literature can be to use an Internet search engine such as Google, Google Scholar, Intute or AltaVista. That is, however, a first step only and certainly should not be the only one.

Areas of Literature

You will need to review the literature in several areas, notably:

- theoretical literature about the topic of your study
- methodological literature about how to do your research and how to use the methods you choose
- empirical literature about previous research in the field of your study or similar fields
- theoretical and empirical literature to help contextualize, compare and generalize your findings.

Let us examine these areas one by one.

Reviewing Theoretical Literature

Theoretical literature means works about the concepts, definitions and theories used in your field of investigation. Reviewing the theoretical literature in your area of research should help you answer such questions as:

- What is already known about this issue in particular, or the area in general?
- Which theories are used and discussed in this area?
- What concepts are used or debated?
- What are the theoretical or methodological debates or controversies in this field?
- What questions remain open?
- What has not been studied yet?

Here you should synthesize the discussion and the concepts and theories that are used in the field you study. The end point should be that it becomes clear which of these have informed your research interest, your study and its design.

We can distinguish several forms of theories. There are those that conceptualize your issue – such as theories of homelessness in our example – and those that define your research perspective, such as social representations (see Flick 1998a). The latter posit that there are different forms of knowledge about an issue linked to different social backgrounds and that these differences are a starting point for analyzing the issue itself.

Reviewing Methodological Literature

Before deciding on a specific method for your study, you should read the relevant methodological literature. If you want to use, say, focus groups (discussed in Chapter 7) in a qualitative study, you should obtain a detailed overview of the current state of qualitative research, for example by reading a textbook or an introduction to the field. Next you should identify the relevant publications about your method of choice by reading a specialized book, some chapters about it, and prior examples of research that has this method. This will allow you to select your specific method(s) with an appreciation of the existing alternatives. It will also prepare you for the more technical steps of planning to use the method and help you to avoid the pitfalls mentioned in the literature. Such understanding will help you to compose a detailed and concise account of why and how you used your method in your study, when you write your report later on.

Overall, reviewing the methodological literature in your area of research should help you to answer such questions as:

- What are the methodological traditions, alternatives or controversies here?
- Are there any contradictory ways of using the methods, which you could take as a starting point?

Reviewing Empirical Literature

In the next step, you should review and summarize the empirical research that has been done in your field of interest. This should allow you to contextualize your approach and, later, your findings and to see both in perspective.

Reviewing the empirical literature in your area of research should help you to answer such questions as:

- What are the methods that are used or debated here?
- Are there any contradictory results and findings, which you could take as a starting point?

Reading Empirical Studies

When you are reading existing studies, it is important to be able to assess them critically – in terms of both their methods and their results. You should consider, in particular, how far the study has achieved its aims, and how far the study meets appropriate methodological standards in collecting and analyzing data. The checklist in Box 3.1 is designed to help you make critical assessments of the literature you read.

BOX 3.1

Landmarks for assessing existing empirical studies

1. Have the researchers or authors clearly defined the aim and purpose of their study and why they conducted it?
2. What is the research question of the study?
3. Did the author review, integrate and summarize the relevant background literature?
4. Which theoretical perspective is the study based on, and has it been explicitly formulated?
5. Which design was applied in the study? Does it fit the research question that was formulated?
6. Which form of sampling was applied? Was it appropriate to the aims and the research question?
7. Which methods of data collection were applied?

---

8. How far have ethical issues been taken into account (for example, informed consent and data protection)?
9. Which methods have been applied for analyzing the data? Is it clear how they were used and maybe modified?
10. Do methods of data collection and analysis fit together?
11. Which approaches and criteria did the researchers apply for assessing their own ways of proceeding?
12. Have the results been discussed and classified through reference to earlier studies and the theoretical literature about the issue of the study?
13. Does the study define its area of validity and its limits? Have issues of generalization been addressed?

Using the Literature

Ways of Argumentation

There are several ways of using the literature you have found. First, we should distinguish between, on the one hand, listing literature and, on the other, reviewing or analyzing it. Merely listing what you found and where will not be very helpful. In a review or an analysis of the literature you will go further than this by ordering the material and producing a critical assessment of it, involving the selection and weighting of the literature.

The outcomes of your analysis may include a synthesis of the range of literature you draw on and some conclusions. These conclusions should lead the readers to your own research question and research plan and provide a rationale for both.

In most cases, it will not be necessary to give a complete account of what has been published in an area. Rather, you should include what is relevant for your project, for justifying and for planning it.

Sometimes it is difficult to decide when to stop working with the literature. One suggestion here is to continue reading and perhaps summarizing new literature while doing the project. You will in any case have to come back to the literature when discussing your own findings. Another suggestion is that you should set up your research plan after reviewing the literature and then, from the moment you start your empirical work, try not to be distracted by new literature and not to revise your project continuously.

A concise definition of a literature review's contents is provided by Hart:

> **The selection of available documents (both published and unpublished) on the topic, which contain information, ideas, data, and evidence written from a particular standpoint to fulfil certain aims or express certain views on the nature of the topic and how it is to be investigated, and the effective evaluation of these documents in relation to the research being proposed. (1998, p. 13)**

You should demonstrate in the way you present the literature used in your study that you have conducted a skillful search into the existing literature. It should also be evident from your literature review that you have a good command of the subject area and that you understand the issue, the methods you use, and the state of the art of the research in your field.

Documentation and Referencing

It is important to develop a way of documenting what you have read – both the sources and the content. For the latter, you should take notes from the major topics of an article or a book you read and derive from your reading some keywords that you can use for further searches. You should always look at the reference list of what you read as an inspiration for further reading. You can take your notes electronically by writing them in a file with your word processor, for example, or by using commercial software tools like Microsoft OneNote (www.office.microsoft.com/en-us/onenote) or the 'free service for managing and discovering scholarly references' called 'citeulike' (http://www.citeulike.org). These tools allow you to store your search results and notes including the sources, that is where you found your information. Alternatively you can make notes manually on index cards. Be sure to note the source of anything you found noteworthy, so that you can come back to the original article and retrieve the context of an argument or concept.

You also need to decide on a system of referencing your literature in your text and in your reference list. You may, for example, take the way I have referred to other sources in this book and the reference list at the end of it as a model for your own use of literature. This means referring to other authors' works *in the text* as in the following examples:

1. As Allmark (2002) holds ….

2. Such an assessment normally considers three aspects: 'scientific quality, the welfare of participants and …' (Allmark 2002, p. 9).

3. Gaiser and Schreiner (2009, p. 14) have listed a number of questions ….

4. Flick et al. (2010, p. 755) hold that ….

More generally, this means that you refer to other authors' works by using the format of author's name, followed by the year of the publication in brackets (as in example 1). When you use a direct quote of the authors (their own words), you will have to add the page number (as in example 2). When you refer to a work by two authors, you mention both authors names linked with 'and', the year of publication and the page number (as in example 3). If you refer to a work of three or more authors, you mention the first author's name and add 'et al.' and the year and page number (as in example 4).

In the *list of references* at the end of your work, you will mention the material you used as follows:

1. *Book.* Name(s) and initials of the author(s), year in brackets, book title in italics, publication place, publisher. Example:

   Gaiser, T.J. and Schreiner, A.E. (2009) *A Guide to Conducting Online Research.* London: Sage.

2. *Book chapter.* Name(s) and initials of the author(s), year in brackets, chapter title, 'in' initial and name of editor, '(ed.)', book title in italics, publication place, publisher, first–last page numbers of the chapter. Example:

   Harré, R. (1998) 'The Epistemology of Social Representations', in U. Flick (ed.), *Psychology of the Social: Representations in Knowledge and Language.* Cambridge: Cambridge University Press. pp. 129–37.

3. *Journal article.* Name(s) and initials of the author(s), year in brackets, article title, journal title in italics, volume number, first–last page numbers of the article. Examples:

   Allmark, P. (2002) 'The Ethics of Research with Children', *Nurse Researcher*, 10: 7–19. Flick, U., Garms-Homolová, V. and Röhnsch, G. (2010) '"When they Sleep, they Sleep": Daytime Activities and Sleep Disorders in Nursing Homes', *Journal of Health Psychology*, 15: 755–64.

4. *Internet source.* Name(s) and initials of the author(s), year in brackets, article title, journal title in italics, volume number, link/URL, date at which you accessed the source. Example:

   Bampton, R. and Cowton, C.J. (2002) 'The E-Interview', *Forum Qualitative Social Research*, 3 (2), www.qualitative-research.net/fqs/fqs-eng.htm (accessed 22 February 2005).

Alternatively, you may use footnotes for references. Which format you use will depend on preferences – your own and those of your supervisor or faculty. The major point here is that you must work systematically: every journal article must be referenced in the same format and every book cited consistently.

You can also use bibliographic software like EndNote (www.endnote.com) or ProCite (www.procite.com) for administering your literature. It will take some time to learn how to use the software, and you should begin using it early in your work and continue to use it while reviewing the literature.

Plagiarism and How To Avoid It

In recent years, the topic of plagiarism has attracted increasing attention in the media and in universities. This is a serious issue, not least as it has become technically much easier to copy and use other people's work.

What Is Plagiarism?

Plagiarism means that you simply use formulations by other authors without acknowledging them and making it evident that you have quoted them. There are three main forms of plagiarism (see Neville 2010, p. 29): (1) to copy other people's work (i.e. ideas and/or formulations) without quoting the authors; (2) to blend your own arguments with the ideas and words of other people without referring to them; and (3) to paraphrase other authors' formulations without referring to them and pretending it was your own work.

Inadvertent Plagiarism

Plagiarism can occur for several reasons (see Birnbaum and Goscillo 2009). The most obvious one is that people intend to use someone else's ideas and/or formulations and to pretend that they were their own ideas or formulations. In this case, they would be aware of their plagiarism. This can also be seen as an intentional deceit. However, there may be other reasons, for example that someone does not know what plagiarism is, or is insecure about how to quote correctly, or is careless in the use of other people's materials. This is referred to as 'inadvertent plagiarism', which in the end will have the same consequences as intentional plagiarism.

Why You Should Avoid Plagiarism

In general, plagiarism offends the rules of good practice in scientific work and it is illegal. Plagiarism detection software is more frequently used now for identifying the use of other authors' formulations without quoting the authors explicitly. Once it is detected, the student or researcher will face very serious consequences, such as failing in their thesis or being removed from the university.

How To Avoid Plagiarism

There are several ways to avoid plagiarism (including inadvertent plagiarism). The first is to pay sufficient attention to including a full list of all the references you have used in writing your thesis. The second is to be very thorough in quoting when you use other people's words. Thus you should put all other authors' wordings you use in quotation marks. You should also use suspension points (ellipsis) when you leave certain words out of a quote, and you should indicate when you add a word by putting it in brackets: for example, 'social research … [is] valuable'. If you take a sentence from another author and paraphrase it, so that the same content and ideas are still the basis of your formulations, and you do not mention the original author and source, this still constitutes plagiarism. If you take a quotation from a text in which another text was already quoted, you should notify this secondary quotation: for example, '(Author 2, as cited in Author 1, pp. 182–93)'. Both should go in the references.

To avoid plagiarism, you should take your own thoughts and formulations as the basis of your thesis, document your sources carefully, and keep notes of where you have found and read something. Finally, you should use more than one source for developing your arguments. (See Birnbaum and Goscillo's 2009 overview of the issues.)

Checklist for Finding, Assessing and Reviewing Literature

In composing a literature review for an empirical project in social research, you should consider the questions provided in the checklist in Box 3.2.

BOX 3.2

Checklist for the use of literature in social research

1. Is your literature review up to date?
2. Is your literature review connected to the issue of your study?
3. Is your literature review and your writing about it systematic?
4. Does it cover the most important theories, concepts and definitions?
5. Is it based on the most relevant studies in your field of research and about your issue?
6. Did you document how and where you searched for literature?
7. Do your research question and design result from your review of the literature?
8. Are they consistent with it?
9. Have you handled quotations and sources carefully?
10. Did you summarize or synthesize the literature you found?
11. Did you take care to avoid plagiarism?

Key Points

- In social research, the search and analysis of existing literature are the most important steps.
- There are several points in the research process where the use of literature can be helpful and necessary.
- In planning research, in analyzing materials, in writing about findings, you should make use of existing literature about (a) other research, (b) theories, and (c) the methods you use in your study.

The first book listed below is the most comprehensive overview of how to do a literature search for your research, where to look, and how to proceed. The second provides the most comprehensive overview of how to do a literature review for your study, which pitfalls to avoid, and how to write about what you find. The third one explains how to use references and avoid plagiarism. The final one provides information about forms of gray literature and how to use it.

Hart, C. (2001) *Doing a Literature Search*. London: Sage.

Hart, C. (1998) *Doing a Literature Review*. London: Sage.

Neville, C. (2010) *Complete Guide to Referencing and Avoiding Plagiarism*. Maidenhead: Open University Press.

University Library (2009) 'Gray Literature', California State University, Long Beach, www.csulb.edu/library/subj/gray_literature/ (accessed 17 August 2010).

PART II
PLANNING AND DESIGN

Part I of this book was designed to help orient you towards doing your research project. Part II guides you through key steps in the early phases of the project itself, whether it be qualitative or quantitative. Chapter 4 offers an overview of the major steps of the research process. This provides the foundations for planning your research project – the subject of Chapter 5. The first practical step in giving your plans a shape is to write a proposal and design a timescale. For this step it will be helpful to know more about which designs, and which forms of sampling, are used in social research – and the implications of these for your project.

Your project plan will become more concrete as you decide which methods you wish to apply. Chapter 6 outlines the decisions you need to take in the research process when choosing your method, the form of sampling, or the type of research. This should lead you to the reflective stage, half-way through the process, in which you consider again the implications of your research plan, before you start actually to apply concrete methods and begin to work with data.

CHAPTER 4

PLANNING SOCIAL RESEARCH: STEPS IN THE RESEARCH PROCESS

Chapter Overview

Chapter Objectives

This chapter is designed to help you:

- develop an overview of the process of social research
- appreciate, from the point of view of planning, what qualitative and quantitative research have in common and also how they differ
- develop an understanding of which steps in the research process you need to take into account when planning your project.

Table 4.1   Navigator for Chapter 4

You are here in your project →	Orientation	• What is social research? • Research question • Literature review
	Planning and design	• Planning research • Designing research • Deciding methods
	Working with data	• Gathering data • Analyzing data • E-research • Integrated research
	Reflection and writing	• Evaluating research • Ethics • Writing and using research

Overview of the Research Process

In quantitative research, the research process is planned primarily in a linear way: one step follows another in sequence. In qualitative research, the process is less linear: some of these steps are more closely interlinked, while some are omitted or located at a different stage of the process. This chapter provides an outline of the research processes for both approaches.

The Research Process in Quantitative Research

Some of the processes outlined in this chapter are rather abstract. To understand them, it will help to have a concrete case. Imagine as an example that members of a hospital have noticed that, in its everyday routines, waiting times are too long. For analyzing when and under what conditions delays occur, and for finding a possible solution for the problem, the institution can go two ways: either it commissions a systematic study of situations in which waiting times are produced by a researcher from outside (e.g. a sociologist or psychologist); or someone on the team is commissioned with this task.

Step 1: selection of a research problem

Every research project begins with the identification and selection of a research problem. We have seen in Chapter 2 that the potential sources of research problems are diverse. In our example here, the motivation for the research is a practical problem.

Step 2: systematic searching of the literature

As the next step, a systematic review of the literature is required. This should cover three areas, namely:

- theories about the issue or theoretically relevant literature (see Chapter 3)
- other studies about this or similar issues
- overviews of the relevant literature on research methods in general or on specific methods (see Chapter 6).

In our example, the researchers should look for theoretical models concerning how waiting times emerge and concerning routines in institutions of this kind. They should also focus on empirical studies about the organization of processes in hospitals and comparable service enterprises.

Step 3: formulation of the research question

It is not enough to identify a research problem. For virtually all research problems, one could study a number of research questions – but not all at the same time. Thus, the next steps are: to decide on a specific research question; to formulate it in detail; and, above all, to narrow it down.

In our example the research question could be either 'When do waiting times occur particularly often?' or 'What characterizes situations in which waiting times occur?' Depending on the research questions, qualitative or quantitative research or a specific qualitative or quantitative method will be (more) appropriate (see Chapter 2).

Step 4: formulating a hypothesis

In standardized research, the next step is to formulate a hypothesis. In our example, a hypothesis could be: 'Waiting times occur more often after the weekend compared to other days in the week.' A hypothesis formulates a relation in a way that can be tested (see Chapter 2).

Step 5: operationalization

To test a hypothesis, you first have to operationalize it. This means that you transform it into entities that can be measured or observed or into questions that can be answered. In our example, you should operationalize the term 'waiting time' and define more concretely how to measure it. How much time (e.g. more than 10 minutes) is seen as waiting time? When should one start to measure waiting time? At the same time, for our hypothesis, we should define what is meant by 'after the weekend' (e.g. the time from 9.00 to 12.00 a.m. on Mondays).

Step 6: developing a project plan or research design

The next step is to develop a project plan and a research design for your study. First you choose one of the usual designs, and then define how to standardize and control the processes in your study so that you can interpret any relations you find in an unambiguous way. In our example, you could test our hypothesis first by comparing waiting times at the beginning of the week with those on days like Thursday and Friday (see Chapter 5).

Step 7: sampling

In the next step, you need to define which groups, cases or fields should be integrated into your study. Such decisions of selecting empirical units are made by applying sampling procedures. In our example, you could take a period of four weeks and include all wards of a hospital on Mondays and Thursdays. To define in which wards you collect the data on both days, you can use a randomized procedure (see Chapter 5).

Step 8: selecting the appropriate methods

Next, you need to select appropriate methods for collecting and analyzing data. Here you have three basic alternatives:

- First you can select one of the existing methods. For example, you may use a questionnaire which has been applied successfully by other researchers.
- Often, you will have to modify an existing method. For example, you may skip some questions of that questionnaire or add new ones.
- If that is not sufficient for the study you are planning, the third option is to develop your own method, such as a new questionnaire, or a new methodology, such as a new form of interviewing (see Chapter 7).

In our example, observations in the selected wards would provide time measures of how long patients wait after admission to the hospital for the beginning of assessment or treatment in each ward. At the same time you may interview team members in the ward using a questionnaire addressing how often such waiting times occur according to their experience and what they see as reasons (see Chapter 8).

Step 9: access to the research site

Once you have finished the planning of your study on the methodological level, the next step – especially if you are conducting applied research – is to find a site in which you can do the study. Here, normally four tasks have to be solved. First, if your research is expected to take place in an institution, you have to organize access to the institution as a whole. Second, you should gain access to individuals in the institution who should participate. Third, you should clarify issues of permission. Fourth, questions of how to protect participants from any misuse of the data and of anonymity have to be answered.

Consider again our example. You have first to find and select appropriate hospitals (i.e. that are relevant for the research question). In each hospital, the director's (and perhaps the staff council's) agreement is required before you can approach single wards and their managers. Once they have agreed to join the study, you must persuade individual members of the institution to participate in the study – according to the sample that is intended (for example, your sample should include not only trainees but also experienced doctors and nurses, maybe even in leading positions). With respect to data protection, you should clarify how to prevent the identification of single participants within the institution and of the institution from the outside. For example, you could develop a system of nicknames or develop a different form of anonymization. Finally, it should be defined who is allowed to see the data and in what form, and who is not allowed.

Step 10: data collection

After finishing these methodological preparations, you are ready to start collecting your data. Basically, you can choose between three main alternatives (see Chapter 7). You may do a survey in one form or another (e.g. with a questionnaire). You may also do observations (in our example with a measurement of waiting times). A third alternative is to analyze existing documents (in our example, documentation of treatment routines could be analyzed for waiting times, which can be found or reconstructed from those documents).

Step 11: documentation of data

Before you can analyze your data, you have to decide how to document them. A survey can be filled in by the participants or alternatively can be completed by the researcher based on the respondents' answers. The form of documentation will have an influence on the contents and the quality of the data. Therefore it should be identical for all participants.

The next step is to edit the data. Take the example of questionnaires. First, the questionnaires themselves need to be entered onto your database. Questionnaires often include questions with open answers and the respondents could write down their answers in their own words. Then, these answers have to be coded. This means the answers have to be summarized into a number of types of answers and each of these types has to be allocated to a number. This elaboration of the data has an influence on their quality and should be done in an identical way for each case (each questionnaire, each observation). This makes the standardization of data and procedures possible (see Chapter 7).

Step 12: analyzing the data

Data analysis constitutes a major step in any project. In standardized studies, the coding of data is essential. This requires filing responses into categories defined into advance or allocated to numerical values (like the alternatives of responding from 1 to 5 in Figure 1.1). If you cannot define the categories in advance, the data (statements, observations) have now to be categorized. This means identical or similar statements are summarized in a category. This leads to the development of a category system (see Chapter 8 for more details).

In a quantitative study, coding and categorization are followed by statistical analysis. In our example, you could refer the average extension of the measured waiting times to the day of the week when they were measured, or differentiate them for the wards in which they were measured. Responses in questionnaires are analyzed for their frequencies and distribution in different professional groups, for example.

Step 13: interpretation of results

Not every statistical analysis produces meaningful results. How you interpret any relations that you found in the data therefore becomes very important. Note that when a statistical analysis shows that certain events occur together or that they correlate in their frequencies or intensities, this does not provide any explanation for why this is the case and what that means in concrete terms. If you show in our example that waiting times on Mondays are much longer than those on Thursdays, this result does not provide any explanation why this is so. If estimations of waiting times differ between nurses and physicians, we need to find an explanation for this finding (see Chapter 8).

Step 14: discussion of the findings and their interpretations

The analysis and interpretation of data and results are followed by their discussion. This means that findings are linked to existing literature about the issue (or the methodology used) and to other relevant studies. Could our study find anything new? Has it confirmed what was known already, or did contradictions to existing results emerge? What does it mean if the hypotheses could not be verified that waiting times occur more often or are more extended after the weekend, and if this result is different from what was found in other studies? How do the team members' perceptions of the problem found here differ from the results of similar surveys by other researchers? In the context of such a discussion you will continue to look for explanations for what you found in your data.

Step 15: evaluation and generalization

From a methodological point of view, this is particularly relevant. You will critically assess your results and the methods that led to them, which means checking their reliability and validity (see Chapter 11 for more details). At the same time you should check what kind of generalization the results justify, asking: can they be transferred to other fields, to other samples, to a specific population (e.g. all nurses, all wards, all hospitals; or all hospitals, physicians etc. of a specific type)? A major element here is to make transparent what the limits of the results are: what could not be found or confirmed, what limits are set for transferability to other institutions, for example (see Chapter 11).

Step 16: presentation of the results and the study

Whether the results of a study are recognized depends mainly on the way in which the results are presented. This means first summarizing the study and its main results and then writing (a report, article, book etc.) about it. Often it is also necessary to select the important information (and to leave out what is less important) due to limits of space and of the reading capacities of potential audiences. In presenting results and the process, it is also important that you manage to make the process of the study transparent for the readers and thus allow them to assess this process and its results (see Chapter 13).

Step 17: using the results

In applied fields of research – such as health – the question arises of how to use the results. This means formulating implications or recommendations. For example, how can you develop suggestions for changing the routines in the ward from analyzing the waiting times in the everyday life of the ward? Using the results can also mean applying them in practical contexts – e.g. that a specific theoretical model (used in the study) is applied in some wards. Finally, 'use' can mean to test the results against the conditions in the practical work and thus to evaluate them critically.

Step 18: develop new research questions

A major outcome of an empirical study is the formulation of new research questions or hypotheses for analyzing the questions that remained unanswered, so that the research in the field can progress.

Step 19: a new study

The new research questions may then lead to a new study.

Summary

These steps of the research process in standardized research can be seen as a linear process as they usually follow one after the other. In practice, however, the process is often more recursive: you will find you often need to go back and revise a step when it becomes evident that an earlier decision does not work in practice. Table 4.2 summarizes the steps of the research process in standardized research. You can use this outline of the research process in standardized or

Table 4.2 Steps of the process in standardized research

1. Selection of a research problem
2. Systematic searching the literature
3. Formulation of the research question
4. Formulating a hypothesis
5. Operationalization
6. Developing a project plan or research design
7. Sampling
8. Selecting the appropriate methods
9. Access to the research site
10. Data collection
11. Documentation of data
12. Analyzing the data
13. Interpretation of results
14. Discussion of the findings and their interpretations
15. Evaluation and generalization
16. Presentation of the results and the study
17. Using the results
18. Developing new research questions
19. A new study

quantitative research for planning your empirical study. It can also be helpful as a framework for reading and assessing existing empirical studies.

The Research Process in Non-standardized Qualitative Research

As we have seen, the process of conducting standardized research may be broken down into a linear sequence of conceptual, methodological and empirical steps. The single steps can be presented and applied one after the other and are more or less independent of each other. In qualitative research, these phases may also be relevant, but they are more closely connected. These connections are illustrated in the following discussion; the step numbers are specified in Table 4.3.

Steps 1–6: selection of a research problem, searching the literature, research question, access

Some of the steps of the process outlined above for standardized research also apply to non-standardized research. In particular, you will have to select a research problem, to formulate a research question, to systematically search the literature and to gain access to the research site here as well before you can collect and analyze data. If we take our example again, you will also formulate a research question if you do a qualitative study: for example, what is characteristic for situations in which waiting times occur (see above). You will review the literature and seek permission for accessing the field. However, you will not formulate a hypothesis to be tested.

Step 7: sampling, collection, documentation and analysis of data

In qualitative research, the remaining parts of the research process tend to be more interrelated than in standardized research. Glaser and Strauss (1967) developed this conception of the research process in their grounded theory approach (see also Strauss and Corbin 1990 and Strauss 1987). The aim of grounded theory within qualitative research makes it very different from standardized research. The aim is to do empirical research in order to use the data and their analysis to develop a theory of the issue under study. Thus theory is not a starting point for research, but rather the intended outcome of the study.

This has consequences for the planning and the steps in the research process. The grounded theory approach gives priority to the data and the field under study over theoretical assumptions. Theories are less applied to the subject being studied. Rather, they are 'discovered' and formulated in working with the field and the empirical data to be found in it. People to be studied are selected according to their relevance to the research topic. They are not (randomly) selected to construct a (statistically) representative sample of a general population. The aim is not to reduce complexity by breaking it down into variables, but rather to increase complexity by including context. Methods also have to be appropriate to the issue under study and have to be chosen accordingly. This approach focuses strongly on the interpretation of data no matter how they were collected. Here the question of which method to use for collecting data becomes minor. Decisions on the data to be integrated and the methods to be used for this are based on the state of the developing theory after analyzing the data already at hand at that moment (see Chapter 8).

In the documentation of data, recording is normally the first step. Interviews, for example, are recorded on tape, mp3 or video. In observations, field notes or protocols are written, sometimes based on video recordings. For interviews, transcription, i.e. making a written text of what was recorded acoustically, is the next step (see Chapter 7).

In qualitative research, interpretation mainly involves analysis of interview statements, events or actions documented in field notes made from observations. Here, you will also look for explanations: why some statements occur in specific contexts together with other statements, or why they occur more often under certain conditions (see Chapter 8).

In our example, researchers would begin with not very structured observations in one ward and talk to members (staff, patients, administrative people etc.) more or less formally. After analyzing their first data, they will select and include another ward and continue observations and conversations there and analyze the resulting materials. They will continue to include further cases and make comparisons among all cases so far included.

Step 8–13: discussion, generalization, use of results and new research questions

As with standardized research, collection and analysis of the data (see Chapters 7 and 8) will lead to a discussion of the results and their validity and reliability (see Chapter 11). However, generalization here is meant less in a statistical than in a theoretical way. Presenting and using the results and developing new research questions will be the final steps here, too.

The Process of Social Research: Quantitative and Qualitative Research Compared

Qualitative research is compatible with the traditional, linear logic of empirical (quantitative or standardized) research only to an extent. Interlinking the empirical steps according to the model of Glaser and Strauss (1967) tends to be more appropriate to the character of qualitative research, which is more oriented towards exploring and discovering what is new. Figure 4.1 summarizes the differences between the two approaches. In quantitative research, you have a linear (step-by-step) process starting from theory and ending with the validation of the theory based on testing it. Sampling is usually finished before data collection begins – which means you have fixed your sampling frame before you send out a questionnaire, for example. It only makes sense to begin interpreting the data – for example a statistical analysis – once the data collection has been finished (see Chapters 7 and 8). Therefore, these steps can be seen as forming a sequence and you will work through them one after the other, as represented in the upper half of Figure 4.1.

In qualitative research, these steps are more interlinked. Sampling decisions are taken during data collection, and interpretation of the data should begin immediately with the first data – for example, the first interview. From analyzing these data, you may arrive at new decisions, such as whom to interview next (thus, in this example, the process of sampling continues). You will also immediately start to compare your data – for example, the second with the first interview and so on. The aim here is to develop a theory from the empirical material and analysis, where the starting point was preliminary assumptions about the issue you want to study. This process is represented in the lower part of Figure 4.1.

Despite this interlinkage of some essential steps in the process of the research, you can also see the qualitative or non-standardized research process to some extent as forming a sequence of decisions (see Flick 2009). These decisions refer to selecting the specific method(s) of data collection and analysis to be applied, the sampling procedure used in the concrete study (see below), and the ways of documenting and presenting the results.

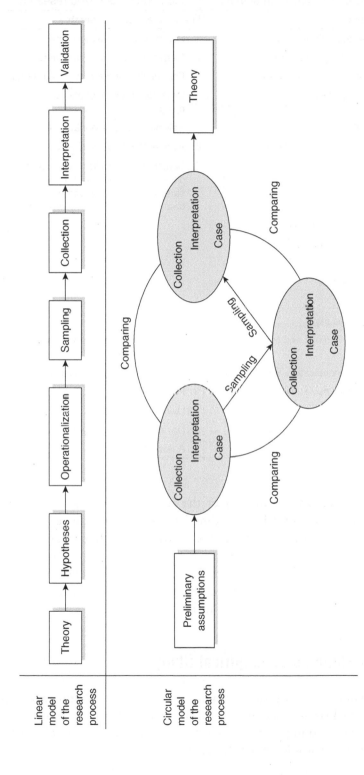

Figure 4.1 Process models of standardized and non-standardized research (Flick 2009, p. 95)

Table 4.3　Steps of the process in standardized and non-standardized research

Standardized research	Non-standardized research
1. Selection of a research problem	1. Selection of a research problem
2. Systematic searching the literature	2. Systematic searching the literature
3. Formulation of the research question	3. Formulation of the research question
4. Formulating a hypothesis	4. Developing a project plan or research design
5. Operationalization	5. Selecting the appropriate methods
6. Developing a project plan or research design	6. Access to the research site
7. Sampling	7. Sampling, data collection, documentation of data, analysis of data, comparison, sampling, data collection, documentation of data, analysis of data, comparison …
8. Selecting the appropriate methods	
9. Access to the research site	
10. Data collection	
11. Documentation of data	
12. Analyzing the data	
13. Interpretation of results	
14. Discussion of the findings and their interpretations	8. Discussion of the findings and their interpretations
15. Evaluation and generalization	9. Evaluation and generalization
16. Presentation of the results and the study	10. Presentation of the results and the study
17. Using the results	11. Using the results
18. Developing new research questions	12. Developing new research questions
19. A new study	13. A new study

Table 4.3 juxtaposes the concepts of the research process of standardized and non-standardized research as outlined in this chapter in a comparative way. This indicates the main differences in the research processes between qualitative and quantitative research. These mainly involve the degree of standardization of procedures. This table also provides a basis for planning the steps of your own project and for developing an adequate design for your study (see Chapter 5 for more detail on this).

Checklist for Planning an Empirical Study

For planning your own empirical project, you should take into account the aspects shown in Box 4.1 and find answers to the questions that arise. This checklist may help you in planning your own study, but you can also use it for assessing the existing studies of other researchers.

BOX 4.1

Checklist for planning an empirical study

1. Be aware which steps in the research process are appropriate for the kind of study you plan.
2. Seek to establish whether the existing knowledge and research about your issue are sufficient for planning and doing a standardized study in which you will test hypotheses.
3. Or seek to clarify whether the empirical and theoretical knowledge about the issue of your study is so limited or has so many gaps that it makes sense to plan and do a non-standardized qualitative study.
4. Check the procedures in your plan for their soundness. Does the methodological plan of your study fit (a) the aims of your study, (b) its theoretical background, and (c) the state of research?
5. Will this kind of research process be compatible with the issue you want to study and with the field in which you intend to do your research?

Key Points

- Quantitative and qualitative studies run through some similar and some different steps in the research process.
- Quantitative research is planned in a linear process.
- In qualitative research, In many cases the steps in the research process will be interlinked.
- Having a firm grasp of the steps that comprise the research process in each case will give you a basis for planning your own study.

Further Reading

Overviews of planning social research in a quantitative approach are discussed in the first and last textbooks, while the other two focus on this issue for qualitative studies.

Bryman, A. (2008) *Social Research Methods*, 3rd edn. Oxford: Oxford University Press.

Flick, U. (2004) 'Design and Process in Qualitative Research', in U. Flick, E. v. Kardorff and I. Steinke (eds), *A Companion to Qualitative Research*. London: Sage. pp. 146–52.

Flick, U. (2009) *An Introduction to Qualitative Research*, 4th edn. London: Sage. Part 3.

Neuman, W.L. (2000) *Social Research Methods: Qualitative and Quantitative Approaches*, 4th edn. Boston: Allyn and Bacon.

CHAPTER 5
DESIGNING SOCIAL RESEARCH

Chapter Overview

Chapter Objectives

This chapter is designed to help you:

- understand how and why to write a proposal and develop a timescale
- develop an overview of the most important research designs
- understand the procedures for selecting study participants
- appreciate the special features of evaluational research.

Table 5.1 Navigator for Chapter 5

Orientation	• What is social research? • Research question • Literature review
Planning and design	• Planning research • Designing research • Deciding methods
Working with data	• Gathering data • Analyzing data • E-research • Integrated research
Reflection and writing	• Evaluating research • Ethics • Writing and using research

You are here in your project →

Chapter 4 provided an outline of the research process. We can now use this to provide a foundation for research planning.

Writing a Proposal for a Research Project

Planning social research becomes more concrete when you are preparing the final thesis in a university program. In most cases, you will need a proposal for enrolling for your thesis as well as for applying for a grant. If this is not required, writing a proposal can nevertheless be an important and helpful step for planning your project and for estimating whether it is realistic under the given conditions like time – but also the skills you have. A proposal for an empirical project should include topics and subitems as follows (see Table 5.2).

In the introduction you should briefly outline the background of the project (why you intend to do it) and the relevance of the topic. In the description of the research problem, you should summarize the state of the art in research and in the literature and derive your own research interest from the gaps that became evident in this summary. What emphasis you should put on each of the points will depend on the type of study you plan. For a quantitative study, the literature review will be more extensive than for a qualitative study. The purpose of the study and the aim of doing it should be briefly described. A major point in any proposal is the research question (see Chapter 2), if possible and necessary divided into major questions and subquestions.

Whether or not it is necessary to formulate a hypothesis will depend on the type of research you intend to do. For a quantitative study, this step should always be included. In any case, you need to describe the methodological procedures you intend to apply. For qualitative research, you should give a short justification of why you will use qualitative methods and why you will work with this specific method. In quantitative research, such a justification is often not seen as necessary. The research strategy – an exploratory, a hypotheses testing or an evaluative approach – should be described as well. In the proposal, you should outline the research design (see below) in its main features: which sample will be included, how big will it be, and on which comparative perspective is it based? In the next step, your proposal should include a short description and justification of which methods you intend to use for collecting your data (see Chapters 6 and 7) and for analyzing them (see Chapters 6 and 8) and how you will assess the quality of your study (see Chapter 11). In many contexts, it is a requirement that a proposal covers the ethical issues (data protection, non-maleficence, informed consent etc.: see Chapter 12) and demonstrates how the researchers intend to take them into account in doing their project.

In this context, you should consider what results you expect from your study and what will be their relevance in the light of earlier results and practical issues (see Chapters 1 and 13). You will elaborate the state of research in writing your thesis or the final report of your research in more detail. Nevertheless, I would strongly recommend that you get a first overview of the literature while planning your project in order to ensure that you don't adopt a research question which has already been answered before to a sufficient extent. Finally, you should briefly discuss the practical conditions of doing your study. For this purpose, it will be helpful to develop a timescale (see below) and to outline your own experience with research. At the end, a preliminary list of references should be added.

Spelling out the topics listed in Table 5.2 is helpful for developing your research project (and the thesis based on it) and should make successful work more likely.

Table 5.2 Model for a proposal structure

1. Introduction
2. Research problem
(a) Existing literature
(b) Gaps in the existing research
(c) Research interest
3. Purpose of the study
4. Research questions
5. Methods and procedures
(a) Characteristics of qualitative research and why it is appropriate here
(b) Research strategy
(c) Research design

Table 5.2   (Continued)

     (i)   Sampling
     (ii)   Comparison
     (iii) Expected number of participants, cases, sites, documents

  (d) Methods of data collection
  (e) Methods of data analysis
  (f) Quality issues

6. Ethical issues

7. Expected results

8. Significance, relevance, practical implications of the study

9. Preliminary pilot findings, earlier research, experience of the researcher(s)

10. Your own experience with doing social research

11. Timeline, proposed budget

12. References

Developing a Timescale

A timescale for your project should outline both the steps required in the research process (see Chapter 4) and the time estimated for each step. You may also indicate milestones, which means the outcomes that are to be expected when each step is completed. In Box 5.1 you will find an example of a timescale for a qualitative study using interviews and participant observation (it comes from our study on homeless adolescents' health concepts, see Flick and Röhnsch 2007). Such a timescale can have two functions. In a proposal forming an application for funding, it will demonstrate how much time is needed and for what in order to convince the funding agency that the budget you ask for is justified. In designing the research (see below), the timescale will help to orient you towards planning the project.

BOX 5.1

Timescale for a research project (Flick and Röhnsch 2007)

Work step	Month of project																							
	[1]	[2]	[3]	[4]	[5]	[6]	[7]	[8]	[9]	[10]	[11]	[12]	[13]	[14]	[15]	[16]	[17]	[18]	[19]	[20]	[21]	[22]	[23]	[24]
Literature research	■	■	■	▨																				
Development of instruments and pre-test		■	■	■																				

Work step	Month of project																							
	[1]	[2]	[3]	[4]	[5]	[6]	[7]	[8]	[9]	[10]	[11]	[12]	[13]	[14]	[15]	[16]	[17]	[18]	[19]	[20]	[21]	[22]	[23]	[24]
Fieldwork: finding participants and data collection (e.g. interviews)						■	■	■	■															
Transcription							■	■	■	■														
Fieldwork: participant observation				■	■	■	■	■	■															
Writing observation protocols				■	■	■	■	■	■															
Analysis of interviews								■	■	■	■	■	■	■	■	■	📖							
Analysis of observation protocols										■	■	■	■	■	■	■	■	■						
Linking back the results to the literature																■	■	■	■	■	■			
Final report and publications																					■	■	■	📖

📖 = Milestones

For making the research (and, beforehand, the proposal) work, the following guidelines should be kept in mind:

- You should try to make the design of your research and the methods as explicit, clear and detailed as possible.

- The research questions, and the relevance of planned procedures and expected data and results for answering them, should also be as explicit and clear as possible.

- The study and the expected results and implications should be placed in their academic and practical contexts.

- Ethics and procedures should be reflected as far as possible.

- Methods should be made explicit not only in the how (of their use) but also in the why (of their selection).
- Ensure that plans, timelines, existing experiences and competences, methods and resources all fit into a sound program for your research.

Designing a Study

A central concept in research planning is the research design, which Ragin defines as follows:

> Research design is a plan for collecting and analyzing evidence that will make it possible for the investigator to answer whatever questions he or she has posed. The design of an investigation touches almost all aspects of the research, from the minute details of data collection to the selection of the techniques of data analysis. (1994, p. 191)

When you construct or use a specific research design, the aims are first to make answering the research question possible and to control the procedures. 'Control' here refers to the means of keeping the conditions of the study constant, so that differences in the replies of two participants can be rooted in their own differences (in their attitudes, for example) and do not result from the fact that the participants were asked in different ways. This in turn requires you to keep the conditions of the study constant and to define your sampling procedures (who is selected and why: see below).

In quantitative research, another aim of research designs is to control external variables. This refers to factors which are not part of the relations that are studied but influence the phenomenon under study. If you study the effects of a medication on the course of a certain disease, you should make sure that other factors (e.g. specific features of some patients, or eating during the treatment) do not influence the course of the disease. One way to control such external variables is to use homogeneous samples (see below). Thus you will select patients who are very similar in their most relevant characteristics (e.g. men of 50–55 years with specific professions). The disadvantage of such a homogeneous sample is that you can only generalize the results to people who also fulfill the criteria of the sample (men of 50–55 years with specific professions). It is more consistent to draw a random sample (see below). The disadvantage here is that the sample will need to be rather sizeable if specific features (of subgroups of people) are to be represented in it.

A second way of controlling external influences is to use consistent methods of data collection. This means that the data are collected from all participants in the same way in order to guarantee that differences in the results come from differences in the participants' attitudes and not from differences in the data collection situation. Some of the most common designs in empirical research will be presented below.

Figure 5.1   Control group design

Research Designs in Standardized Research

Control group designs

Let us again begin with an example. In the practice of a hospital, it might be observed that for patients who received a certain medication, the symptoms are reduced and have disappeared by the end of the treatment. This indicates that healing has occurred. To discover whether the improvement of the patients' state is caused by the medication under study, control group designs are often applied. In such a design the medicament is labeled the independent variable. The improvement in the patient's state that it produces is the dependent variable. Note that the term 'dependent' variable refers to the variable which is caused or changed by another variable (the independent variable). In our example, the healing depends on giving the medication. Thus the medication is labeled independent, as it is not influenced by the other variable in this setting; the healing has no effect on the medication.

To find out whether such a relation really exists – that the healing depends on the medication (and not on something else) – you will apply a control group design. Two groups of patients are selected; the members of these groups are comparable in features like diagnoses, age and gender. The intervention group receives the medicament under study. The control group is not given the medicament or receives a placebo (a pill without substance and effects). After the end of the treatment in the first group, you can compare the two groups for whether the treatment was more successful here than in the control group. If in the end both groups show the same changes, the effect cannot be attributed to the medication (see Figure 5.1).

Experimental designs

Control group designs also form the basis of experimental research. Here, to continue our example, the aim is less to find out the effects of a medicament than to test the effects of taking it. Experiments consist of goal-directed acts upon study groups in order to analyze the effects of these acts. An experimental design includes at least two experimental groups, to which the participants are randomly allocated. The independent variable is manipulated by the researcher (Diekmann 2007, p. 337).

In an experimental study, in contrast to a control group design, the medication (independent variable) is given or changed for research purposes. In order to be sure that an observed effect (of healing for example – dependent variable) does not come from the patient knowing 'I am treated', participants are not informed in such a study as to whether they are given the medication or a placebo without effect. Because the patient does not know whether he or she has received medication or a placebo, this design is also called a blind test.

If, in our example, a clear difference becomes evident – that the healing effects in the intervention group can be documented for significantly more patients than in the control group – this could still be due to another influence. It might not be the medication in itself that produces the healing effect, but rather the attention by nurses or doctors associated with the administration of the pill. To be able to exclude this influence, in many medication trials a double blind test is applied. Here both groups receive treatments, the intervention group with the medication and the control group with a placebo, which look identical. To avoid any influence by the nurses or doctors giving the medication – for example, any subconscious signals sending the message that the placebo is without effect anyway – you would not inform the doctors and nurses which is the pill and which the placebo. Neither patients nor doctors and nurses know who has received the medication and who was given the placebo. Thus this design is called a double blind test.

To exclude the influences of other variables as far as possible, experiments are often conducted in laboratories. They are run not in the service routines or in the everyday life of the hospital, but in an artificially designed surrounding. This allows control or exclusion of any external influences as far as possible. The disadvantage is that the results are difficult to transfer to contexts outside the laboratory – i.e. to everyday life.

Pre–post design

Another way of excluding external influencing variables is to do a pre–post measurement with both groups. First the initial situation is measured in both groups (pre-test measurement). Then the study group is given the treatment (intervention). Afterwards, in both groups, the post-test situation is documented. A problem here is that the first measurement might influence the second one, for example due to a learning effect. This means that experience with the tests, measurements or questions might facilitate the reaction in the second measurement – e.g. a question can be answered more easily (see Figure 5.2).

Cross-sectional and longitudinal studies

The designs presented so far aim at controlling the conditions of the study. This allows capturing the state at the moment of the study. Most studies are planned to take a picture of the moment: interviews or surveys, say, are done at one moment in time, for example to analyze the attitude of a specific group

| Pre-test | Intervention | Post-test |

Figure 5.2   Pre–post design

(the French) towards a specific object (a political party). Such picturing is based on a cross-sectional design: a measurement is done to capture the state at a specific moment. In most cases you take a comparative perspective, for example by comparing the attitudes of several subgroups – e.g. those who voted for one political party and those who voted for another party in an election.

However, if processes, courses or developments form the focus of the study, such a cross-sectional design will not be sufficient. Instead you should plan a longitudinal study for documenting a development – for example the attitudes of one or more groups over the years. This attitude is measured repeatedly: for example, the same instruments are used every two years with the same samples in order to find out how attitudes towards a specific political party have changed. If you repeat such surveys not just once but several times, you can produce time series or trend analyses for documenting long term changes in political attitudes.

Longitudinal studies are also interesting if you want to study the influence of a specific event on attitudes or the life course. An example is how the mental illness of a family member develops and how it influences the other family members' attitude to mental illness in general over the years. A problem in this context could be that this process of changing attitudes can only be covered in a comprehensive way when the attitude has been measured for the first time before the event occurred. If this is not possible, often a retrospective study is done instead: after the disease has been diagnosed, the family members are asked about which changes in their attitude to mental illness they had before the illness and which they have now.

Non-standardized Research Designs

Qualitative or non-standardized research pays less attention to research designs and even less to controlling conditions by constructing specific designs. In general, the use of the term 'research design' here refers to planning a study: how to plan data collection and analysis and how to select empirical 'material' (situations, cases, individuals etc.) in order to be able to answer the research question in the available time and with the available resources.

The literature on research designs in qualitative research (see also Flick 2004b, 2008b or 2009, Chapter 12) addresses the issue from two angles. Creswell (1998) presents a number of basic models of qualitative research from which the researchers can select one for their concrete study. Maxwell (2005) discusses the parts of which a research design is constructed. (See Flick 2009, Chapter 12 for more details of what follows.)

Case studies

The aim of case studies is precise description or reconstruction of cases (for more detail see Ragin and Becker 1992). The term 'case' is understood rather broadly here. You can take persons, social communities (e.g. families), organizations, and institutions (e.g. a nursing home) as the subject of a case analysis. Your main problem then will be to identify a case that would be significant for your research question and to clarify what else belongs to the case and what methodological approaches its reconstruction requires. If your case study is concerned with the chronic illness of a child, you have to clarify, for instance, whether it is enough to observe the child in the treatment environment. Do you need to integrate an observation of the family and its everyday life? Is it necessary to interview the teachers and/or fellow pupils?

Comparative studies

Often, rather than observe some single case as a whole and in all its complexity, you will instead observe a multiplicity of cases, focusing on particular aspects. For example, you might compare the specific content of the expert knowledge of a number of people in respect of a concrete experience of illness. Or you might compare biographies of people with a specific illness and the subsequent course of life. Here arises the question of the selection of cases in the groups to be compared.

A further problem is what degree of standardization or constancy is required for those conditions that you are not focusing on. For example, to be able to show cultural differences in the views of health among Portuguese and German women in one study we conducted, we selected interview partners from both cultures. We had to ensure that in as many respects as possible they lived under at least very similar conditions (e.g. big city life, comparable professions, income and level of education) in order to be able to relate differences to the comparative dimension of 'culture' (see Flick 2000b).

Retrospective studies

Case reconstruction is characteristic of a great number of biographical investigations that examine a series of case analyses in a comparative, typology-oriented or contrastive manner (see Chapter 8). Biographical research is an example of a retrospective research design in which, retrospectively from the point in time when the research is carried out, certain events and processes are analyzed in respect of their meaning for individual or collective life histories. Design questions in relation to retrospective research involve the selection of informants who will be meaningful for the process to be investigated. They also involve defining appropriate groups for comparison, justifying the boundaries of the time to be investigated, checking the research question, and deciding which (historical) sources and documents (see Chapter 7) should be used in addition to interviews. Another issue is how to consider the influences of present views on the perception and evaluation of earlier experiences.

Snapshots: analysis of state and process at the time of the investigation

Qualitative research will often focus on snapshots. For example, you might collect different manifestations of the expertise that exists in a particular field at the time of the research in interviews and compare them to one another. Even if certain examples from earlier periods of time affect the interviews, your research does not aim primarily at the retrospective reconstruction of a process. It is concerned rather with giving a description of circumstances at the time of the research.

Longitudinal studies

Qualitative research may involve longitudinal studies, in which one returns to analyze a process or state again at later times of data collection. Interviews are applied repeatedly and observations are extended over sometimes a very long period.

Figure 5.3 presents the basic designs of qualitative research again.

In what follows, I will examine one aspect of planning empirical studies in more detail, namely the question of how to select the participants for a study so that the insights produced will be (generally) valid and representative. Either you start from a big group (e.g. German youth) which cannot be studied empirically in its entirety, and select the cases you study so that the results can later be generalized to the original group or population. This addresses the issue of statistical sampling in quantitative research. Or you want to select those cases which are particularly relevant for answering your research question. This addresses the issue of purposive sampling in qualitative research.

Sampling

Most empirical studies involve making a selection from a group for which propositions will be advanced at the end. If you study the professional stress of nurses, you will address a selection from all the nurses (in the UK, for example) which is too big a group to be studied. All the nurses are the basic population, from which you will draw a sample for your study.

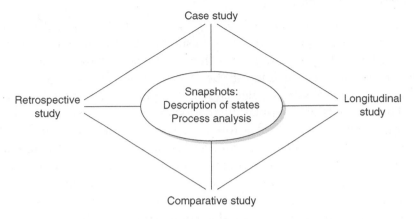

Figure 5.3   Basic designs in qualitative research (Flick 2009, p. 140)

The population is the mass of individuals, cases, events to which the statements of the study will refer and which has to be delimited unambiguously beforehand with regards to the research question and the operationalization. (Kromrey 2006, p. 269)

In exceptional cases you can use the strategy of complete collection, which means all cases of a population are included in the study. The other extreme is to select and study one person in a single case study (see above). In most studies, a sample will be drawn according to one or other of the procedures described below and the results are then generalized to the population. Arguments against complete collection and for sampling are that the latter saves you time and money and allows more accuracy.

Here you should distinguish between sampling elements and the empirical units. The latter refers to the units which you include in your data collection. For example, the sampling elements are several hospitals in which you want to study the emergence of waiting times. The empirical units are specific situations in these hospitals in which waiting times occur or are to be expected, e.g. situations of preparing for surgery. The problem of sampling arises in qualitative and in quantitative studies in a similar way, but it is addressed differently: statistical sampling is typical of quantitative research, while qualitative researchers apply procedures of purposive or theoretical sampling.

Sampling in Quantitative Research

There are a number of requirements for a sample. The sample should be a minimized representation of the population in terms of the heterogeneity of the elements and the representativeness of the variables. The elements of the sample have to be defined. The population should be clear and empirically defined. This means the population has to be clearly limited. Here, we find two alternatives for sampling: random and non-random procedures.

Simple random samples

Often you do not know enough about the constitution or features of the population to make a purposive selection such that the sample is a minimized representation of the population. In such cases it is suggested to draw a random sample. Here, we can distinguish between simple and complex random sampling. An example of simple random sampling is selecting from a card index. The elements of a population are documented in a list or a card index; for example, all inhabitants of a town are registered in a card index at the residents' registration office. You can use this card index for drawing a simple or a systematic random sample. A simple random sample results when every element in the sample is drawn independently in a random process from the population. One example here is to use a lottery drum: all postcards in a competition are in a lottery drum and are drawn one after the other. Each time the cards are mixed again before the next is drawn. If we transfer this principle to drawing a sample from a residents' registration file, you would give a number to every entry in this file and make a ticket for each number. All the tickets are mixed in a lottery drum. One after the other you would draw numbers until your sample is complete. This process can be simulated with a computer.

For very large populations, systematic sampling is suggested. The first choice (the first case, the first index card) is selected randomly (by having a throw or by randomly picking a number from a random number table). The other elements to be included in the sample are defined systematically. For example, from a population of 100,000, you draw a sample of 1000 elements. The first number is selected randomly between 1 and 100, e.g. 37. Then, you include systematically every 100th case in the sample (i.e. the cases 137, 237, 337, ..., 99,937).

One disadvantage of such a simple random sample is the difficulty in representing relevant small subpopulations in the sample. In such sampling you will also neglect the context of the single case, i.e. its features beyond the main criterion for its selection, and will lose that for the analyses. To give an example for the first disadvantage: in a population of nurses from which you want to draw a sample, you find an ethnic minority which could be of particular interest for your study. In simple random sampling, the chances are very limited that members of that subgroup will be included at all or in sufficient number. Context information (concerning, say, ethnic minorities) cannot be taken into account systematically in a simple random sample without neglecting its principle.

Systematic random sampling: stratified and cluster sampling

Therefore, more complex or systematic forms of random sampling may be applied by drawing a stratified sample. The intention often is to be able to analyze the data in the sample separately for specific groups – e.g. to compare the data of the ethnic minority with those of all participants. Accordingly, you will divide the population into several subpopulations (in our example according to the members' ethnic background). From each of these subpopulations you will then draw a (in most cases simple) random sample. In our example, you would divide the population of the nurses according to their ethnic backgrounds and then draw a random sample from the subgroups of the British, Turkish, African, Korean etc. nurses. If you apply the same sampling procedure to every group and if you take into account the proportion of each subgroup in the population, you will receive a proportionally stratified sample. In the sample, the percentage of each subgroup is exactly the same as in the population. In our example: if you know that the proportion of Turkish nurses is 20% of all nurses and that of the Koreans is 5%, you will draw random samples for each of these groups in the population until you have 20% Turkish and 5% Korean nurses in your sample.

In small samples, the consequence here is that the real number of cases with a Korean background will be very small – for example, one case in a sample size of $n = 20$. This is not sufficient for statistical analyses comparing Korean and other nurses. As a solution, you could extend the sample so that in every subsample there will be enough cases, which will increase the financial and time resources necessary for the study. An alternative is to build a disproportionate stratified sample; this would balance the under representation of a subsample. The sample is drawn in such a way that for every subsample the same number of cases is included. In our example, you would aim at a sample size of 20 cases and in each subgroup you would apply random sampling until you have five cases for each group (British, Turkish, African, Korean nurses).

For taking contexts more strongly into account than in simple random samples, cluster sampling can be applied. In research in schools, you will select the students not as empirical elements but in subgroups like school classes, in which you will collect data and make statements for every member (the individual students). The students are the empirical elements (to whom you apply a questionnaire), the classes are the sampling elements. You will only talk of a cluster sample when the empirical units are not the clusters themselves (i.e. the classes) but their single members (the pupils).

You can also draw samples in stages, working on a number of levels. For example, you will first make an overview of the location of all schools for nursing, from which you draw a simple random sample. Then you will divide the selected schools into units roughly of the same size, e.g. classes. From all of these classes, you draw another random sample. This sample is then divided into subgroups according to their performance, for example (such as all students with an average grade of better than 5, all with grades between 4 and 2, and all with 2 and worse). From these subgroups you will again draw a random sample, which finally constitutes the group of those treated with a questionnaire.

The big advantage of random sampling is that the samples drawn in this way are representative for all features of the empirical elements. A non-random sample can only claim to be representative for the features according to which it was drawn.

Non-random sampling: haphazard, purposive and quota sampling

It is not always possible or even desirable to draw a random sample. Nevertheless, sampling should be as systematic as possible. A relatively unsystematic method of sampling is haphazard sampling. Here we do not have a defined sampling plan or framework, according to which we decide which elements of the population are integrated in the sample. An example is the person-on-the-street interview, in which everyone passing by at a specific moment and ready to be interviewed is integrated in the sample. The decision is taken haphazardly, i.e. not according to defined criteria.

A different strategy is purposive sampling. For example, you do a study in which experts will be interviewed, and define criteria according to which someone is an expert for the issue of the study or not. Then you will search for individuals who meet these criteria. If their number is big enough, you can apply a questionnaire to them, which will be analyzed statistically. The sampling from the population of all experts for this issue is not random. Due to the applied criteria, this is not a haphazard sampling either. In most cases, however, you have to assume that the experts are typical cases (of experts). Then the problem arises, how to decide whether the individual case is a typical case or not. Often, this definition is set by the researchers. For this definition, they need enough knowledge about the population to be able to decide whether a case is typical or not. Whether experts are typical experts for this issue can often only be decided at the end of the study by comparing them with other experts. Therefore the sampling here is often done by using substitute criteria – e.g. professional experience in a specific position. But this again assumes a link between expertise and professional experience.

In addition, you may apply the concentration principle. This means you focus in the sampling on those cases which are particularly important for the issue of the study. The cases are selected according to their relevance – either the very rare cases, which have the strongest influence on the process under study, or those cases that can be found most often, for example.

Survey research often uses the technique of quota sampling. Here, specific features (e.g. age and gender) are defined by which the participants should be characterized. For these features, you will then define quotas of the values of these features, which will be represented in the sample at the end. For example, the distribution of gender might be four to six, i.e. in 10 interviews four men and six women will be included. Age groups might be distributed in a way that in 10 interviews two participants are younger than 30 years, three are older than 60, and five are between 30 and 60 years. In these quotas, you will then search participants haphazardly – i.e. not randomly. If this procedure works, some conditions should be specified. The distribution of the quota features (in our example age and gender) in the population has to be known. A sufficient relation between the quota features and the features to be studied (e.g. health behavior) has to be given or assumed. The quota features have to be easy to assess.

Finally, you can use the principle of snowballing: that is, you ask your way from the first participant to the next ('Who do you think could be relevant for this study, too?'). Often, for practical reasons, this is the best or only way to arrive at a sample. The representativity of this sample, however, is rather limited.

Sampling Strategies in Qualitative Research

In qualitative research, some of the sampling strategies discussed in the previous paragraphs are applied. Others, however, such as random sampling, are seldom found. Here as well you can use quotas (of age or gender) or haphazard or purposive sampling (of experts for example). Principles of snowballing or of concentration are used as well. Some unique principles can refine and systematize these approaches for the specific aims of qualitative research.

Theoretical sampling

If the aim of the research is to develop a theory, strategies of sampling are likely to be based on 'theoretical sampling' as developed by Glaser and Strauss (1967). Decisions about choosing and putting together empirical material (cases, groups, institutions etc.) are made in the process of collecting and interpreting data. Glaser and Strauss describe this strategy as follows:

> **Theoretical sampling is the process of data collection for generating theory whereby the analyst jointly collects, codes and analyses his data and decides what data to collect next and where to find them, in order to develop his theory as it emerges. This process of data collection is controlled by the emerging theory. (1967, p. 45)**

Here you select individuals, groups and so on according to their (expected) level of new insights for the developing theory in relation to the state of theory elaboration so far. Sampling decisions aim at the material that promises the greatest insights, viewed in the light of the material already used, and the knowledge drawn from it. The main question for selecting data is: '*What* groups or subgroups does one turn to *next* in data collection? And for *what* theoretical purpose? … The possibilities of multiple comparisons are infinite, and so groups must be chosen according to theoretical criteria' (1967, p. 47).

Sampling and the integration of further material are complete when the 'theoretical saturation' of a category or group of cases has been reached (i.e. nothing new emerges any more). In contrast to a statistically oriented sampling, theoretical sampling does not refer to a population whose extent and features are already known. You also cannot define in advance how big the sample to

Table 5.3 Theoretical and statistical sampling

Theoretical sampling	Statistical sampling
Extent of the basic population is not known in advance	Extent of the basic population is known in advance
Features of the basic population are not known in advance	Distribution of features in the basic population can be estimated
Repeated drawing of sampling elements with criteria to be defined again in each step	One-shot drawing of a sample following a plan defined in advance
Sample size is not defined in advance	Sample size is defined in advance
Sampling is finished when theoretical saturation has been reached	Sampling is finished when the whole sample has been studied

Source: Wiedemann 1995, p. 441

be studied has to be. The features of both the population and the sample can only be defined at the end of the empirical study on the basis of the theory that was developed in it.

The main features of theoretical and statistical sampling strategies are compared in Table 5.3.

Purposive sampling

Patton (2002) suggests the following variants of purposive sampling:

- Extreme cases, which are characterized by a particularly long process of development or by the failure or success of an intervention.

- Typical cases, which are typical for the average or the majority of potential cases. Here, the field is explored rather from the inside, from the center.

- Maximum variation sampling includes a few cases which are as different as possible, for analyzing the variety and diversity in the field.

- Intensity sampling includes cases which have a different intensity of the relevant features, processes or experiences or for which you assume such differences. Either way, you will include and compare cases with the highest intensity or with different intensities.

- Critical cases, which show the relations under study particularly clearly or which are very relevant for the functioning of a program under study. Here, you often look for advice from experts about which cases to choose.

- Politically important or sensitive cases can be useful for making positive results widely known.

- Convenience sampling refers to choosing those cases that are most easily accessible under given circumstances. This can reduce the effort in sampling. Sometimes this is the only way to do a study with limited resources of time and with difficulties in applying a more systematic strategy of sampling.

Summary

Sampling refers to strategies for assuring that you have the 'right' cases in your study. 'Right' means that they allow generalization from the sample to the population because the sample is representative of the population. For example, the results from a questionnaire study with a sample of youth should be able to be generalized to youth in Germany. 'Right' can also mean that you have found and included the most instructive cases in your interviews – that you have the range of health experiences of homeless adolescents, rather than that your results are valid for youth in Germany in general (see the examples in Chapter 2).

These sampling strategies are a major step in research planning. Some research designs will need one or the other form of sampling. Experiments, control group or double blind studies need random sampling to be successful. For a non-standardized, theory developing qualitative study, strategies of theoretical or purposive sampling are more appropriate. The same is the case for the models of the research process that we discussed earlier: random and similar forms of sampling are more suitable for the process model of quantitative research; theoretical and purposive sampling are better suited to the qualitative research process.

Evaluation

What has been said so far refers to empirical research as a whole. Let us now focus on one specific area of social research, namely evaluation. Here, the focus is on the assessment of interventions with empirical methods. Evaluation research was developed in the context of social politics in the US and has since been extended to education, health, therapy and politics in general. Several phases can be distinguished (see Guba and Lincoln 1989). The first phase (early twentieth century) was strongly oriented towards measurement (of performance in school, similar to natural science research). The second phase (1920–1940) focused on the exact description of processes (e.g. of promoting pupils' performance). The third phase (1950s–1970s) saw evaluation essentially as assessment and made it an instrument of the state's welfare and social policy. The focus was extended to the use and usefulness of the results obtained in this way, in addition to the scientific quality of the evaluation. The fourth phase (since the 1980s) has been characterized by the concept of responsivity, with a shift in emphasis from scientific quality (as a main criterion) to usefulness of evaluation.

This shift is embedded in a turn to qualitative and more dialogical methods of evaluation:

> **Evaluation practices based in a value-critical framework decenter [the] conception of the aim, nature, and place of social inquiry in social life. They do so by redefining social inquiry as a dialogical and reflective process of democratic discussion and philosophical critique. (Schwandt 2002, p. 151)**

Evaluation in general still addresses the question of how and with what efforts the aims (of an intervention, for example) are reached, and which undesirable side effects occur. Thus evaluation is the use of research methods with the aim of empirically grounded assessments of interventions and their success and consequences. Evaluations are often commissioned to researchers. Commissioned evaluations aim at answering the issue of assessment in a transparent and unambiguous way. An essential here is that the results are elaborated and presented in such a way that non-experts (of research) can also understand them (see Chapter 13).

We can distinguish between self-evaluation and external evaluation. In the first case an institution organizes the evaluation of one of its programs or departments by hiring employees for this purpose. In external evaluation, an independent research team or institute will be asked to do the evaluation, which may lead to more reliable and independent results. If you intend to do an evaluation, you will not only need skills in research methods but also have communicative competencies for successfully negotiating your way in and through the institution. A further distinction here is between summative and formative evaluation. The first is located after the end of a program and focuses on its outcomes; the latter addresses the introduction and proceedings of the program.

Checklist for Designing an Empirical Study

For planning your own empirical project, you should take into account the aspects shown in Box 5.2 and find answers to the questions that arise. This checklist may help you in planning your own study and also for assessing the existing studies of other researchers

---

BOX 5.2

Checklist for designing an empirical study

1. Write a proposal for your project to indicate which steps it should run through.
2. Develop a timescale for your project in order to ascertain whether you can manage it in the available or given timeframe.
3. Do the proposal and the timescale cover the main steps of your project?
4. Is the design you chose adequate for the aims of your study and for the conditions in the field you study?
5. Is the form of sampling you want to apply appropriate for reaching the goals of your study and also for reaching the target groups of your study?
6. If you do an evaluation – is your research plan adequate for this purpose?

■ ■ Further Reading ■

Issues of designing social research in a quantitative approach are discussed by the first and last textbooks, while the other two focus on this issue for qualitative studies.

Bryman, A. (2008) *Social Research Methods*, 3rd edn. Oxford: Oxford University Press.

Flick, U. (2008) *Designing Qualitative Research*. London: Sage.

Flick, U. (2009) *An Introduction to Qualitative Research*, 4th edn. London: Sage. Part 3.

Neuman, W.L. (2000) *Social Research Methods: Qualitative and Quantitative Approaches*, 4th edn. Boston: Allyn and Bacon.

CHAPTER 6
DECIDING ON YOUR METHODS

Chapter Overview

Chapter Objectives

This chapter is designed to help you:

- understand the series of decisions required in the research process
- appreciate that selecting a specific method of data collection is an important decision – though only one of many
- see how your decisions concerning methods are related to more general issues concerning (a) your research, (b) the conditions in the field, and (c) available knowledge about the issue.

Table 6.1 Navigator for Chapter 6

Orientation	• What is social research? • Research question • Literature review
Planning and design	• Planning research • Designing research • Deciding methods
Working with data	• Gathering data • Analyzing data • E-research • Integrated research
Reflection and writing	• Evaluating research • Ethics • Writing and using research

You are here in your project →

Decisions in the Research Process

In Chapter 4, I outlined the steps involved in quantitative and qualitative research processes. In the chapters that follow, the most important methods will be discussed in more detail (see Chapters 7 and 8). Both qualitative and quantitative research entails a series of decisions you will need to take – from defining your research question to collecting and analyzing data and finally to presenting your results. Each decision will have implications for subsequent stages in your research project.

Overviews of methods in social research rarely provide much advice on the choice of specific research methods. This chapter aims to make good that lack.

Decisions in Standardized Research

Selecting the Research Problem

The first decision you need to make concerns the selection of a research problem. This will have major implications for the subsequent procedures. Bortz and Döring (2006) have formulated a number of criteria for evaluating research problems or ideas for studies. These can be used to inform your decision. Their criteria are:

- Precision in the formulation of the problem: how vaguely or exactly is the idea articulated? How clear are the concepts on which it is based?

- Can the problem be studied empirically? Can the ideas be addressed empirically, or are they based on religious, metaphysical or philosophical content (e.g. concerning the meaning of life)? And how likely is it that sufficient potential participants can be reached without excessive effort?

- Scientific scope: has the topic already been studied so comprehensively that no new insights can be expected from further investigations?

- Ethical criteria: would the study violate any ethical principles (as discussed in Chapter 12) or, seen the other way around, is the study ethically justified?

These criteria will help both to assess your research ideas and to justify your selection.

BOX 6.1

Decision quant-1: research problem

Your decision at this point concerns the research problem as such and those aspects of it that will be in the foreground of your study. They should be oriented to your interests and to how far you can formulate them empirically. Furthermore, you should assess whether the existing knowledge about the problem is sufficient for doing a standardized study and whether you will be able to access a sufficient number of participants. Decisions at this stage will subsequently have an influence on your methodological decisions.

Aims of the Study

Quantitative studies usually aim at testing an assumption that has been formulated in advance in the form of a hypothesis. Here the aim will be to assess the connections between variables or to identify the causes of specific events. One should be careful here not to assert a relationship or causal link between variables without evidence to justify the assertion. Thus there will need to be a strong emphasis, when planning and designing the study, on standardizing as many conditions as possible and on defining variables.

It is important to distinguish between independent and dependent variables (see also Chapter 5). The 'causing' condition is labeled the 'independent variable' and the consequences the 'dependent variable'. For example, an infection will be the cause of certain symptoms. The symptoms occur due to the infection. Thus they depend on the existence of the infection and are therefore treated as dependent variables. The infection is independent of the symptoms: it just occurs. It is therefore treated as the independent variable. Sometimes this relation is not so immediate. Other factors may play a role: for example, not everyone exposed to an infection falls ill; some people have more dramatic symptoms due to an infection; and others have less dramatic symptoms despite the same infection. Thus one must suppose that other variables are relevant. These are called intervening variables. This term is a label for those other influences on the connection between independent and dependent variables. In our example, the social situation of the infected persons can be such an intervening variable. (For example, socially disadvantaged people may be more likely to develop stronger symptoms than people in better living situations.) Testing the relationship between the independent and dependent variables can be your aim – in our example, the relation between infection and disease (as seen from the symptoms) and thus the identification of the infection as the cause of the disease. In this example it will be important to control the influence of the intervening variable.

Another aim of a quantitative study can be to describe a state or situation – e.g. the frequency of a disease in the population or in various subpopulations. Such studies are known as 'population description studies', as distinct from 'hypothesis testing studies' (Bortz and Döring 2006, p. 51). When the state of research and the theoretical literature are not sufficiently developed for you to formulate hypotheses that you can test empirically, you may first conduct an exploratory study. In this kind of study you may develop concepts, explore a field, and end up by forming hypotheses based on the exploration of the field.

BOX 6.2

Decision quant-2: aims

Your decision on the type of study you will pursue should be determined by your research interest and the state of the research before your study. The relevant question at this stage is: how far is your decision determined by the issue and the field you study? Or is it (mainly) influenced by your general methodological orientation?

Theoretical Framework

Theoretical questions can become an issue for decisions on a number of levels. You should take as your starting point a specific theoretical model of the issue that you intend to study. Often a number of alternative models will be available. For example, if your study concerns coping behavior in the case of a disease, there are several different models of coping behavior to select from. Moreover, the study can be planned within the framework of a general theoretical model or a research program. For example, in the case of studying coping behavior, one might adopt a rational choice approach.

Formulating the Research Question

For the success of any study, it is important to limit the chosen research problem to a research question that is manageable. For example, if you are interested in the research problem 'Health of senior citizens', this is not yet a research question, as it is too vast and vague. To turn it into a research question, you will have to focus on the parts of the problem formulation. Which aspect of health do you want to study? What kind of senior citizens are the focus of your study? What is the link between health and older people? Then you may arrive at a question like: 'Which factors delimit the autonomy of people over 65 with depression living in big cities and in rural contexts?' Here the elements of your research question are clearly defined and you can start to consider how you will do your sampling and data collection for approaching this question empirically. If you want to do a quantitative study, you should reflect on whether there will be enough people for you to address and whether they will be capable of filling in a survey etc., and how this survey will cover issues of autonomy, of limitations, of living conditions (city, countryside) and of depression (see Chapter 2 for more examples and distinctions between good and bad research questions).

At this stage, it is important that the formulation of your research question helps you to orient your research. It is also important how far your research question is helpful for stimulating new insights about your research issue so that your study does not simply reproduce knowledge already available from other research.

Resources

A key factor is the cost of a study. Without detailed knowledge about the project, an estimate of the cost will be difficult to make. In general, the higher the methodological standards, the greater the cost. Denscombe (2007, p. 27) mentions in this context that commercial survey institutes in Britain inform their customers that for a certain price a specific level of exactness in measurement and sampling can be expected, and that higher levels will incur higher prices. Accordingly, Hoinville et al. state in the case of sampling that 'In practice, the complexity of the competing factors of resources and accuracy means that the decision on sample size tends to be based on experience and good judgment rather than relying on a strict mathematical formula' (1985, p. 73).

BOX 6.5

Decision quant-5: resources

Your decision in this context generally refers to weighing your available resources (money, time, experience, wo/manpower) against methodological claims (of exactness and scope of the sampling, for example) so that you can make your project work with realistic claims.

Sampling and Building of Comparative Groups

Sampling in quantitative research mostly rests on concern for the representativeness of the studied persons, situations, institutions or phenomena for the wider population. Often one will construct comparative groups so that they match each other as far as possible (for example, the study group will be constructed like the control group as much as possible). The aim here is to control and standardize as many features of the group as possible; then differences between groups can be traced back to the variable that you are studying. The most consistent approach is random sampling, in which the allocation to the study group or the control group is also done randomly (see Chapter 5). However, strictly random sampling is not always the best or most appropriate way. Depending on the issue and field you study, quota or cluster sampling may be more appropriate (see Chapter 5), as the focus of strictly random sampling may be insufficiently specific.

BOX 6.6

Decision quant-6: sampling and comparison

Your decisions here are related to the question of the appropriateness of a specific form of sampling. How far does this allow taking specific target groups of your study sufficiently into account?

Methods

Decisions concerning methods need to be made on a series of levels. The first concerns the character of the data you wish to work with. Ask yourself whether you can use existing data (e.g. routine data on health insurance) for your own analysis. Here, one has to consider the question of accessibility of data (for example, not every health insurance company is ready to make its data available for research purposes). Sometimes data protection issues also form obstacles. There will also be questions about the suitability of the data: in particular, you should check whether the issue you are interested in is indeed covered by the data and whether the way the data are classified permits the necessary analysis (see Chapter 7).

Next you should decide between survey and observation. For example, when collecting data about the relevant phenomena, are you interested more in knowledge and attitudes or in practices?

The next decision to be made is whether for data collection you use an existing instrument or develop a new one. The advantages of the first alternative are that these methods are mostly well tested and that you can more easily link your data to other studies. For example, in quality of life research, existing questionnaires are often used; similarly, in attitude research, interactions are often analyzed with available inventories in observations. However, you should check whether the existing instrument covers the aspects that are relevant for your own study and whether it is appropriate for your specific target group.

Developing your own instrument enables you to adapt it to the concrete circumstances of your study. In this case, you should reflect on whether the existing theoretical or empirical knowledge is developed enough for you to formulate the 'right' questions or observational categories. Finally, pre-testing and checking the reliability and validity (as discussed in Chapter 11) of the instrument are necessary before you can actually apply it.

In analyzing quantitative data, existing statistical packages like SPSS are most often used. Here you should decide which kinds of relational analyses are best for answering your research question. Also you should check in advance which tests you should apply to your data – for example, plausibility checks (are there contradictory responses in the dataset, like 20-year-old pensioners?) or checks for missing data (see Chapters 7 and 8)

BOX 6.7

Decision quant-7: methods

Your decision here is between using existing data or instruments and collecting your own data, perhaps with instruments developed specifically for your study. This decision should be related to your research questions, the conditions in the field, and the existing knowledge about the issue under study. Finally, your decisions can be a matter of your resources – such as the time available.

Degree of Standardization and Control

Quantitative research is based on (a) standardizing the research situation and the research procedures and (b) controlling as many conditions as possible. In most cases, variables are defined that are linked in hypotheses for testing these connections. Analytic units are defined (for example, every patient attending a general practitioner's surgery). Concrete measures are defined for the single variables (for example, the time that each patient waits before he or she is called into the treatment room to see the doctor). These are defined before entering the field and are then applied to every case in an identical way. This is intended to ensure the standardization of the research and the control over the conditions in the research situation as far as possible.

BOX 6.8

Decision quant-8: standardization and control

Your decisions in this context refer to how far you can or should advance with standardizing and controlling. Experimental studies are most systematic when seen from a methodological point of view. However they cannot be applied to every field and every issue. Other study forms are less standardized and controlled, but can more easily fit the conditions in the field under study. The decisions you take in this context concerning more or less standardization and control should be defined both by the conditions in the field and by the aims of your study.

Generalization

Generalization usually involves inference from a small number (of people in the study) to a larger number (of people that could have been studied). Accordingly, generalization may be seen as a numerical or statistical problem. It is closely linked to the question of the (statistical) representativeness of the sample that you have studied for the population that you assumed (as discussed in Chapters 5 and 11). Note here that the 'population' does not necessarily refer to the whole population of a country; in many studies, the term will refer to rather more limited basic populations.

BOX 6.9

Decision quant-9: generalization

Deciding on the specific target population for the purposes of generalization will have consequences for the research design and for the methods that you apply. This decision should be driven by the aims of your study in general and by the conditions in the study field. The general question here is how appropriate is the intended generalization to (a) the issue of your study, (b) the field, and (c) the participants.

Presentation

Who do you want to address with your research and its results? What will be the audience and target group when it comes to presenting your findings? Here, we can distinguish between (a) academic, (b) general, and (c) political audiences. If your study will in the end be presented in a thesis (a master's thesis for example), it will be more important that you demonstrate specific methodological competences than if the results are meant to draw the attention of the general public to a social problem. If your research and its results are intended to have an influence on political decision-making, their presentation will need to be concise, easily understandable, and focused on the essential results (see Chapter 13).

BOX 6.10

Decision quant-10: presentation

Your decisions at this stage concern what kinds of information you should select for the audience you want to address. A second issue is what style of presentation is appropriate for this purpose.

Decisions in Qualitative Research

Selection of the Research Problem

Many factors affect the choice of research problem in qualitative research. It may be that the theoretical literature or empirical research to date is lacking in some way. Alternatively, one might choose a qualitative approach because the participants in question would be difficult to reach through quantitative methods. Another factor influencing the choice may be that the number of potential participants (e.g. people with a specific but rare diagnosis) is small (though not too small). Or one may wish to explore a field to discover something new. The decision over the choice of problem will also involve a consideration of ethical issues (discussed in Chapter 12).

BOX 6.11

Decision qual-1: research problem

Questions you should focus on here are: what is new about the problem under consideration; which aspects of it can be researched empirically and discovered; the limitations of existing research; and whether a sufficient number of participants can be accessed. Your decisions at this stage will influence the methodological steps that you take later in the project.

Aims of the Study

Maxwell (2005, p. 16) has distinguished different types of research aims. There are (a) personal aims such as completing a master's or doctoral thesis; (b) practical aims such as finding out whether a specific program or service works; and (c) research aims concerning the desire for general knowledge on a specific issue.

Qualitative studies often have the aim of developing grounded theory according to the approach of Glaser and Strauss (1967). However, this is an ambitious and demanding aim. If you are writing a bachelor degree thesis, this aim may well be unrealistic: you may not have the time or experience required. It may be more realistic to aim instead to provide a detailed description or evaluation of some ongoing practices. Overall, qualitative research may aim to provide description or evaluation or to develop theory.

BOX 6.12

Decision qual-2: aims

Your decision concerns which aims you can *realistically* pursue with your study.

Theoretical Framework

In qualitative research, it may be that you do not use a theoretical model of the issue under study to provide a starting point for determining the actual questions you use (or those you ask in an interview). Nevertheless, studies should be related to previous theoretical and empirical work on the issue in question. The current state of extant research should influence your subsequent methodological and empirical procedures. In qualitative research there may be a number of frameworks for studying an issue: for example, it may be that you can analyze either (a) subjective views and experiences or (b) interactions related to the topic in question.

BOX 6.13

Decision qual-3: theoretical framework

When you decide the research perspective and the substantive points of the research, you will in effect be committing yourself to proceeding in certain ways. In doing so, you should take as your points of reference the knowledge available to you and the conditions in the field you study.

Formulating the Research Question

We can distinguish between (a) research questions where the answers focus on the possible confirmation of an assumption or a hypothesis, and (b) questions designed to discover new aspects. Strauss (1987) calls the latter 'generative questions'. He defines them as 'Questions that stimulate the line of investigation in profitable directions; they lead to hypotheses, useful comparisons, the collection of certain classes of data, even to general lines of attack on potentially important problems' (1987, p. 22).

In qualitative research, Maxwell (2005) has proposed alternative distinctions. He distinguishes first between generalizing and particularizing questions, and second between questions that focus on distinctions and those that focus on the description of processes. Generalizing questions place the issue under study in a wider context – for example, as the biography of a person or a group could be understood against the background of a political turmoil. Particularizing questions foreground some specific aspect – for example, a specific event, such as the onset of illness. Questions focusing on distinction address differences in the knowledge of people – say several patients' differences in knowing about their illness. Questions focusing on describing a process look at how such knowledge develops in a group of patients in the progress of their illness.

BOX 6.14

Decision qual-4: research question

Selecting a research question entails decisions about both what exactly you will be studying and also what you will be excluding from your study. This will have implications subsequently for your choice of methods for data collection and analysis.

Resources

When one is elaborating a research design, the resources required (time, persons, technologies, competencies, experiences) are often underestimated. In research proposals, it is common to see a mismatch between work packages envisaged and the personal resources that have been requested. To plan a project realistically, you need to assess accurately the work to be undertaken.

For example, for an interview lasting 90 minutes, it is recommended that you allow an equivalent amount of time for recruiting the interviewee, organizing the appointment etc. For calculating the time needed for transcribing the interviewees, estimates vary according to the degree of exactness of the transcription rules that are applied. Morse (1998, pp. 81–2), for example, suggests that for fast-writing transcribers, the length of the tape containing the interview recording be multiplied by a factor of four. If checking the finished transcript against the tape is also included, the length of the tape should be multiplied by a total of six. For the complete calculation of the project she advises doubling the time, to allow for unforeseen difficulties and 'catastrophes'. Example plans for calculating time schedules or empirical projects may be found in Marshall and Rossman (2006, pp. 177–80) and Flick (2008b).

BOX 6.15

Decision qual-5: resources

In decisions in this context, you should above all take the relation of available resources and the aims or the planned efforts of the study into account. This should help you to ensure that the data you collect is not too complex and differentiated for you to be able to analyze them in the time available.

Sampling and Building of Comparative Groups

Decisions about sampling in qualitative research above all refer to persons or situations in data collection. Sampling decisions become relevant again for the parts of the collected material that you will address with extended interpretations when analyzing your data. For the presentation of your research, sampling concerns what you present as exemplary results or interpretations (see Flick 2009, p. 115). Sampling decisions here are not normally taken according to abstract criteria (as in random sampling), but rather according to substantive criteria referring to concrete cases or case groups.

A major task for the sampling decisions is to build comparative groups. Here you need to decide on what level you want to do your comparisons. For example, will your focus be the differences and similarities between persons and institutions, or between situations and phenomena?

BOX 6.16

Decision qual-6: sampling and comparison

Here you make decisions about the persons, groups or situations that you will include in your study. The decisions should be oriented on the relevance of who or what you select for your study. They should also be oriented on having enough diversity in the phenomena you study. If that is your topic, you should look for people with a *specific* illness experience (and not just people who are sick in some way or another). At the same time your selection should provide for some diversity, for example people living in different social circumstance with this illness experience and not just people living under the same conditions.

Methods

The central distinction here is between (a) direct analysis of what occurs and (b) analysis of reports about what has occurred. The former will involve (participant) observation or interaction studies. In the latter case, you will work with interviews with or narratives of the participants. You can decide between different degrees of openness or structuredness: data collection can rely on questions formulated in advance or on narratives; observation is either structured or open and participant. The analysis of data can be oriented on categories (sometimes defined in advance) or on the development of the text (of the narrative or of the interaction protocol: see Chapters 7 and 8).

BOX 6.17

Decision qual-7: methods

Your decision here concerns the level of the data (report or observation) and the degree of openness or structure in the data collection and analysis. Other points of reference – besides your research question and the particular conditions in the field – will be the aims of your study and the resources available.

Degree of Standardization and Control

Miles and Huberman (1994, pp. 16–18) distinguish between tight and loose research designs in qualitative research. Tight research designs involve narrowly restricted questions and strictly determined selection procedures. The degree of openness in the field of investigation and the empirical material will remain limited. The authors see such designs as appropriate when researchers lack experience of qualitative research, when the research operates on the basis of narrowly defined constructs, or when it is restricted to the investigation of particular relationships in familiar contexts. In such cases, they see loose designs as a detour to the desired result. Loose designs are characterized by less defined concepts and have, in the beginning, hardly any fixed methodological procedures. Tight designs make it easier to decide which data are relevant for the investigation. They make it easier to compare and summarize data from different interviews or observations.

BOX 6.18

Decision qual-8: standardization and control

In qualitative research, standardization and control play a minor role compared to the case in standardized research. However, you can try to reduce the variety in your material and try to focus your approach as far as possible (producing tight designs). Alternatively, you can reduce standardization and control if you decide on a more open and less defined approach (loose design). Both have their advantages and disadvantages.

Generalization

With qualitative research, aims may vary – for example, between (a) providing a detailed analysis of a single case in as many of its aspects as possible, or (b) comparing several cases, or (c) developing a typology of different cases. The generalization involved is likely to be theoretical rather than numerical. The important consideration is more likely to be the diversity of cases considered or the theoretical scope of the case studies than the number of cases included. To develop a theory can be a form of generalization on various levels as well. This theory can refer to the substantive area that was studied (e.g. a theory of trust in counseling relationships). Generalization can be advanced by developing a formal theory focusing on broader contexts (e.g. a theory of interpersonal trust related to various contexts). This distinction between substantive theory and formal theory was suggested by Glaser and Strauss (1967).

BOX 6.19

Decision qual-9: generalization

Your decision concerning the kind of generalization that you aim for will have implications for planning your study and in particular for your selection of cases. This decision should take account of the aims of your study and at the same time the question of what is possible in the field that you study. It should take account of the situation of the possible participants. More generally, the question arises of how appropriate the type of generalization that you are aiming at will be for the field under study.

Presentation

Finally you should take into account in your planning the questions of presentation. Will the empirical material form the basis for an essay or a narrative with a more illustrative function? Or is your aim to provide a systematic study of the cases under study and the variations between them? You need to consider here the assessment criteria that will be applied for your thesis. In general, the question will be how to relate concrete statements and evidence to more general or deepening interpretations so that your inferences are substantiated in a clear and convincing way. (Questions of presentation will be discussed in more detail in Chapter 13.)

BOX 6.20

Decision qual-10: presentation

You should carefully decide how you will present your research. It is important that you not only present some results. You should also make transparent how you entered the field, how

---

you got in touch with the relevant people, and how you arrived at gathering the data you needed for your analysis. It is also important that your readers have access to the way you gathered your data and to how you analyzed them. The path from the original data to the more general (comparative, analytic) statements and conclusions should be elucidated with examples in the methods section of your report and with enough original material (quotes) in its results section. Illustrations with sample materials but also with charts or tables can be very helpful here.

Figure 6.1   Decisions in the research process

Decisions within Quantitative and Qualitative Research

In standardized research, the decision process outlined in the first part of this chapter is intended to help select the alternatives in the procedure and to apply them to a greater or lesser extent to the issue of your study. Each of the decisions delimits the perspective you take on what you study and defines which parts of this issue you can cover in your data and in their analysis. In qualitative research as well as in quantitative research, we can describe the process as a series of decisions. Planning a research project involves making a series of decisions that serve to foreground some aspects and exclude others. The decisions require consideration of interrelated questions concerning your field of study, the issue to be researched, the theoretical context, and the methodology involved.

The decisions discussed in this chapter so far are summarized in Table 6.2. These decisions (displayed in Figure 6.1) will inform the shaping of the research design and of the research process in its further steps.

Table 6.2   Decisions in quantitative and qualitative research

Decision	Quantitative study	Qualitative study
Research problem	Enough existing knowledge? Enough participants accessible?	What is new about the problem? Enough participants accessible?
Aims	Study type Research interest State of the research	Knowledge interest and practical aims?
Theoretical framework	Model as a basis for operationalization?	Research perspective taken?
Research questions	Helpful for working with the research problem?	Delimiting the research question?
Resources	Methodological claims in relation to money, time etc.	Is it possible to analyze the collected data in the time framework?
Sampling and comparison	Appropriateness of sampling: are your target groups sufficiently taken into account?	Diversity of the phenomena in the sample?
Methods	Your own or existing methods? New or existing data?	Openness and structure of the data coming from the methods?
Standardization and control	Limits of standardization in the field	Comparability of the differences in groups or fields?
Generalization	How far is a generalization intended?	How far can a generalization be intended?
Presentation	Condensation of the essential aspects?	Understandability and transparency of the procedures?

Deciding between Qualitative and Standardized Research

The following factors provide starting points for deciding between qualitative and quantitative approaches to your empirical project:

- The issue you study and its features should be your major points of reference for such a decision.
- Theoretical approaches have implications for selecting your methodological approaches.
- Your concrete research question will play a major role in defining how you focus your issue conceptually and how you cover it empirically.
- Methodological decisions between qualitative and quantitative methods and designs should be derived from the points of reference just mentioned above. They should not be based simply on the belief that only one or the other version of social research is scientific, acceptable or credible.

- A main reference should be the resources available. (With regard to time, however, note that doing a qualitative analysis consistently and carefully in most cases takes as long as a quantitative study.) Under 'resources' here are included your own methodological knowledge and competences.

Overall, your decision between qualitative and quantitative methodologies should be driven more by your research interest and the features of the field and issue you study than by prior methodological preferences. If it is not possible to decide unequivocally between the two approaches, there may be a case for using a combination of the two (as is discussed further in Chapter 10).

Deciding between Doing Research On-site or Online

As will be discussed further in Chapter 9, quantitative and qualitative approaches may take the form of e-research. You may, for example, conduct a survey, not by mailing out copies of a questionnaire and waiting for them to be returned by post, but doing it on the Internet. You may also consider doing your interviews online instead of face to face. The arguments outlined in the literature concerning the advantages and disadvantages of doing research projects online compared to the traditional way are discussed in detail in Chapter 9.

Deciding on Specific Approaches to Research

Textbooks on social research often provide little help concerning the choice between specific methods for a project. Most books treat each single method or research design separately and describe their features and problems in isolation. In most cases, they fail to provide a comparative presentation, either of methodological alternatives or of the bases for selecting methods appropriate for the research issue in question.

In medicine or psychotherapy, it is usual to check the appropriateness of a certain treatment for specific problems and groups of people. This raises the question of 'indication': one asks whether a specific treatment is 'indicated' (i.e. is appropriate) for a specific problem in a specific case. Similarly in social research we can ask when (in terms of, for example, the research question, field and issue) qualitative methods are indicated and when quantitative methods are indicated instead. For example, it is common practice to study 'quality of life' for people living with a chronic illness. You will find a number of established instruments to measure quality of life (e.g. the SF-36) which are regularly applied for measuring

Table 6.3 Indication of research methods

Psychotherapy and medicine			Social research		
Which disease, symptoms, diagnosis, population	**indicate**	which treatment or therapy?	Which issue, population, research question, knowledge of issue and population	**indicate**	which method or methods?

1. When is a particular method appropriate and indicated?
2. When is which combination of methods appropriate and indicated?
3. How do you make a rational decision for or against certain methods?

quality of life of different populations. The question of indication becomes relevant if you want to use this instrument to study the quality of life of say a population of very old people living in a nursing home who are suffering from a number of diseases (and not just one) and are somewhat disoriented. Then you will see that this well-established instrument finds its limits in the specific features of this target groups: as Mallinson (2002) has shown, the application of this instrument is not at all clear for such a population and the concrete situation in which they are living. The research question – 'What is the quality of life of old people with multiple morbidity in nursing homes?' – is an appropriate one. However, to answer it you may need other methods than the established SF-36 due to the concrete conditions under which you will study it. For this population, a different method (e.g. an open interview) may be more indicated than the common method. This may be different if you study the question of quality of life for a more general population. Then there may be no need to use very open methods and to start from a very open approach in order to develop theories and instruments. Here, enough knowledge about the issue and the population is available to apply standardized and well-established methods. Table 6.3 illustrates this comparison diagrammatically (for more details about this in qualitative research see Flick 2009, Chapter 29).

Reflection Halfway through the Process

Before considering in detail the most common methods available for doing a research project, you might be advised to step back for a moment and reflect on the process of planning so far. Table 6.4 provides a list of guideline questions for examining the consistency and adequacy of your planning to date. Reflecting on these questions will provide a solid foundation for choosing your methods for collecting and analyzing your data.

Table 6.4 Guideline questions for reflecting on your own research project

Issue	Guideline questions	Relevant aspects
Relevance	What is your study important for?	• What theoretical and empirical progress of knowledge do you expect from your results? • What practical relevance do you see for your results?
Clarity	How clearly is your study conceptualized?	• How clear are the aims of your study? • How clearly is the research question formulated?
Background knowledge	What are the bases of your study and of doing it?	• Did you check the state of research and the knowledge about the issue of your research? Do both justify a standardized, hypotheses testing study? Or is there enough of a gap for justifying a qualitative study? • Which methodological skill do you have for doing the study?
Feasibility	Can the study be realized?	• Are your resources (e.g. time) sufficient for doing the study? • Did you clarify the access to the field and the participants? How likely is the possibility of organizing this access? • Are there (enough) people who can answer your questions?
Scope	Is the approach planned too narrowly?	• Will you include cases, groups, events etc. in sufficient diversity? • Will the response rate and the readiness to participate be great enough? • Which generalization can you achieve with your results?
Quality	Which quality claims can be formulated for the results?	• Will you be able to apply the methods consistently? • Will the participants' statements be reliable? • Will the data be sound enough to do the intended analysis with them?
Neutrality	How can you avoid biases and being one-sided?	• Can you approach the field and the participants in an unbiased way, even if you do not share their points of view? • Can you avoid acting for or against certain participants in a one-sided way? • Can you accept the limits of your methodological procedures?
Ethics	Is your research ethically sound?	• Can you proceed in your research without deceiving the participants or doing harm to them? • How can you guarantee anonymity, data protection and confidentiality?

Checklist for Choosing a Specific Method

For selecting your concrete methods, you can take the points in Box 6.21 as an orientation. These questions can be relevant for planning your own project and for assessing the existing studies of other researchers.

Checklist for choosing a specific method

1. How far does your methodological approach fit the aims and theoretical starting points of your study?
2. Do your methods of data collection fit those of analyzing your data?
3. Do your data fit the level of scaling and the calculations you will do with them?
4. Are the methods of analysis to be used appropriate to the level of complexity of the data?
5. What implications do the methods (from sampling to collection and analysis) selected have for the issue of the study and on what is covered in it?
6. Is your decision on certain procedures grounded in the issue and field you study or based on your methodological preferences?
7. Have you assessed which approach(es) are 'indicated'?

Key Points

- In doing social research, whether qualitative or quantitative, you face decisions at each of the steps outlined in Chapter 4.

- The decisions are interrelated. The method of data collection should be taken into account when you decide how to do your analysis.

- The aims of your research – for example, who you want to reach and maybe convince with your results – and the framework conditions (e.g. the resources available and the characteristics of the people or groups and fields you study) also play a role.

- Decisions between qualitative and quantitative approaches should be driven by the issue you study and by your resources.

- The same applies to the decision of whether to conduct your project online or not.

- Checking the 'indication' of research methods provides a starting point for the decisions discussed in this chapter.

Further Reading

The first and last texts listed below take a more integrative approach to the selection of research methods, while the second and third references adopt a qualitative perspective.

Bryman, A. (2008) *Social Research Methods*, 3rd edn. Oxford: Oxford University Press.

Flick, U. (2009) *An Introduction to Qualitative Research*, 4th edn. London: Sage.

Miles, M.B. and Huberman, A.M. (1994) *Qualitative Data Analysis: An Expanded Sourcebook*, 2nd edn. Thousand Oaks, CA: Sage.

Punch, K. (1998) *Introduction to Social Research*. London: Sage.

PART III
WORKING WITH DATA

The central part of a research project consists of collecting and analyzing data. This third part of the book explains these processes.

Chapter 7 introduces three main forms of data collection. The first is the use of questionnaires or interviews; the second is the use of observation; and the third is documentary research. Chapter 8 focuses on three major forms of data analysis. The first is content analysis; the second is descriptive statistics; and the third is interpretative analysis for qualitative data. Case studies are discussed at the end. And Chapter 9 considers the use in research of the Internet, especially for online surveys and interviews and virtual ethnography.

Every method has its limitations and so it can be fruitful to combine methods. Chapter 10 outlines ways to do this through mixed method research, triangulation, and integrated research.

CHAPTER 7
GATHERING DATA: QUANTITATIVE AND QUALITATIVE APPROACHES

Chapter Overview

Chapter Objectives

This chapter is designed to help you:

- understand a range of social research methods for collecting data
- appreciate the similarities and differences, with regard to methods, between qualitative and quantitative research
- assess the methods available to you and what you can achieve with them.

Table 7.1   Navigator for Chapter 7

Orientation	• What is social research? • Research question • Literature review
Planning and design	• Planning research • Designing research • Deciding methods
Working with data	• Gathering data • Analyzing data • E-research • Integrated research
Reflection and writing	• Evaluating research • Ethics • Writing and using research

You are here in your project →

In social research, there are three main forms of data collection: you can collect data through asking people (through surveys and interviews), observing, or studying documents. This chapter outlines each of these methods in turn.

Surveys and Interviews

By way of preparation for understanding the alternatives for asking people, please respond to the questionnaire given in Box 7.1.

BOX 7.1

Questionnaire

Please fill in the following excerpt of a questionnaire for assessing the stress caused by studying according to the following instruction:

'We ask you to answer some questions about your personal situation and about features of your university. Please circle without hesitation how far each of the areas mentioned in the questions is stressful and satisfying for you. Very stressful is indicated by the value 5 in the stress scale, very satisfying by the value 5 in the satisfaction scale. Not stressful or satisfying is indicated by 1 on the respective scale. If one of the areas for you is only stressful or only satisfying, please circle only one of the scales (stressful or satisfying).' If you circle 0, that means this area is neither stressful/nor satisfying for you.

Stressful   Satisfying
   5----4----3----2----1----0----1----2----3----4----5

	Stressful	Satisfying
To study at this university means a limitation of my behavior for me	5----4----3----2----1----0----1----2----3----4----5	
To do exams is for me	5----4----3----2----1----0----1----2----3----4----5	
At the university, contacts often happen	5----4----3----2----1----0----1----2----3----4----5	
At the university, contacts rarely happen	5----4----3----2----1----0----1----2----3----4----5	
The professors and lecturers hardly bother about my studies or my work	5----4----3----2----1----0----1----2----3----4----5	
To spend much (leisure) time for my studies is for me	5----4----3----2----1----0----1----2----3----4----5	
Often I have to decide between family/friends and studying	5----4----3----2----1----0----1----2----3----4----5	
Sometimes I have to do things at the university I do not agree with	5----4----3----2----1----0----1----2----3----4----5	
Much is expected from me	5----4----3----2----1----0----1----2----3----4----5	

Now – again by way of preparation – please use the material in Box 7.2 to interview one of your peer students.

BOX 7.2

Interview about everyday life and studying

I would like to do an interview with you about the issue 'everyday life and studying'. It is important that you answer according to your subjective point of view and express your opinions. I will ask you several questions concerning situations in which you have experience with studying and ask you to recount those situations for me.

First of all I would like to know …

1. What was your first experience with studying here? Could you please give me a concrete example about this?
2. Please tell me about the course of your day yesterday and when your studies played a role in it.
3. When you look at what you do in your time off, what role does your study play in it? Please give me a concrete example for this.

4. If you look at your life in general, do you have the feeling that studying takes a bigger part of it than you expected? Can you outline this by giving me an example?
5. What do you link to the word 'stress'?
6. When you look back: what was your first experience with stress as a student? Could you tell me about' this situation?

What do you find are the differences between these two experiences? Which exercise do you feel would cover the respondent's situation better? Which form gave more room for the respondent's own views? Which one do you think produces the clearer data?

The two research instruments in Boxes 7.1 and 7.2 are adapted from a questionnaire often used for studying stress at the workplace and an episodic interview. They represent contrasting forms of asking people about their situation. The main difference lies in the degree of standardization of the procedure: the questionnaire comes with a predefined list of questions and answers, while the interview is more open ended. In the interview, the questions can be varied in their sequence and interviewees can use their words and decide what they want to refer to in their responses. Below, we discuss both methods in more detail.

Standardized Surveys: Questionnaires

Most surveys are based on questionnaires. These may be answered either in written form or orally in a face-to-face interrogation with a researcher noting the answers. A characteristic of questionnaires is their extensive standardization. The researchers will determine the formulation and sequencing of questions and possible answers. Sometimes a number of open or free text questions, which the respondents may answer in their own words, are included too.

Questionnaire studies aim at receiving comparable answers from all participants. Therefore, the questions as well as the interview situation are designed in an identical way for all participants. When one is constructing a questionnaire, rules for formulating questions and arranging their sequence should be applied.

Question wording

Here, there are three main issues: how to formulate a question, which kinds of question and possible answers are appropriate, and the purpose for asking the questions. Questions should collect, directly or indirectly, the respondents' reasons for a specific behavior or attitude and show their state of information concerning the issue under examination.

How instructive is the information received will depend both on the type of question and on its position in the questionnaire. It will also depend on whether (a) the questions fit the respondent's frame of reference and (b) the respondent's and the interviewer's frames of reference correspond. Finally, the situation, in which a question is asked and should be answered, plays a major role.

If you wish to identify the interviewee's frame of reference, you should ask for reasons to be given (e.g. 'Why did you choose this issue for your studies?'). You will need to take the interviewee's state of information into account: if questions are too complex, they are likely to be misunderstood and produce diffuse answers. Accordingly you should translate complex issues into concrete, clearly understandable questions. Where possible, use colloquial language. Note here that it may not make much sense to incorporate the language of your hypothesis directly into your questions.

Be careful to avoid multidimensional questions, for example: 'How and when did you discover that … ?'. If questions include several dimensions, their comparability will be reduced, because respondents may pick up different dimensions in a question. Also avoid questions with a bias, which suggests a specific answer (suggestive questions), or with certain assumptions. For example, if you are studying burnout processes, the question 'How burnt out by your job do you feel?' assumes that the respondent already feels burnt out. Instead, you should find out through a prior question whether this is in fact the case. Questions should be as short and simple as possible and aligned to the respondent's frame of reference as closely as possible. Double negations should be avoided. So too should unclear or technical terms. For example, rather than ask 'What is your subjective definition of health?', ask 'What do you associate with the word "health"?'.

You should also recognize that the features of the event you are studying will influence the quality of the answers provided. The further in the past an event is, the less exact the answers will be. The more respondents are interested in an issue, the more detailed and accurate the answers will be. The more frightening an event has been for respondents, the more likely it is they will have forgotten it. The more something is linked to social rejection (e.g. times spent in psychiatric wards), the less a person will talk or make statements about it. The higher the value of something (e.g. income, status), the more likely it is that the responses will include overestimates. For closed questions with two possible answers, it is more likely that the second will be given. For questions with a list of possible answers ('list questions'), a person who does not know the answer is likely to select an answer from the lowest third of the list: this is known as the 'position effect'. These and other problems of how to formulate and position a question are dealt with in detail by Neuman (2000, Chapter 10).

		Degree of agreement				
		Not at all				Full
A	Science and technology will be able to solve environmental problems	1	2	3	4	5
B	More economic growth is the most important precondition for solving environmental problems	1	2	3	4	5

Figure 7.1   Five-step answer scale (excerpt from Diekmann 2007, p. 212)

Some texts (e.g. Bortz and Döring 2006, pp. 244–6) provide checklists for assessing standardized oral or written questions. Such checklists include guiding points such as:

- Are all the questions necessary?
- Does the questionnaire include redundant questions?
- Which questions are superfluous?
- Are all the questions formulated easily and clearly?
- Are there negative questions, with answers that could be ambiguous?
- Are the questions formulated too general?
- Will the interviewee be potentially able to answer the questions?
- Is there a risk that the questions will be embarrassing for the interviewee?
- Might the result be influenced by the position of the questions?
- Are questions formulated in a suggestive way?
- Are the opening questions adequately formulated and has the questionnaire a properly reflected end?

Types of questions and of possible answers

Questions can be distinguished according to how they can be answered. Open questions do not come with answers defined in advance, while closed questions already specify the alternatives for answering them. Such alternatives may be specified in the wording of the question (e.g. 'Are most nurses satisfied or unsatisfied by their work?'), which permits only a limited number of answers (in our example, two). A closed question may limit the number of possible answers by use of a scale of agreement, as shown in Figure 7.1. An alternative is to present different possibilities for answering, as illustrated in Box 7.3.

BOX 7.3

Ways of defining possible answers

1. The first alternative is to use a scale. One example is the Likert scale, which includes five possible answers, one of which is neutral ('don't know'). This might be used for the statement, 'Most nurses are unhappy with their work.'

Totally correct	Correct	Don't know	Not correct	Not at all correct
○	○	○	○	○

2. Often, simple questions are presented and multi-step rating scales presented for answering them: 'How happy are you with your work?'

Very satisfied		A bit satisfied		A bit unsatisfied		Very unsatisfied
○	○	○	○	○	○	○
	Satisfied		Neither		Unsatisfied	

3. A third option is to present several possible answers to the question, 'What do you think? Why are nurses unhappy with their work?' (multiple answers possible).

- Unfavorable hours of working   ☐
- Poor pay   ☐
- Emotional stress   ☐
- Stress with colleagues   ☐

It is also possible to present a situation. Here you would list several possible answers to the question, 'What would you do in such a situation?' Or you could ask questions relating to how some other person would react in this situation. Sometimes questionnaires include control questions, which readdress the issues of earlier questions using a different wording. Questions can also be asked indirectly: for example, 'Many people think that nursing as a profession is underrated in our society. Do you think this, too?' Thus you can avoid a direct confrontation with a possibly delicate issue whilst still receiving the interviewee's opinion.

Positioning of questions

Questions may influence each other. That is, how some question is answered may be influenced by the question asked immediately before. This is known as the 'halo effect'. The links between two questions are not necessarily designed deliberately. In general, it is suggested that you group questions from the most general at the start to the most concrete at the end.

Suggestions for how to formulate questions

Porst (2000) has provided '10 commandments' of question wording for surveys. These are given in Box 7.4. His starting point is as follows:

> **Why questions have to be 'good', i.e. methodically and technically faultless, should be self-evident: bad questions lead to bad data and no procedure of weighing and no method of analyzing the data can make good results from bad data. (2000, p. 2)**

The 'commandments' are designed to ensure that questions are clearly formulated and do not over-challenge or confuse respondents. Porst intends these rules to provide an orientation only: 'most of the rules leave room for interpretation and sometimes … are even in competition to each other and thus cannot be applied a hundred percent at the same time' (2000, p. 2).

BOX 7.4

The '10 commandments' of question wording (Porst 2000)

1. You shall use simple unambiguous concepts which are understood by all respondents in the same way!
2. You shall avoid long and complex questions!
3. You shall avoid hypothetical questions!
4. You shall avoid double stimuli and negations!
5. You shall avoid assumptions and suggestive questions!
6. You shall avoid questions aiming at information many respondents presumably will not have available!
7. You shall use questions with a clear reference to time!
8. You shall use answer categories which are exhaustive and disjunct (free of overlap)!
9. You shall assure that the context of a question does not impact on answering it!
10. You shall define unclear concepts!

Practical issues

Often questionnaires are distributed and recipients are asked to send them back within a certain time. In this case, the questionnaire will need to be accompanied by a letter providing sufficient information about the study, explaining its importance, and encouraging the recipient to participate. A major problem is the response rate (i.e. the number of questionnaires which are actually filled in and sent back). It is not only necessary that enough questionnaires are returned (50% would be quite a good ratio here); in addition, enough of those returned must have been filled in *completely*.

Finally you should check how far the distribution of the returned questionnaires corresponds to the distribution in the original sample. To use a simple example: the proportion of men to women in a population is two to one. The selection of the sample and the mailout of the questionnaires have taken this proportion into account. If the proportion that characterizes the distribution in the returned questionnaires is completely different from the proportion in the original sample, the results of the study can be generalized to the population in only a very limited way. An alternative is to decide not to mail out the questionnaires, but instead to do a standardized survey with an interviewer, who visits the participants. This may improve the return of questionnaires, though it will be much more time consuming and expensive.

Example: a youth health survey

The youth health survey has already been described in Chapter 2. It is based on a questionnaire covering the topics in Box 7.5 (see Richter 2003).

BOX 7.5

Topics in the youth health survey

- Demographic information: gender, age, family structure, location, form and grade of school, socioeconomic status, ethnic background.
- Subjective health: psychosomatic complaints, mental health, allergies, life satisfaction etc.
- Risk of accidents and violence: accident injuries, mugging (perpetrator and victim), participation in fights, use of substances (tobacco, alcohol, illegal drugs).
- Eating behavior and diets: eating habits, body-mass-index diets etc.
- Physical activity: sports, physical efforts, inactivity because of television and computer etc.
- Social resources: number of friends, support by parents and peers, family situation, living conditions etc.
- School: performance requirements, quality of teaching, support by parents, fellow students and teachers, friends at school, involvement in the school etc.
- Peer group and leisure activities: frequency of meetings, use of media, membership in associations and organizations etc.

Summary

Questionnaires are appropriate for a study when (a) the knowledge about the issue allows you to formulate a sufficient number of questions in an unambiguous way, and (b) a large number of participants will be involved. Questionnaires are highly standardized. The sequence and formulation of questions are defined in advance, as are the possible answers. Questionnaires are often sent out which may produce problems with the response rates.

Non-standardized Inquiries: Interviews and Focus Groups

We turn now to consider alternative forms of interviews. There are semi-structured interviews: these are based on an interview guide with (sometimes different types of) questions to be answered more or less openly and extensively. There are also narrative-based interviews, which focus on inviting the interviewees to recount (aspects of) their life history. Also we find interviews mixing both questions and narrative stimuli. Finally, there are interviews applied to groups rather than single participants. Focus groups are another form of collecting verbal data. Below we consider some of these types in more detail.

Semi-structured interviews

For semi-structured interviews, a number of questions are prepared that between them cover the intended scope of the interview. For this purpose, you will need to develop an interview guide as an orientation for the interviewers. In contrast to questionnaires, interviewers can deviate from the sequence of the questions. They also do not necessarily stick to the exact formulation of the questions when asking them. The aim of the interview is to obtain the individual views of the interviewees on an issue. Thus questions should initiate a dialogue between interviewer and interviewee. Again in contrast to questionnaires, in an interview you will not present a list of possible answers. Rather, the interviewees are expected to reply as freely and as extensively as they wish. If their answers are not rich enough, the interviewer should probe further.

In constructing an interview guide and doing the interview, four criteria are helpful. These have been provided (initially for focused interviews) by Merton and Kendall (1946). They focus on:

- non-direction in the relation with the interviewee
- specificity of the views and definition of the situation from their point of view
- covering a broad range of meanings of the issue
- the depth and personal context shown by the interviewee.

For this purpose, in most cases a variety of questions are applied. Questions may be open ('What do you link to the word "health"?') or semi-structured ('If you think about what you eat, what role does health play in this context?'). Only rarely are structured questions used, which present a statement that the interviewee is expected to agree with or to reject (e.g. 'Many children are eating in too unbalanced a way. In your everyday life as a teacher, is this your impression too?'). Such statements almost have a suggestive character, though they are used sometimes in this context to stimulate the interviewees to reflect about their position or maybe also to make them explicitly express their distinction from the question or statement. Other elements in a semi-structured interview – such as presenting a fictitious case story with questions referring to it (also known as the 'vignette' technique) – can have a similar function.

Decisive for the success of a semi-structured interview is that the interviewer probes at apposite moments and leads the discussion of the issue into greater depth. At the same time, interviewers should ask all the questions in the interview that are relevant for its issue. Open questions should allow room for the specific, personal views of the interviewees and also avoid influencing them. Such open questions should be combined with more focused questions, which are intended to lead the interviewees beyond general, superficial answers and also to introduce issues that the interviewees would not have mentioned spontaneously.

The construction of an interview should of course be linked closely to the aims and the target group of the research. Expert interviews (see Bogner et al. 2009), for example, focus not so much on the personalities of the interviewees, but rather on the need to retrieve their expertise in a specific area. In contrast, if you interview patients about their illness, the people themselves and their personal experiences will be of greater interest. Accordingly, in the first case the experts will be asked more focused questions, while in the second case the patients will be asked more open questions. In all applications of semi-structured interviews, it is only in the interview situation that you can decide when and how extensively to probe. For this purpose, it can be helpful first to do interview training before the data collection. This will consists of role-plays of practice interviews and of comments by others.

Narrative interviews

A different path to discovering the subjective views of participants is found in the narrative interview. Here, it is not questions that are central. Instead, the interviewees are invited to present longer, coherent accounts (say, of their lives as a whole, or of their disease and its course) in the form of a narrative. The method is prominent in biographical research. Hermanns describes its basic principle of collecting data as follows:

> **In the narrative interview, the informant is asked to present the history of an area of interest, in which the interviewee participated, in an extempore narrative ... The interviewer's task is to make the informant tell the story of the area of interest in question as a consistent story of all relevant events from its beginning to its end. (1995, p. 183)**

The narrative interview comprises several parts – in particular (a) the interviewee's main narrative, following a 'generative narrative question', (b) the stage of narrative probing in which narrative fragments that were not exhaustively detailed before are completed, and (c) the final stage of the interview (known as the 'balancing phase'), consisting of questions that take the interviewees as experts and theoreticians of themselves.

If you aim to elicit a narrative that is relevant to your research question, you must formulate the generative narrative question broadly yet at the same time sufficiently specifically to produce the desired focus. The interest may relate to the informant's life history in general. In this case, the generative narrative question will be rather generalized: for example, 'I would like to ask you to begin with your life history.' Or the interest may lie in some specific, temporal and topical aspect of the informant's biography, e.g. a phase of professional reorientation and its consequences. An example of the type of generative question required here is:

> **I want to ask you to tell me how the story of your life occurred. The best way to do this would be for you to start from your birth, with the little child that you once were, and then tell all the things that happened one after the other until today. You can take your time in doing this, and also give details, because for me everything is of interest that is important for you. (1995, p. 182)**

It is important to ensure that the first question really is a narrative generative question and that the interviewer does not impede the interviewee's storytelling with questions or directive or evaluating interventions. A major test of validity here is the question of whether a narrative really was presented by the interviewee. Here you should take into account that 'It is always only "the story of" that can be narrated, not a state or an always recurring routine' (1995, p. 183).

There is a problem presented here by the role expectations of the parties involved. They include a systematic violation of the usual expectations surrounding an 'interview', because the main part of the narrative interview does not consist of questions in the traditional way. At the same time, expectations pertaining to the situation 'everyday narrative' are also violated, as the extensive space for narration that the interviewee is given here in a unilateral way hardly ever occurs in everyday situations. This can produce difficulties for both parties involved. Here, interview training focused on active listening and a clarification of the specific character of the interview situation for the interviewee is necessary.

The narrative interview aims to access interviewees' subjective experiences through three means, namely:

1. The opening question, which aims to stimulate not simply a narrative, but specifically a narrative about the interesting topical area and period in the interviewee's biography.

2. The orientation of the scope for the interviewees in the main narrative part, which enables them to tell their stories perhaps for several hours.

3. The postponing of concrete, structuring, thematically deepening interventions in the interview until the final part, when the interviewer is supposed to pick up issues briefly mentioned and to ask focused questions. This means that any structuring activities of the interviewer are located at the end of the interview and even more so at the beginning.

The episodic interview

Both methods presented so far choose one approach – either questions and answers, or narrative stimulus and telling life histories – as the major approach to an issue under study. For many research questions, however, it is necessary to use a method that combines both principles – narratives and interrogation – equally. The episodic interview (see Flick 2008a; 2009) starts from the assumption that individuals' experiences about a certain area or issue are stored in the forms of narrative-episodic and semantic knowledge. While the first form is focused closely on experiences and linked to concrete situations and circumstances, the second form of knowledge contains abstracted, generalized assumptions and connections. In the first case, the course of the situation in its context is the central unit, around which knowledge is organized. In the second case, concepts and their interrelations form the central units. In order to cover both parts of knowledge about an issue, the method collects narrative-episodic knowledge in narratives and semantic knowledge in concrete and focused questions.

The aim is systematic connection of the two kinds of data (i.e. narratives and answers) and thus of the two kinds of knowledge they make accessible. The episodic interview gives space for context-related presentations in the form of narratives, as they address experiences in their original context more immediately compared to other forms of presentation. At the same time, narratives can elucidate more about processes of constructing realities on the part of the interviewees than other approaches that focus on more abstract concepts and answers.

The focus in the interview is on situations and episodes, in which the interviewee has had experiences that are relevant for the issue of the study. Which form of presentation (description or narrative) is chosen for the single situation, as well as the selection of situations, can be decided by the interviewees according to their subjective relevance for the issue. The aim of the episodic interview is to permit the interviewee for each substantial area to present experiences in a general or comparative form, and at the same time to recount relevant situations and episodes. Planning, doing and analyzing episodic interviews includes the following steps (see Flick 2000a). As a preparation, you should develop an interview guide, which includes narrative stimuli and questions for the areas and aspects you see as relevant for the issue of your study. At the beginning of the interview, you should introduce the principle of the interview, explaining that you will repeatedly invite the interviewee to recount specific situations. The general problem of interviews based on narratives is relevant here, too; some people have more problems with narrating than others. Therefore it is very important that you explain the principle of recounting situations to the interviewees. Interviewees should be encouraged to recount relevant situations, rather then merely mention them. You should take care that the interviewee has understood and accepted the method. An example of such an introduction to the interview principle is: 'In this interview, I will ask you a number of times to tell me situations in which you have had experiences with the topic of health.'

With the opening questions, you invite the interviewees to present their subjective definition of the issue of the research and to recount relevant situations. Examples of such questions are: 'What does "health" mean for you? What do you link with the word "health"?', or 'What has influenced your ideas of health in a particular way? Could you please tell me a situation which makes this clear for me?' Which exemplary situation they choose and recount for this purpose is always a decision of the interviewees. You can subsequently analyze both the selection and the account of the situation that each interviewee focuses on.

The next part of the interview will focus on the role or relevance of the issue under study for the participants' everyday lives. For this purpose, you can ask them to recount how a day (e.g. yesterday) went and what relevance the issue had on that day. If a multitude of situations is mentioned, you should pick up the most interesting ones and probe for a more detailed presentation. Again it is interesting for the analysis to identity which situations the interviewees pick up themselves for recounting. An example of a question addressing changes in the relevance of the issue is: 'Do you have the impression that your idea of health has changed during your professional life? Could you please recount a situation for me which shows this change?'

Next you will ask the interviewees to outline their personal relation to major aspects of the issue under study. For example, 'What does it mean for you to promote health as part of your work? Could you please tell me a situation of this kind?' You should ask the interviewee to illustrate these examples of personal experiences and subjective concepts as substantially and comprehensively as possible by probing if necessary.

In the final part of the interview, you will ask the interviewees to talk about more general aspects of the focal issue and to present their personal views in this context. This is meant to extend the scope of the interview. You should try as much as possible to link these general answers with the more personal and concrete examples used before so that possible discrepancies and contradictions become visible. An example of such a generalizing question is: 'Who do you think is responsible for your health? Is there a situation for which you can outline this?'

As in other interviews, the final question should ask the respondent for aspects missing from the questions or ask whether there is anything that should be added (e.g. 'Is there anything else ...?').

Immediately after the interview, you should complete a sheet on which you document socio-demographic information about the interviewee and features of the particular interview situation. Any disturbances and anything mentioned about the issue of the interview after the recording device was turned off should be noted as well, provided that is ethically acceptable (see Flick 2009, p. 299 for an example of such a documentary sheet).

Example: health concepts of homeless adolescents

In Chapter 2, the study on the health concepts of homeless adolescents was described. Our interviews with the adolescents were based on the episodic interview and covered the areas in Box 7.6, for which some examples of questions and narrative stimuli are presented.

BOX 7.6

Excerpts from an interview guide for an episodic interview

Health concepts: general and individual definition of health, relevance, possible influences

- First of all, I would like to ask you to tell me what life in your family was like. What made you turn to living on the street? Can you tell me of a situation which explains this for me?
- Now let's turn to our topic. What is that for you – health?
- How do you decide that you are healthy? Can you please tell me about a situation which helps me to understand this?

Links of factors and risks in the life world to health concepts and practices

- If you think of how you live these days, is there anything which influences your health? Can you tell me about a situation which explains this for me?
- Do you see any relation between your current housing situation and your health? Can you tell me about a situation which explains this for me?
- How do you deal with illness? Can you tell me of a situation which explains this for me?
- Do you think that your financial situation has an influence on your health? How? Can you give me a situation for this?

Risk behavior and secondary prevention as part of health practices

- Do you think that you sometimes risk your health by what you do? Is there a situation you can tell me about?
- If you think of drugs and alcohol, what do you use? Please give a situation when you do this.

Illness experiences and dealing with them

- When you do not feel well, what are your major problems? How do you think this problem [mentioned by the interviewee] comes about?

Focus groups and group discussions

An alternative to interviewing individuals is to use group interviews in which several participants are asked the same question and they answer one after the other. Alternatively – and more commonly – a group may be used as an interaction community. Since the 1950s, group discussions have been used mainly in German speaking areas and, in parallel, focus groups were used in the Anglo-Saxon world. In both cases, data collection is based on inaugurating a discussion in a group about the issue of the study. For example, pupils discuss their experiences with violence and how they deal with it, or students evaluate the quality of their courses and of the teaching in focus groups.

The starting point for using this method is that these discussions can make apparent how attitudes or evaluations are developed and changed. Participants are likely to express more and go further in their statements than in single interviews. The dynamics of the groups become an essential part of the data and of their collection.

For group discussions, a variety of forms of group can be used. You can start from a natural group (i.e. a group that exists in everyday life beyond the research), or from a real group (which is confronted in its everyday life by the issue of the study), or from artificial groups (set up for the research according to specific criteria). You can also distinguish between homogeneous and heterogeneous groups. In homogeneous groups, the members are similar in essential dimensions with respect to the research question: for example, they may have a similar professional background. In heterogeneous groups, the members should differ in the features that are relevant for the research question. Focus groups and group discussions can be moderated in different ways. You can refrain from any form of moderation, or do some formal steering (setting up a list of speakers), or do a more substantial moderation (by introducing topics or intervening with some provoking questions). One starts a focus group or a group discussion with a discussion stimulus, which can be a provoking question, a comic or a text, or the presentation of a short film.

In general you should be aware that running focus groups may require a lot of organizational effort (in coordinating the date of the meeting, for example). Afterwards it is the various groups that can be compared rather than all participants across the groups. Thus you should compare the various groups with each other, rather than the single members. You should use this method only if you have good reasons because of the research question and not because you expect to save some time compared to single interviews (see also Chapter 11).

Conclusion

The methods presented so far aim at collecting verbal data – whether by interviewing individuals, by inviting them to recount autobiographical experience, or by having groups discussing an issue. These methods make the knowledge about practices and processes accessible, but do not give immediate access to practices and processes in their course.

Observation

More direct access to practices and processes is provided by the use of observations. Here we can also distinguish several concepts regarding the role of the researcher:

- Covert and overt observation: how far are the observed persons or fields informed that they are observed?

- Non-participant and participant observation: how far do the observers become active parts of the field that is observed?

- Systematic and unsystematic observation: is a more or less standardized observation scheme applied or are the processes observed more openly?

- Observation in natural or artificial settings: do the researchers enter the relevant fields, or do they 'transfer' the interactions to a specific room (a laboratory) for improving the quality of the observations?

- Introspection or observation of others: in most cases, observation will focus on other people. What role does the researcher's reflecting introspection have in making the interpretations of the observed more solid?

- Standardized and non-standardized observation: in most cases, complex situations are now observed with open and adapted methods. However, approaches using observation categories defined in advance for observing a sample of situations are also applied.

- Experimental and non-experimental observation: in the first case, you will intervene specifically and observe the consequences of such an intervention.

Standardized Observations

Bortz and Döring describe this approach as follows:

> **The observation plan of a standardized observation exactly defines what to observe and how to protocol what was observed. The events to observe are known in principle and can be dismantled in single elements or segments, which are exclusively the issue or the observer's attention. (2006, p. 270)**

For standardized observation, you will draw a sample either of events or of time. The first alternative is oriented to certain events (e.g. a certain activity) in their frequency in the period of observation or in the frequency of occurrence in combination with other events: how often do girls answer in a mathematics class, or how often do they do so after a specific question is asked? To answer these questions, a whole class is observed and the frequency of the events is noted. An alternative is to draw a time sample. Here, the observation is segmented in fixed periods in which you observe or maybe change the object of observation – for example, in five minute intervals, which are randomly sampled from the observation period (mathematics class). The observations are done with a standardized observation scheme, often after training for the observers in dealing with the situation and the instrument. Observations can be documented with video and then be noted off the tape. A problem can be that the camera (or the observation scheme) does not cover the essentials of the situation. In time sampling, the relevant events may occur outside the selected periods.

This basic situation of social science observation – the researchers observe the field, and the people in it, by using a sample and confine themselves to noting the processes – can be extended in several directions in research practice.

Experiments

In experimental research, especially in psychology, observation may be focused on a deliberate intervention in one group, which is then compared to a second group in which this intervention is absent. For example, in school observations, the teacher may apply an intervention reducing aggression in one group – e.g. a teaching unit about de-escalation in situations of conflict. Then, in a second group, this intervention is not applied. Both groups will then be observed in their behavior in the next situation of conflict that occurs and compared. If the groups are set up by random sampling, this will be an experimental study. If the groups already exist (two seventh grades) this is a quasi-experimental study. The observation is applied according to the principles mentioned earlier – e.g. in sampling times or persons. The researchers will do a non-participant observation and use an observation protocol for documenting behaviors defined as relevant in advance. In our example, the data will still be collected in a field observation (in class). This will make standardization of the research situation more complicated. Therefore observation in the laboratory, i.e. an artificial situation under controlled conditions, is the alternative to observing in the natural context of teaching situations.

Participant Observation

A contrasting form of data collection is provided by participant observation. Here, the researcher's distance from the observed situation is reduced. Their participation over an extended period in the field that is studied becomes an essential instrument of data collection. At the same time, the observation is much less standardized. Here, you will also do some sampling of the situations that are observed, but not in the sense of time sampling as described above. Rather, you will select situations, persons and events according to how far the interesting phenomenon becomes accessible in this selection. The principal procedure can be summarized in Jörgensen's words by 'a logic and process of inquiry that is open-ended, flexible, opportunistic, and requires constant redefinition of what is problematic, based on facts gathered in concrete settings of human existence' (1989, p. 13).

Participant observation can be understood as a two-part process. First, the researchers are supposed to become participants and find access to the field and the persons in it. Second, the observation itself becomes more concrete and more strongly oriented to the essential aspects of the research question. Here we can distinguish three phases (see Spradley 1980, p. 34). First, descriptive observation for orienting in the study field is supposed to provide rather unspecific descriptions, to cover the complexity of the field as far as possible and to make research questions more concrete. Second, focused observation is more and more limited to the processes and problems that are particularly relevant for the research question. Selective observation at the end of data collection is supposed to find further evidence and examples for the processes identified in the second step. The documentation mostly consists of detailed field notes of protocols of situations. Whenever possible, research ethics (see Chapter 12) demand that observations are conducted openly, so that the observed people know that they are observed and have agreed beforehand to being observed. Third, for (participant) observation, the problem often is that certain issues are not immediately accessible at the level of practice, but only or mainly become 'visible' in interactions when people talk about the issues. Some topics are only an issue in conversations with the research or in *ad hoc* interviews. However, the results of a participant observation will be more fruitful when more insights come from protocols of activities and fewer come from reports about activities. Nevertheless, conversations, interrogations and other data sources will always comprise a big part of the knowledge process in participant observation.

Ethnography

Recently, the more general strategy of ethnography has tended to replace participant observation. However, observation and participation are interlinked with other procedures in this strategy as well:

> **In its most characteristic form it involves the ethnographer participating, overtly or covertly, in people's daily lives for an extended period of time, watching what happens, listening to what is said, asking questions – in fact, collecting whatever data are available to throw light on the issues that are the focus of the research. (Hammersley and Atkinson 1995, p. 1)**

This strategy will help you adapt data collection to your research question and to conditions in the field most consistently. Methods are subordinated to the research practice in the field. There is a strong emphasis on exploring a field or phenomenon. You will collect mostly unstructured data instead of using categories defined in advance and an observation scheme. For this purpose, a few cases are involved (or even a single case). Data analysis focuses on interpretation of meanings and functions of practices, statements and processes (see Hammersley and Atkinson 1995, p. 110–11). Lüders sees the central defining features of ethnography as follows:

> **first [there is] the risk and the moments of the research process which cannot be planned and are situational, coincidental and individual ... Second, the researcher's skillful activity in each situation becomes more important ... Third, ethnography ... transforms into a strategy of research which includes as many options of collecting data as can be imagined and are justifiable. (1995, pp. 320–1; see also Lüders, 2004a)**

Conclusion

The observational methods described above vary in the distance the researchers maintain to the field that is observed; the alternatives are to participate or just to observe from the outside. Furthermore the methods differ in the degree of control of the conditions of the study exerted by the researchers. Control is strongest in the laboratory experiment and weakest in participant observation. They can also be distinguished by the standardization of the research situations – again, most limited in participant observation and strongest for the experiment. In general, for observation, the idea guiding data collection is that it provides more immediate access to practices and routines compared to interviews and surveys. However, in most cases, conversations, statements and questions or sometimes *ad hoc* interviews are involved in observations.

Working with Documents

The methods presented so far have in common that you will *produce* data with them – data such as answers in a survey, or a narrative in an interview, or the observations and descriptions in the field or laboratory. As an alternative, you can use already *existing* materials, e.g. documents resulting from an institutional process. These can be texts or images, which can be analyzed in a qualitative or quantitative way depending on the research question. The analysis of documents can refer to existing materials – like diaries – which have not yet been used as data in other contexts. Sometimes they refer to existing datasets from other contexts – like official statistics, which have been produced not for research but for purposes of documentation.

The term 'secondary analysis' means that you analyze data that were not collected for your own research project. Instead, you use existing datasets that were produced for other purposes.

Kinds of secondary analyses

Here we can distinguish between reanalyzing data from other research projects and data produced for purposes other than research. In the second category, we find data from federal bureaux of statistics which are collected, elaborated and analyzed for monitoring purposes. They can be used for a number of research questions. In the first category, you will find data produced and analyzed by other researchers in studying a specific issue that now can be used again by other researchers for their own research questions. This can be organized through the direct cooperation of researchers with other researchers. But there are also several institutions which collect datasets from research projects and provide them for other researchers, who pay for the right to use these data. Examples of such institutions are GESIS in Germany and GALLUP in the US. In several contexts, datasets are elaborated as 'public use files' and made available to interested researchers for further work with them.

Selecting and weighting secondary data

The advantage of analyzing secondary data is that you do not need to collect data and so can save time. However, you should consider some questions and problems arising when you use secondary data. First, you should check whether these data fit your research question: do they include the information necessary to answer it? Second, you should assess whether the form of elaboration in which the data are available corresponds to the aims of your study. A simple example will illustrate: if your research question refers to a distribution of age in one-year steps but the available dataset has classified the studied people in age groups (for example in five-year steps) and if this classification cannot be traced back to the single value in years, this might produce problems in the usability of the data for your purpose. A second example: many epidemiological studies have been based on death cause statistics in local health authorities for reconstructing the frequencies of certain diseases as death causes. Here, in many cases, it was not the single death certificate which was used as data but the classification done by the single health authority. Here again the problem results that the classification of different death causes (or diseases) in categories will not necessarily be the same as the researchers needed or would have applied for their study and research question. Mistakes made in allocating a single case to a category cannot be assessed in such a dataset (see Chapter 8). The more general problem is that the data are available in aggregated form only, i.e. elaborated and processed, and that the original raw data are not accessible.

Qualitative Analysis of Documents

Alternatively, you may use existing documents for a qualitative analysis. The following definition outlines what is generally understood as 'documents':

> **Documents are *standardized artifacts*, in so far as they typically occur in particular *formats*: as notes, case reports, contracts, drafts, death certificates, remarks, diaries, statistics, annual reports, certificates, judgments, letters or expert opinions. (Wolff 2004, p. 284)**

Again you can use documents produced for your study. For example you might ask a group of people to write a diary over the next 12 months and then analyze and compare what was noted in these diaries. Or you might use existing documents, for example the diaries written by a specific group of people (e.g. patients with a specific diagnosis) in their everyday lives independent of the research. Documents are mostly available as texts (in printed form) and more and more also or exclusively in electronic form (e.g. in a database).

Many official or private documents are meant only for a limited circle of recipients who are authorized to access them or who are addressed by them. Official documents allow conclusions about what their authors or the institutions they represent do or intend, or how they evaluate. Documents are produced for a certain purpose – e.g. for substantiating a decision or for convincing a person or an authority. But that also means that documents represent issues only in a limited way. When analyzing them for research purposes, you should always consider who has produced a document, for whom, and for what purpose. How documents are designed is a part of their meaning; how something is presented influences which effects are produced with a document.

From a practical point of view, the first step is to identify the relevant documents. For analyzing official records, you have to find out where they are stored and whether they are accessible for research purposes. Then you have to make the appropriate selection: which of the existing records will you concretely use and why (see also Rapley 2008)?

Visual Data: Photo and Film

Visual data, such as photos, film and videos, have attracted increasing attention as documents to be used in research (see Knoblauch et al. 2006). Again, we can distinguish two approaches: cameras can be used as instruments for data collection and images can be produced for research purposes; or existing images can be selected for the research and analyzed. An approach can be to analyze the photos in family albums and the family's or the individual's history as documented in these photos over time. In research with families or institutions, the analysis of self-presentations in photos or images of the members displayed on the walls of rooms can give insights into the structures of the social field (see Banks 2008). Media analyses also address films or TV series for analyzing the presentation of certain problems and how a society deals with them (see Denzin 2004 for this).

Conclusion

When you use existing materials (texts, images, datasets) for your study, you will save time at the data collection stage, since this is limited to selecting from the existing material. But you should not underestimate the obstacles arising from such material: photos, texts and statistics have their own structure that is often strongly influenced by who produced them and for what purpose. If this structure is not compatible with the demands for data arising from your own research question, this may produce selectivity problems. To solve these problems can sometimes be more expensive and time consuming than to collect your own data. Thus, to use secondary data in particular and existing materials in general is only suggested if the research question gives you good reasons to do so.

Obtaining and Documenting Information

Social research is based on data collected with empirical methods. In general we can distinguish two major groups of methods. Quantitative methods aim at covering the phenomena under study in their frequencies or distributions and therefore work with big numbers of cases in data collection. Numbers are in the foreground. For example, you could collect how often waiting times in the hospital occur, what the average time is that a patient waits (unnecessarily) before a treatment, and how this is distributed over the week.

Qualitative methods are more interested in an exact description of processes and views and therefore often work with small numbers of cases. In the foreground are texts – e.g. transcribed interviews. In our example you would collect data about how situations occur in which patients wait (unnecessarily), what subjective explanations the staff have for this, or how single patients experience these situations of waiting.

Data collection in qualitative research pursues different aims, and is grounded on different principles, from quantitative research. Quantitative research is devoted to the ideals of measurement and works with numbers, scales and index construction. Qualitative research is more oriented to producing protocols of its research issues and to documenting and reconstructing them. Before we turn to methods of analyzing data (see Chapter 8), we will briefly consider these aims and principles.

Measurement

For quantitative methods, a measurement is assumed; in a time measure, for example, the duration of an event is identified with a measurement instrument (a watch). This is fairly unproblematic if there is an established unit (e.g. a minute, a centimetre) and a means of measurement to identify how many of these units are given in the concrete case (e.g. 15 minutes of waiting time). However, often this unit does not exist for the objects social science is interested in and has to be defined by the researcher. To measure then is to allocate a number to a certain object or event. Three problems are linked to this allocation. First, the number comes to represent the object or its feature in the further progress of the research – in other words, the object itself is no longer part of the process. In addition, different numerical values represent differences and relations between the objects. For example, extensions of waiting time before an operation are measured in minutes. In this case, you can assume that two minutes are always two minutes and four minutes are twice as long as two minutes. Another example illustrates the other two problems, namely unambiguousness and significance. The subjective distress of the patient has to be translated into a numerical value first. If 'extremely stressful' equals 4, 'very stressful' equals 3 and 'stressful' equals 2 on a scale, you can assume neither that the distance between 2 and 3 is as big as that between 3 and 4, nor that a value of 2 always represents the same degree of subjective distress. This is the question of the unambiguousness of measurement values. Finally, you cannot assume in this example that a value of 4 here represents double the value of 2. This is the problem of significance. That raises questions about which mathematical operations make sense based on the measurements made.

Scaling

The allocation of numerical values to an object or an event leads to the construction of a scale. Here, four kinds of scales are distinguished.

A nominal scale allocates objects with identical features to identical numerical values. For example, male as gender might be labeled with 1, female as gender with 2. A relation between the values does not exist.

In ordinal scales, a relation of ordering exists between the values. If, in our example, the degree of the patients' subjective distress is labeled as 4 when the situation is extremely stressful, 3 when it is very stressful and 2 when it is stressful, this represents an order between the different degrees of subjective distress. But here, the distances between the values are not necessarily the same.

In an interval scale, in contrast, the distances between two values are always the same. An example is the Fahrenheit temperature scale.

Table 7.2 Kinds of scale

Kind of scale	Possible statements	Examples	Answers and values
Nominal scale	Equality differences	Gender	☐ Male ☐ Female
		Professional groups	☐ Physician ☐ Teacher
		Satisfied by the treatment	☐ Yes ☐ No
Ordinal scale	Bigger–smaller relations	Social status	☐ Upper class ☐ Middle class ☐ Working class
		School grades	☐ Very good ☐ Good ☐ Satisfying ☐ Sufficient ☐ Failed
Interval scale	Sameness of differences	Temperature (°F)	☐ 36 °F ☐ 37 °F ☐ 38 °F
		Calendar, time intervals (e.g. of sickness leave per year)	☐ One day ☐ Two days ☐ Three days
Ratio scale	Sameness of relations	Weight	☐ One kilogram ☐ Two kilograms ☐ Three kilograms
		Length	☐ One centimetre ☐ Two centimetres ☐ Three centimetres

A ratio scale is given if not only the distances between values are the same, but you can assume that two units of distance represent twice the distance of one unit. Examples are measurements of length or weight: the distance between 2 kg and 3 kg is the same as the distance between 5 kg and 6 kg, and 6 kg is twice as heavy as 3 kg. A ratio scale furthermore has a fixed point zero. Ratio scales are seldom found in the social sciences and their research.

The kind of scale determines which calculations are justified for each scale (see Chapter 8). Table 7.2 summarizes the various kinds of scale.

Counting

If you want to count certain objects, this assumes that the objects to be counted are equal in their major features: that is, that you are not 'comparing apples and oranges'. If you want to count people, activities or situations, the sameness as a precondition of the countability has to be produced in advance. People are characterized by strong individuality and diversity. They can be counted if they can be classified according to specific features – e.g. their ages. The age is already defined as a number. For other, more qualitative features, first a classification in numerical form has to be done beforehand. Someone is either male or female. People can be helpful in varying degrees (not at all, a bit, average, very or extraordinarily helpful). To be able to count such a feature, the characteristic has to be classified and labeled with a numerical value (not at all helpful is classified as 1, a bit helpful as 2 etc.). Then you can count these features and relate them to others using numerical values. A precondition is that a feature like helpfulness can be classified with such categories. For this purpose, it must be possible to define categories exactly (e.g. what does 'a bit helpful' or 'not all helpful' mean?). Categories should be able to describe the feature in an exhaustive way (it must be possible to allocate all possible forms of helpfulness to these categories).

Constructing an Index

For quantitative features like age, all persons with a certain value (age) are summarized (e.g. all 25-year-olds) or allocated to specific age groups (e.g. the 20- to 30-year-olds). Often, more complex features have to be counted. Many studies start from the social status of a person (e.g. for finding out whether people with a high social status fall ill less often than people with low social status). The social status is constructed from various single features – the state of education, the profession, the income, the situation of housing. This means an index is constructed in which these single features are combined. Counting then is applied to this index. The parts of the index can have the same weight or can be weighted differently, e.g. when income counts twice as much as the other parts of the social state. In the research on quality of life (see for example Guggenmoos-Holzmann et al. 1995) a variety of quality of life indices have been established.

Protocols

While quantitative research is based on measurement and counting, qualitative research tends to refrain from using such numerical values. Rather, the first step is to produce a protocol of the events and of the context in which they occurred. The protocol should be as detailed, comprehensive and exact as possible. For observations, you will produce detailed descriptions of situations and of their contexts. Interviews are recorded on tape or on mp3 players and this is complemented by memory protocols of the interview situation. Interactions are documented on audio or video tape in order to make possible a repeated and more or less unfiltered access to the raw data. Whereas in interviews the data are produced with methods (questions lead to answers or narratives, which are produced specifically for the research), several other approaches in qualitative research, like ethnography or conversation analysis (see Chapter 8 and Flick 2009 for more details), restrict themselves to recording and proto-colling everyday life situations, without intervening with questions for example. Quantitative research produces a specific condensation of the data already in the data collection by delimiting them to specific questions and possible answers. Qualitative research is first interested in less condensed data. Reduction of the information here is part of the analysis. The original data should remain available in an unfiltered way and accessible repeatedly.

Documentation

Documentation of the data has a specific relevance here. A comprehensive recording is seen as most important for qualitative research. Therefore audio or video recording has priority over making notes of answers or practices only at a glance. Only where technical recording devices are in the way of the method – when they prevent the researcher from participating and from integrating into the field in participant observation, for example – is the preference still for field notes and protocols made after the observation (see Flick 2009, Chapter 22 for more details). A detailed and comprehensive recording leads in most cases to a similarly exact transcript of the data. This should include as much as possible of the context information for the interviewees' statements. Here again, an unobstructed view of the reality under study is seen as highly relevant.

Exactness in documenting the events is a precondition for a detailed inter-pretation of the statements and occurrences grounded in the data.

Reconstruction

In the analysis and interpretation of the data, it becomes possible to recon-struct – asking, for example, how does or did something occur, or what views the participants had on this occurrence. In a detailed reconstruction of case trajectories, data are obtained which then will be the subject of comparison. This comparison does not work with numbers, but nevertheless is intended to arrive at generalizing statements. For example, reconstructions of single trajec-tories lead to constructing types of processes and detailed descriptions of these types. Here it is less important how often these types can be identified. Rather the question is how far these types cover the range of existing trajectories and allow inferences about when and under what conditions each type is relevant.

Summary

The two kinds of methods – quantitative and qualitative – are often character-ized as 'standardized' and 'non-standardized methods' respectively because an essential difference is their degree of standardization of the procedures. Analyzing data from a questionnaire in a quantitative and statistical way makes sense only when the data collection was standardized by uniform question wording and sequence and uniform alternatives for answering them. This requires that every participant is under exactly the same conditions in answering the questions. Qualitative studies in contrast are often most fruitful when the procedures are less standardized and are applied in a flexible way so that new and unexpected aspects become relevant. At the same time, specific attention is paid to including context information: the participants' answers are not meant to speak as facts for themselves. Rather they should be embedded in a longer narrative or extended presentation. This will then allow insights into the subjective meaning of what has been presented and thus make clear in which contexts the interviewees themselves understand their statements.

Checklist for Designing Data Collection

In doing your empirical project in social research, you should consider the points in Box 7.7 for selecting and conceptualizing methods of data collection. These questions can be helpful for doing your own study and also for assessing the studies of other researchers.

BOX 7.7

Checklist for designing data collection

1. What are the major aspects that should be covered by the data collection?
2. Is the focus more on practices referring to an issue or more on knowledge about it?
3. Do existing data already include the relevant information, so that it is not necessary to collect your own data?
4. Do the existing data and their content, their degree of detailing, fit your own research question?
5. What is the intention for the data in their later analysis? Are the data provided by the actual method of data collection appropriate for this kind of analysis (in their exactness, structure and level of scaling)?
6. What scope for idiosyncrasies (of the contents or the way of presenting them by the participants) do the selected methods offer, and what scope is necessary for answering the research question?
7. What degree of exactness in documenting and transcribing qualitative data is necessary for answering the research question?

■ ■ Further Reading ■

The first and fourth of the texts listed below provide a comprehensive overview of social research methods with a stronger focus on quantitative methods; the second and third concentrate more on qualitative methods.

Bryman, A. (2008) *Social Research Methods*, 3rd edn. Oxford: Oxford University Press.

Flick, U. (2009) *An Introduction to Qualitative Research*, 4th edn. London: Sage.

Flick, U. (ed.) (2007) *The Sage Qualitative Research Kit*, 8 vols. London: Sage.

Neuman, W.I. (2000) *Social Research Methods: Qualitative and Quantitative Approaches*, 4th edn. Boston: Allyn and Bacon.

CHAPTER 8
ANALYZING QUANTITATIVE AND QUALITATIVE DATA

Chapter Overview

Chapter Objectives

This chapter is designed to help you:

- understand some major methods of data analysis in social research
- understand the similarities and differences between the procedures of qualitative and quantitative data analysis
- be able to assess which methods are available for your research and what they can provide.

Table 8.1   Navigator for Chapter 8

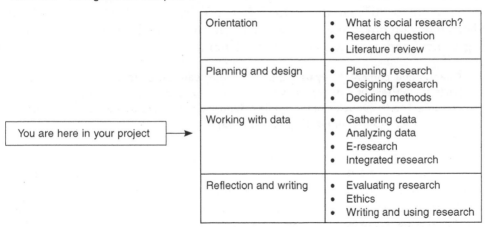

You are here in your project →		
Orientation	• What is social research? • Research question • Literature review	
Planning and design	• Planning research • Designing research • Deciding methods	
Working with data	• Gathering data • Analyzing data • E-research • Integrated research	
Reflection and writing	• Evaluating research • Ethics • Writing and using research	

The previous chapter discussed selected methods of data collection. In this chapter, we turn to describing methods for analyzing the data that has been collected. We first consider quantitative and qualitative content analysis. We then focus on quantifying analyses for standardized data. Finally, we look at interpretative methods for analyzing qualitative data from interviews and participant observations.

Content Analysis

Content analysis is a classical procedure for analyzing text material of whatever origin, from media products to interview data. It is 'an empirical method for systematic, inter-subjectively transparent description of substantial and formal features of messages' (Früh 1991, p. 25). The method is based on using categories derived from theoretical models. One normally applies such categories to texts, rather than develop them from the material itself – though one may of course revise the categories in the light of the texts under analysis. Content analysis aims at classifying the content of texts by allocating statements, sentences or words to a system of categories.

Below we distinguish quantitative and qualitative content analyses.

Quantitative Content Analysis

Analyzing newspaper articles

While *qualitative* content analysis is seen as a method of *analyzing* for example data from interviews, some sources see *quantitative* content analysis rather as a specific method for *collecting* data (e.g. Bortz and Döring 2006). Schnell et al. (2008, p. 407) see the method as 'a mixture of "analytic technique" and data collection procedure'. It is used for collecting and classifying information, e.g. in newspaper articles. We find as a definition:

> **Quantitative content analysis captures single features of text by categorizing parts of the text in categories, which are operationalizations of the interesting features. The frequencies of the single categories inform about the features of the analyzed text. (Bortz and Döring 2006, p. 149)**

In the foreground of such analyses are the questions: (a) what characterizes the communication about a specific issue in certain media, and (b) what impact does this have on the addressees? Communication according to this model can be defined according to the formula of Laswell (1938): WHO (communicator) SAYS (writes, mentions in form of signs …) WHAT (message) in WHICH CHANNEL (medium) to WHOM (receiver) and WITH WHAT EFFECT?

The methodological core of content analysis is the category system used to classify the materials you study. The allocation of a passage in the text to a category is described as coding. A crucial step is that you select the right materials (the sample that is drawn from the text) and the correct units for your analysis. Which texts from which newspaper and on which publishing days should you select? Will you analyze single words, or will you allocate whole sentences or paragraphs to the categories?

Analytic strategies

We can distinguish several analytic strategies. In simple frequency analyses, you ask how often certain concepts are mentioned in the texts you analyze. This method is used for inferring the medial presence of a topic in the daily newspapers: e.g. how often was the topic 'health fund' an issue in the most important German press releases in the period under study (see Table 8.2)?

In a contingency analysis, you do not seek only the frequency of concepts (and thus of topics) in the relevant period in the press. Contingency analysis is interested in which other concepts appear at the same time: for example, how often is the issue 'health fund' mentioned together with 'caring deficits' or 'costs' (see Table 8.3)?

Quantitative content analysis of other texts

Quantitative content analysis is often used for analyzing newspaper articles. However, you can use it as a method for analyzing interviews or other materials that have been produced for research purposes.

Steps in quantitative content analysis

We can distinguish several steps in the analysis. First you will decide which texts are relevant for the purpose of your study. The next step is to draw a sample from

Table 8.2 Frequency analysis in content analysis

	Health fund
Newspaper A 20.10.2008	
Newspaper B 20.10.2008	
Newspaper A 21.10.2008	
Newspaper B 21.10.2008	
Newspaper A 22.10.2008	
Newspaper B 22.10.2008	
Newspaper A 23.10.2008	
Newspaper B 23.10.2008	

Table 8.3 Contingency analysis in content analysis

	Health fund	Caring deficits	Costs	Interest of health insurers
Newspaper A 20.10.2008				
Newspaper B 20.10.2008				
Newspaper A 21.10.2008				
Newspaper B 21.10.2008				
Newspaper A 22.10.2008				
Newspaper B 22.10.2008				
Newspaper A 23.10.2008				
Newspaper B 23.10.2008				

these texts before you define the counting unit (all or certain words, groups of words, sentences, complete articles, headlines etc.). From the research question and from its theoretical background, you will next derive a system of categories. These should be (a) mutually exclusive (clearly distinguishing), (b) exhaustive, (c) precise, (d) based on discrete dimensions, and (e) independent of each other.

The classification of texts with categories aims mainly at reducing the material. The category system can consist of concepts and subconcepts. Often, a dictionary is established that includes the names of categories and the definitions and rules for allocating words to categories. For applying the categories to texts, coding rules are defined. Coders collect the analytic units by applying the categories that were defined before. Coders are trained for this purpose and the coding system is checked in a pre-test for its reliability (correspondence of allocation by different coders). Then statistical analyses are applied for identifying how often certain words in total or in connection with other words appear in the text and for analyzing the distribution of categories and contents (see below).

Problems of quantitative content analysis

Problems in quantitative content analysis arise from the necessary isolation of single words or passages, which are thus taken out of their context. Texts are decomposed in their elements, which then can be used as empirical units. This makes it more difficult to grasp any meaning or coherence of and in texts.

For example, there have been attempts to identify changes in attitudes towards the elderly by analyzing newspaper articles using the frequencies with which certain words (e.g. 'frail' or 'experience') appear together with 'age' or 'old people'. If the concepts or the frequencies in which they are used together with 'age' and 'old people' are changing, this is used to infer changes in attitudes towards aging.

Thus the application of content analysis is often rather reductionist. This may result from strong standardization and the use of small analytical units (e.g. a single word) in order to provide repeatability, stability and exactness of the analysis. Repeatability refers to the degree to which classifications of the material are completed in the same way by several analysts. Stability means that the method of classification of content does not vary over time. Exactness indicates how far the coding of a text corresponds with the norm of coding or the standard coding.

A strength of quantitative content analysis is that you can analyze large amounts of data with it. The procedures can be standardized to a high degree. Frequencies and distributions of statements, attitudes etc. can be calculated. The weakness of quantitative content analysis is that one rules out the analysis of single cases right from the beginning: the single text and its structure or particularity as a whole are not taken into account. The context of words is rather neglected. How far the analysis of frequencies or topics in texts is sufficient for answering substantive research questions has been debated since the early days of research with content analysis.

Qualitative Content Analysis

Against the background of the limitations of quantifying approaches, Mayring (1983) has developed his approach of a qualitative content analysis.

The procedure of qualitative content analysis

The first step here is to define the material (e.g. to select the interviews or those parts that are relevant for answering the research question). Then you will analyze the situation of data collection (how was the material generated, who was involved, who was present in the interview situation, where the documents to be analyzed come from, and so on). You will continue by formally characterizing the material (was the material documented with a recording or a protocol? Was there an influence on the transcription of the text when it was edited? and so on). Then, you will define the direction of the analysis for the selected texts and 'what one actually wants to interpret out of them' (1983, p. 45).

In the next step, the research question is further defined on the basis of theories. A precondition is that the 'research question of the analysis must be clearly defined in advance, must be linked theoretically to earlier research on the issue and generally has to be differentiated in sub-questions' (1983, p. 47). After that, you will select the analytic technique (see below) and define the units. The 'coding unit' defines what is 'the smallest element of material which may be analyzed, the minimal part of the text which may fall under a category'; the 'contextual unit' defines what is the largest element in the text which may fall under a category; the 'analytic unit' defines which passages 'are analyzed one after the other'. Now you conduct the actual analyses before you interpret their final results with respect to the research question. In the end, you will ask and answer questions of validity (see Figure 8.1).

Techniques of qualitative content analysis

The concrete methodical procedure essentially involves three techniques. In *summarizing content analysis*, you will paraphrase the material so that you can skip less relevant passages and paraphrases with the same meanings (this is the first reduction) and bundle and summarize similar paraphrases (the second reduction). For example, in an interview with an unemployed teacher, the statement 'and actually, quite the reverse, I was well very, very keen on finally teaching for the first time' (1983, p. 59) was paraphrased as 'quite the reverse, very keen on practice' and generalized as 'rather looking forward to practice'. The statement 'therefore, I have already waited for it, to go to a seminar school, until I finally could teach there for the first time' was paraphrased as 'waited to teach finally' and generalized as 'looking forward to practice'. Owing to the similarity of the two generalizations, the second one then is skipped and reduced with other statements to 'practice not experienced as shock but as big fun' (1983, p. 59).

Explicative content analysis works in the opposite way. It clarifies diffuse, ambiguous or contradictory passages by involving contextual material in the analysis. Definitions taken from dictionaries or based on the grammar are used or formulated. 'Narrow context analysis' picks up additional statements from the text in order to explicate the passages to be analyzed, whereas 'wide context analysis' seeks information outside the text (about the author, the generative situations, from theories). On this basis, an 'explicating paraphrase' is formulated and tested.

Definition of the material

↓

Analyzing the situation in which it was produced

↓

Formal classification of the material

↓

Direction of the analysis

↓

Theoretical differentiation of the research questions

↓

Definition of the analytical technique(s) and of the concrete process model

↓

Definition of the analytical units

↓

Analytical steps with the category system

Summary   Explication   Structuration

↓   ↓   ↓

Reassess the category system against theory and material

↓

Interpretation of the results according to the main research questions

↓

Application of the content analytic quality criteria

Figure 8.1   General content analytic process model (Source: Mayring 1983, p. 49)

For example: in an interview, a teacher expressed her difficulties in teaching by stating that she – unlike successful colleagues – was no 'entertainer type' (1983, p. 109). In order to find out what she wished to express by using this concept, definitions of 'entertainer' were assembled from two dictionaries. Then the features of a teacher who fits this description were sought from statements made by the teacher in the interview. Further passages were consulted. Based on the descriptions of such colleagues included in these passages, an 'explicating paraphrase can be formulated: an entertainer type is somebody who plays the part of an extroverted, spirited, sparkling, and self-assured human being' (1983, p. 74). This explication was assessed again by applying it to the direct context in which the concept was used.

With *structuring content analysis,* you look for types or formal structures in the material. You can look for and find four kinds of structures. You may find specific topics or domains which characterize the texts (content structures) – for example, xenophobic statements in interviews are always linked to issues of violence and crime. Or you find an internal structure on a formal level which characterizes the material – for example, every text begins with an example and then an explanation of the example follows. Scaling structuring means that you find varying degrees of a feature in the material – e.g. texts which express xenophobia in a stronger way than other texts in the material. Finally you may find typifying structures – e.g. that interviews with female participants are systematically different from those with male participants in how the main questions are answered.

Structuring *content analysis* has been described as follows:

> According to formal aspects, an internal structure can be filtered out (formal structuring); material can be extracted and condensed to certain domains of content (structuring as regards content). One can look for single salient features in the material and describe them more exactly (typifying structuring); finally, the material may be rated according to dimensions in the form of scales (scaling structuring). (1983, pp. 53–4)

Problems of qualitative content analysis

The schematic elaboration of the procedures makes this method look more transparent, less ambiguous, and easier to handle than other qualitative methods of analysis. This is because of the reduction it allows, as outlined above. The method is mainly suitable for reducing large amounts of text and analyzes on their surface (What is said in them?). Often, however, the application of the rules given by Mayring proves at least as time consuming as in other procedures. The quick categorization of text based on theories may obscure the view of the contents, rather than facilitate analyzing the text in its depth and underlying meanings. Interpretation of the text (How is something said? What is its meaning?) is applied rather schematically with this method, especially when the technique of explicative content analysis is used. Another problem is the use of paraphrases, which are used not only to explain the basic text but also to replace it – mainly in summarizing content analysis. The more quantitative a content analysis is oriented and applied, the more it reduces the meaning of the text to frequencies and parallel appearance of certain words or word sequences.

Example of a Content Analysis

The example in Box 8.1 is a thematic content analysis of journals.

BOX 8.1

Age and health in journals: example of a content analysis

In this study (Walter et al. 2006), four journals, two medical and two nursing journals, were content analyzed. We selected articles which focused on the topics of health, age, aging, old or very old people, and prevention and health promotion for the elderly. For this purpose, (1) the content of the title of the articles, (2) the abstract and (3) the whole article were analyzed.

The number of selected articles shows that representations of health, of aging and of old people as well as the areas of prevention and health promotion for the elderly are hardly an issue in the four journals. Of the 3028 issues of the journals in the years 1970–2001, only 83 articles explicitly address representations of health; 216 (7.1%) address representations of aging and old people, and 131 (4.3%) mention prevention and health promotion for the elderly, over a period of three decades and in four major journals.

For a more detailed content analysis, 283 publications from 1970 to 2001 were available. The relevance of the issues of aging and of the elderly in the medical and nursing journals was rather low. The distribution of the 216 publications over the period 1970–2001 shows in particular that the general practitioners journal and the nursing journal pick up this topic, whereas the other two refer to it more seldom. In the 1970s only 37 (17.1%) articles could be identified which addressed aging; in the 1980s 71 (32.9%) and in the 1990s 91 (42.1%) referred to that topic. Three of the journals paid more attention to it over time, and only the second nursing journal picked it up in the 1970s more frequently.

In the majority of the 131 identified articles, prevention and health promotion for the elderly are mentioned according to the distinction of primary, secondary and tertiary prevention. Only 12% of the 131 articles address health promotion according to the Ottawa Charta of the World Health Organization (1986).

The quantitative part of prevention and health promotion for elder people in most of the articles is below 10%. This means that the topic mostly is only mentioned in one to three sentences. This already shows the marginal relevance of prevention and health promotion in the journals that were studied.

Often, prevention and health promotion are not mentioned explicitly in the selected medical and nursing journals in Germany. This applies in particular to the nursing journals, which use prophylactic aids as a term instead.

All in all, the distribution of the identified publication over the decade shows the following. Representations of health were an issue in the medical and nursing journals in the 1990s less frequently compared to the 1970s. Images of aging and of old people have been increasingly an issue over the decades, but without having much relevance. Also the issues of prevention and health promotion are mentioned more and more. This shows the growing importance of these topics over time but also that they are still mentioned in a very limited way.

Quantitative Data Analysis

In the first part of this chapter, quantitative and then qualitative approaches to content analysis have been presented. In the next step we will consider

Table 8.4   Data matrix 1

| Study unit | Variable | | | | | |
	Gender	Age	Profession	School degree	Question 1: grade of consent	Question 2: grade of consent
Case 1	M	21	Student	High school	5	3
Case 2	F	28	Sales person	Grammar school	3	4
Case 3	M	–	Taxi driver	Public school	1	1
Case 4	F	25	Physician	Without	2	5
...						

Table 8.5   Data matrix 2

| Study unit | Variable | | | | | |
	V1	V2	V3	V4	V5	V6
01	2	21	4	4	5	3
02	1	28	1	2	3	4
03	2	999	3	3	1	1
04	1	25	5	1	2	5
...						

general aspects of quantitative data analysis, before I then turn to qualitative interpretative analyses.

Elaboration of the Data

Before you can analyze questionnaire data, you have first to elaborate them. This includes constructing a data matrix, i.e. a compilation of all variables for every study unit, more specifically of all responses for every case (see Table 8.4), which you will transform into numerical values (see Table 8.5). The questionnaire in our example begins with four questions about the demographic characteristics of the respondents (gender, age, profession, school degree) before substantive questions follow. A code plan was developed in advance, showing which number is code for which possible answer. For gender, female is coded with 1, male with 2. School degree is coded from 'without' to 'high school' with values of 1–4, and the current profession in a similar way. For the answers to questions 1 and 2, the values are taken from the scale (see the example in Figure 7.1). The cases are given an identification number and the variables are labeled with numbers (e.g. age in Table 8.4 becomes variable V2 in Table 8.5).

In this context, coding means allocating numerical values to answers. In this data matrix, you will enter all responses from every questionnaire. If open questions (without a defined scale of answers) are used, the answers (the text noted by the participant at this point) have to be allocated to categories, which then can be labeled with numerical values.

Cleaning the Data

In the next step, one needs to clean the data. First, you should test in the first frequency calculation whether data have be entered in the wrong column. If, for example, only 10 possible values were defined for 'profession' but several cases have values of 25 or 35, this indicates that maybe age values were coded in the column for profession. Such mistakes in columns have to be checked and corrected. Then, missing data have to be checked. In Table 8.4, for case 3, the age is missing and was coded with '999' for missing value in Table 8.5. You should also do a plausibility check for the data. In Table 8.4, you will find entries in case 4 which are at least unlikely (a physician without a school degree and with an age of 25). Here you should also check whether this is a coding error or if a combination of these answers really can be found in the questionnaires. Perhaps these answer have to be treated as 'missing'. After this assessment of the data, which can be quite time consuming for big datasets, and after correcting all identified errors, you can analyze the data on various levels of complexity.

Univariate Analyses: Referring to One Variable

A common way of demonstrating commonalities and differences for a certain feature or for a variable is to calculate its distribution in the sample that is studied.

Frequencies

If there are, say, four possible answers, you can first calculate their relative frequencies by dividing the number of cases in one category by the number of cases in the sample. If you want to calculate the percentage of the frequency, the result of this division is multiplied by 100. If, say, 27 of a sample of 100 people ticked 'public school' as highest degree, the relative frequency of public school as school degree is 0.27 and the percentage is 27%. Finally, you can calculate the cumulated relative percentage. If in our example another 33 persons have indicated 'grammar school' and 20 persons 'no degree' and 20 persons 'high school', you can rank order the values according to the level of the degrees. From cumulating (or adding) the single values, you can see for example that here the relative frequency of people with not more than a grammar school degree is 0.80 and the relative percentage is 80% (see Table 8.6).

Table 8.6 Frequency distribution of the variable 'school degree'

	Category	Number of cases	Relative frequency	Percentage	Cumulated relative frequency	Cumulated percentage
No degree	1	20	0.20	20%	0.20	20%
Public school	2	27	0.27	27%	0.47	47%
Grammar school	3	33	0.33	33%	0.80	80%
High school	4	20	0.20	20%	1.00	100%

For demonstrating the distribution of answers in a sample, you can go two ways: on the one hand you can identify the central tendency, or on the other hand the dispersion.

Central tendency

The most prominent measure for the central tendency is the arithmetic mean, which is calculated by dividing the sum of the observed values by the number of cases. A familiar example is school grades. A student has the grades 1, 1, 4, 3 and 5 in his degree. For calculating the mean, you will add the single grades and divide that by the number of subjects (the sum is 14, the number of subjects is 5, which makes a mean of 2.8). For calculating means, you need data on the level of interval scales (the distances between the values have to be equal – see Chapter 7). If your data only consist of an ordinal scale, you can calculate the central tendency with the mode or with the median.

The mode is the value that occurs most frequently. The mode in our grades example is 3 (as it occurs most often). The median is the midpoint of a distribution, which means where the cumulated relative frequency reaches 50%. This means the distribution is separated such that 50% of the values are under and 50% are over the median. In our example of the school degrees (see Table 8.6), the median would be a little higher than 'public school' as almost 50% of the respondents have the values 'public school and less' and a little more than 50% have 'grammar school and more'.

Dispersion

Measures of central tendency will not tell you everything about a distribution. The example of the mean of two school grades may demonstrate this. A grade of 3 and a grade of 4 have a mean of 3.5. The same applies to the grades of 1 and 6. The dispersion of the grades is much lower in the first case (both values are close to each other) than in the second case (where the distance between the values is much bigger). For taking this dispersion into account, the first way is to calculate the range of the values. This is the difference between the minimum and the maximum value. For this purpose, you will subtract the minimum from the maximum values. In our example, in the first case (grades of 3 and 4), the range is 1. In the other case (grades of 1 and 6), it is 5.

The range is still strongly influenced by outliers, as it is only based on minimum and maximum values; it does not take the frequency of the values between those outliers into account. By defining the quartiles and the distance between quartiles you can analyze the distribution of the values more exactly. Quartiles define the limiting points which distinguish the quarters of a value distribution. Accordingly, there are the quartiles Q_1–Q_4: 25% of the values are less than or equal to the value of the first quartile Q_1, 50% are less than or equal to the second quartile Q_2, and 75% are less than or equal to the third quartile Q_3. The second quartile is equivalent to the median and separates the second and third quarters of the values. The interquartile range is the difference between the third and the first quartiles.

If the measured values are expressed on an interval or a ratio scale, you can calculate the dispersion by calculating the *standard deviation* and the *variance*. The standard deviation is the average amount of variation around the mean and the variance is the squared value of the standard deviation. These measures shed light on the distribution of the single values in the sample. With the calculations discussed so far, you can identify the central tendency in the data, what are the average values in a variable, and how the values are distributed in the dataset.

Analyses Referring to Two Variables: Correlations and Bivariate Analyses

If you want to identify the connections between two variables, you may calculate their correlation. Correlation means that a change in the value of one variable is associated with a change in the other variable. Three forms of correlation can be distinguished: a positive correlation (when variable 1 has a high value, variable 2 also has a high value); a negative correlation (when variable 1 has a high value, variable 2 has a low value and vice versa); and the absence of a correlation (you cannot say what will be the value of variable 2 if the value of variable 1 is high or low). The correlation coefficient varies between −1 (a strongly negative correlation), and +1 (a strongly positive correlation), and a value of 0 indicates the absence of a correlation. For example, you will find a correlation between education and income (more education is associated with higher income).

Correlations need to be interpreted: a correlation does not by itself indicate which of the variables is causal (for example, does more education lead to more income, or does a higher income make more education more likely?). Furthermore, a correlation does not establish a causal connection. In our example, perhaps another variable (e.g. the social status of the family of origin) is the reason for the high values for education and income: the two are consequences of the third variable and are not in a causal relation with each other. On the level of calculations, you may find meaningless connections in calculations (e.g. links between good weather and income).

Table 8.7   Bivariate analysis

Civil rights	Middle class	Working class
High	37%	45%
Low	63%	55%
N	120	120

Source: Schnell et al. 2008, p. 446 (Copyright: Methoden der empirischen Sozialforschung, p. 446, Tabelle 9-4, Schnell et al., 3rd edn (2005) Oldenbourg Wissenschaftsverlag GmbH)

Table 8.8   Multivariate analysis

| Civil rights | Colored | | White | |
	Middle class	Working class	Middle class	Working class
High	70%	50%	30%	20%
Low	30%	50%	70%	80%
N	20	100	100	20

Source: Schnell et al. 2008, p. 447 (Copyright: Methoden der empirischen Sozialforschung, p. 447, Tabelle 9-5, Schnell et al., 3rd edn (2005) Oldenbourg Wissenschaftsverlag GmbH)

Often the issues under study are more complex than can be represented through bilateral correlation. Schnell et al. (2008, pp. 446–7) demonstrate this by using an example of Rosenberg (1968). Here attitudes towards civil rights were surveyed and linked to the social class of the respondents: middle class versus working class, and liberal attitude (given a high value) versus conservative attitude (a low value). A survey of 240 people (half of them working class and half of them middle class) led to the values in Table 8.7. This gives the impression that working class people, more than members of the middle class, have a positive attitude to civil rights.

Analyses with More Than Two Variables: Multivariate Analyses

If you intend to show the relations between more than two variables, you should apply a multivariate analysis. If we take our last example and further differentiate for the respondents' color, this study leads to the distributions shown in Table 8.8.

Here we see that taking the third variable (color) into account leads to a different picture. The differences between the two classes in both parts of the table are stronger (20% and 10%) than in the first table which did not consider color (only 8%). Furthermore, the relation in both groups is inverted. In Table 8.7, in both subgroups, a bigger portion of the middle class members gave a higher value to civil rights than the working class. Now, in Table 8.8, the relation is different in both subgroups: the higher the social class, the more positive the attitude to civil rights. We see a higher estimation of civil rights in 70% of 'coloured' middle class compared to 50% of working class, and in 30% in white middle class compared to 20% in working class instead of 37% of middle class compared to 45% of working class in Table 8.7.

Discovery of relations

Methods of multivariate analysis can also be used for testing relations, especially differences between groups, if the data are on interval or ratio levels. Multiple regression, for example, starts by analyzing the differences between means in groups and shows how far a set of variables explains the dependent variable, in the sense of predicting values of the dependent variable on the grounds of information about independent variables. In addition, the regression measures the direction and strength of the effect of each variable on a dependent variable (see Neuman 2000, p. 337).

Software packages like SPSS facilitate such multivariate analyses. Nevertheless, the following should be borne in mind:

> **It is typical for this and other multivariate methods that they hardly produce unambiguous solutions; rather, there are a number of models and parameters to choose in a cluster analysis, which can lead to differing results also independent of the optimal numbers of clusters to be defined. That leads to the general problems that these procedures now can be used quite easily with the current software packages for statistical analyses. However the question of which model to choose and the interpretation of the results that are produced still require firm methodological skills and refined theoretical considerations referring to the issue of the studies. (Weischer 2007, p. 392)**

Testing Associations and Differences

To find relationships between variables in the data is often not sufficient for answering a research question. Rather it becomes necessary to test whether the observed relationships occur by chance and how strong the observed relationships between two variables are. It might be also necessary to know whether one variable is the cause of the other or if both are mutual conditions for each other. For answering such questions you can apply a significance test. Then you basically test whether a result was to be expected or whether it represents a relationship between two variables that is above chance.

If, say, you want to study pupil absence from school because of illness and to find out whether there is a relationship to gender, you can count the frequencies of absence for boys and girls. If you find that 76% of the documented absences occur for female students, this may be remarkable at first sight and seems to indicate a relationship between gender and absence. However, if in the school that is studied and in the sample that was drawn three-quarters of the students are girls, it can be expected that also 75% of the absences apply to girls. That means that you should test whether there is enough difference between the measured value (in our example 76%) and the expected value (in our example 75%) that you can derive a relationship between the variables – here gender and times of absence. By comparing the expected and the observed values you will test the null hypothesis: there is no relation between the variables above chance. If in our example the value of 76% has been observed, you can test in a significance test (e.g. the chi-square test) whether the difference between expected and observed values is big enough for confirming a relation between gender and absence. For this purpose, several significance tests are available that can be applied depending on the type of data that were measured. These include the *t*-test and Mann–Whitney test.

In the *t*-test, two datasets are compared for their differences – e.g. measures at two times or measures of two subgroups, such as either (a) the grades of a school class at the beginning and at the end of a term or (b) the grades of two classes at the end of term. With the *t*-test, a statistical significance test is applied, in which the means and the standard deviations of both datasets are taken for calculating the probability that the differences between the two datasets are accidental. Here also you will assume that the null hypothesis is correct – that there are no real differences and that observed differences occur by chance – until the statistical test demonstrates that the probability is big enough that the differences found are above chance. The latter is the case when you can show that there is a probability of less than 5% that differences are accidental. The *t*-test can be applied to small samples and also to samples with different sizes – like school classes of 18 and 25 students in our example. This test requires interval data.

The Mann–Whitney *U*-test can be applied to ordinal data. Here, you will do a rank ordering of the cases in both groups and an overall ranking of all cases in both groups. The position of the members of each group in this overall ranking will be the basis for calculating and testing the statistical significance of the differences between the two groups.

Quantitative Analyses of Relations: A Conclusion

The procedures for analyzing relations outlined above highlight either the central tendency in the data or the distribution of values in the data. They also calculate the relations between two or more variables and test the significance of the relations that were found.

Table 8.9 summarizes the approaches of quantitative analysis, the types of variables that each requires, and the usual tests for relations that can be applied.

The above overview has presented only some basic principles of quantitative analyses. For applying and studying them more extensively, you should consult a more comprehensive textbook of quantitative research and of statistics (e.g. Bryman 2008 or Neuman 2000).

Interpretative Analysis

Interpretations are also relevant in quantitative analysis. Interrelations, which can be found through calculations, e.g. correlations of two variables, are

Table 8.9   Variable types and appropriate descriptive-statistical tests

Variable types	Central tendency	Dispersion	Statistical tests
Nominal	Mode	Frequency distribution	Chi-square
Ordinal	Median	Range	Mann–Whitney U-test
Interval	Mean	Standard deviation	t-test

Source: after Denscombe 2007, p. 271

interpreted by looking for a substantive explanation for these numerical relations. However, the subject of the interpretations is not so much the data themselves but rather the calculations made with them and their results. In the methods that are presented in what follows, interpretation refers immediately to the data and is the actual analysis (see Flick 2009 for more details).

Analyses for Generating Theories Coding in Grounded Theory Research

In the development of a grounded theory from empirical material, coding is the method for analyzing data that have been collected for this purpose. This approach was introduced by Glaser and Strauss (1967) and further elaborated by Glaser (1978), Strauss (1987) and Strauss and Corbin (1990/1998/2008) or Charmaz (2006). In the process of interpretation, a number of 'procedures' for working with text can be differentiated. They are termed 'open coding', 'axial coding' and 'selective coding'. You should see these procedures neither as clearly distinguishable procedures nor as sequential phases in a linear process. Rather, they are different ways of handling textual material between which the researchers move back and forth if necessary and which they combine (see also Chapter 31 in Flick 2009).

Whereas the process of interpretation begins with open coding, towards the end of the whole analytical process *selective* coding comes more to the fore. Coding here is understood as representing the operations by which data are broken down, conceptualized, and put back together in new ways. It is the central process by which theories are built from data (Strauss and Corbin 1990/1998, p. 3). According to this understanding, coding includes the constant comparison of phenomena, cases, concepts and so on and the formulation of questions that are addressed to the text. Starting from the data, the process of coding leads to the development of theories through a process of abstraction.

Open coding aims at expressing data and phenomena in the form of concepts. For this purpose, data are first disentangled ('segmented'). 'Units of meaning' classify expressions (single words, short sequences of words) in order to attach annotations and 'concepts' (codes) to them.

This procedure cannot be applied to the whole text of an interview or of an observation protocol. Rather, you will use it for particularly instructive or perhaps extremely unclear passages. Often the beginning of a text is the starting point for the coding. This procedure serves to elaborate a deeper understanding of the text. Possible sources for labeling codes are concepts borrowed from social science literature (*constructed* codes) or taken from interviewees' expressions (*in vivo* codes). Of the two types of codes, the latter is preferred because codes then are closer to the studied material. The categories found in this way are then further developed. To this end the properties belonging to a category are labeled and dimensionalized. This means they are located along a continuum in order to define the category more precisely regarding its content. Open coding may be applied in various degrees of detail. You can code a text line by line, sentence by sentence, or paragraph by paragraph. A code can also be linked to a whole text (a protocol, a case etc.).

For open coding, and indeed for the other coding strategies, it is suggested that you regularly address the text with the following list of so-called basic questions (Strauss and Corbin 1998):

- *What?* What is the issue here? Which phenomenon is mentioned?
- *Who?* Which persons or actors are involved? Which roles do they play? How do they interact?
- *How?* Which aspects of the phenomenon are mentioned (or not mentioned)?
- *When? How long? Where?* Time, course, and location.
- *How much? How strong?* Aspects of intensity.
- *Why?* Which reasons are given or can be reconstructed?
- *What for?* With what intention, to which purpose?
- *By which?* Means, tactics, and strategies for reaching the goal.

By asking these questions, you may open up the text. They may be applied either to particular passages or to entire texts.

After a number of substantive categories have been identified, the next step is to refine and differentiate the categories that result from open coding. As a second step, Strauss and Corbin suggest completing a more formal coding for identifying and classifying links between substantive categories. In *axial coding,* the relations between categories are elaborated. In order to formulate such relations, Strauss and Corbin (1998, p. 127) suggest a coding paradigm model, which is symbolized in Figure 8.2.

This serves to clarify the relations between a phenomenon, its causes and consequences, its context, and the strategies of those involved. The coding paradigm outlines possible relations between phenomena and concepts. It is used to facilitate the discovery or establishment of structures of relations between phenomena, between concepts, and between categories. Here, as well,

Figure 8.2   The paradigm model

the questions addressed to the text and the comparative strategies mentioned above are employed once again in a complementary way. You will move continuously back and forth between inductive thinking (developing concepts, categories and relations from the text) and deductive thinking. The latter means testing the concepts, categories and relations against the text, especially against passages or cases that are different from those from which they were developed.

In the third step, i.e. *selective coding*, you will focus on elaborating the potential core concepts or core variables. This leads to an elaboration or formulation of the *story of the case*. In any case, the result should be *one* central category and *one* central phenomenon. You should develop the core category again in its features and dimensions and link it to other categories (all of them, if possible) by using the parts and relations of the coding paradigm. The analysis and the development of the theory aim at discovering patterns in the data as well as the conditions under which these apply. Grouping the data according to the coding paradigm gives specificity to the theory and will enable you to say, 'Under these conditions (listing them) this happens; whereas under these conditions, this is what occurs' (Strauss and Corbin 1990, p. 131).

Finally, you will formulate the theory in greater detail and again check it against the data. The procedure of interpreting data, like the integration of additional material, ends at the point where *theoretical saturation* has been reached. This means that further coding, enrichment of categories, and so on no longer provide or promise new knowledge. At the same time, the procedure is flexible enough that you can re-enter the same source texts and the same codes from open coding with a different research question and aim at developing and formulating a grounded theory of a different issue.

Box 8.2 provides a case study of this method in operation.

BOX 8.2

Example: 'awareness of dying'

The following represents an important early example of a study that pursued the goal of developing theory from qualitative research in the field. Barney Glaser and Anselm Strauss worked from the 1960s as pioneers of qualitative research and of grounded theory in the context of medical sociology. They did this study in several hospitals in the United States around San Francisco. Their research question asked what influenced various people's interaction with dying people and how the knowledge that the person would die soon determined the interaction with that person. More concretely, they studied which forms of interaction between the dying person and the clinical staff in the hospital, between the staff and the relatives, and between relatives and the dying person could be noted.

The starting point of the research was the observation that, when the researchers' relatives were in the hospital, the staff in hospitals (at that time) seemed not to inform patients with a terminal disease and their relatives about the state or the life expectancy of the patient. Rather the possibility that the patient might die or die soon was treated as a taboo. This general observation and the questions it raised were taken as a starting point for a more systematic observation and interviews in one hospital. These data were analyzed and used to develop categories. That was also the background for deciding to include another hospital and to continue the data collection and analysis there.

Both hospitals – as cases – were directly compared for similarities and differences. The results of such comparison were used to decide which hospital to use next, until finally six hospitals were included in the study. These included a teaching hospital, a Veterans' Affairs hospital, two county hospitals, a private Catholic hospital, and a state hospital. Wards included among others geriatrics, cancer, intensive care, pediatrics and neurosurgery, in which the fieldworkers stayed two to four weeks each. The data from each of these units (different wards in one hospital, similar wards in different hospitals, hospitals amongst each other) were contrasted and compared in order to show similarities and differences.

At the end of the study, comparable situations and contexts outside hospitals and health care were included as another dimension of comparison. Analyzing and comparing the data allowed a theoretical model to be developed, which then was transferred to other fields in order to develop it further. The result of this study was a theory of awareness contexts as ways of dealing with the information and with the patients' need to know more about their situation.

This method aims at a consistent breaking down of texts. Combining a consistently open coding with more and more focused procedures can contribute to a more profound understanding of the contents and meanings of text – one that goes beyond paraphrasing and summarizing it (which were the main approaches of qualitative content analysis discussed above). The advantage is that the interpretation of texts here becomes methodologically realized and manageable. It differs from other methods of interpreting texts because it leaves the level of the pure texts during the interpretation in order to develop categories and relations, and thus theories.

One problem with this approach is that the distinction between method and art becomes hazy. This makes it in some places difficult to teach or learn as a method. Often, the extent of the advantages and strengths of the method becomes clear only whilst applying it. If the numbers of codes and possible comparisons become too great, it is suggested to set up lists of priorities: which codes have to be further elaborated in all cases, which appear to be less instructive, and which can be omitted when you take your research question as a point of reference?

Thematic Coding

If you want to keep the reference to interviewees, for example, as a (single) case when using a coding procedure, the alternative is to use thematic coding (see Flick 2009, Chapter 23). Here you start your analysis with case studies for which you will develop a thematic structure (what characterizes across several substantive areas how the interviewee deals with health? Can you identify issues running through these ways of handling the areas?). In thematic coding you will first analyze the cases in your study in a number of case studies. For a first orientation you should develop a short description of each case, which you can continually check and modify throughout the further interpretation of the case if necessary. This description will include a statement which is typical for the interview, a short characterization of the interviewee with respect to the research question (e.g. age, profession, number of children, if relevant for your issue of research), and the major topics mentioned in the interview with respect to the issue under study. This short description first is a heuristic tool for the following analysis.

In Strauss's (1987) procedure, you will code material also across single cases in a comparative way from the beginning. In thematic coding, you will go more into the depth of the material by focusing on the single case in the next step (for example, looking at a single interview as a whole). This single-case analysis has several aims: it preserves the meaningful relations that the respective person deals with in the topic of the study, which is why a case study is done for all interviews; and it develops a system of categories for the analysis for the single case.

In the further elaboration of this system of categories (similar to Strauss), first apply open coding and then selective coding. With selective coding here you will aim less at developing a grounded core category across all cases than at generating thematic domains and categories for the single case first.

After the first case analysis, you will cross-check the categories you have developed with the thematic domains that are linked to the single cases. A thematic structure results from this cross-check, which underlies the analysis of further cases in order to increase their comparability.

The structure you developed from the first cases should be continually assessed for all further cases. You should modify it if new or contradictory aspects emerge and use it to analyze all cases that are part of the interpretation. For a fine interpretation of the thematic domains, single passages of the text (e.g. narratives of situations) are analyzed in greater detail. The coding paradigm suggested by Strauss (1987, pp. 27–8; see above) is taken as a starting point. The result of this process complemented by a step of selective coding is a case-oriented display of the way it specifically deals with the issue of the study, including constant topics (e.g. strangeness of technology) that can be found in the viewpoints across different domains (e.g. work, leisure, household).

The thematic structure developed will also serve for comparing cases and groups (that is, for elaborating correspondences and differences between the various groups in the study). Thus, you analyze and assess the social distribution of perspectives on the issue under study.

This procedure is helpful above all for studies in which theoretically based group comparisons are conducted in relation to a specific issue. Therefore, the scope for a theory to be developed is more limited than in Strauss's (1987) procedure.

Hermeneutic Procedures

In qualitative research, one makes great efforts when collecting the data to be able to understand and analyze statements in their context afterwards. Therefore, in interviews, open questions are asked. In analyzing the data, open coding is used for this purpose, in the first step at least. The analytic methods just discussed, as well as qualitative content analysis, increasingly depart from the original wording of the text: statements assume a new order according to the categories or – in Glaser and Strauss's method – the theories that are developed. More consequently oriented to the Gestalt of the text are methods guided by the principle of sequential analysis.

Narrative analyses

For analyzing narrative interviews, Schütze suggests as a 'first analytic step [i.e. formal text analysis] … to eliminate all non-narrative passages from the text and then to segment the "purified" narrative text for its formal sections' (1983, p. 286). A structural description of the contents follows, specifying the different parts of narratives ('temporally limited process structures of the life course on the basis of formal narrative connectors': Riemann and Schütze 1987, p. 348), such as 'and then' or pauses. The analytic abstraction – as a third step – moves away from the specific details of the life segments. Instead its intention is to elaborate 'the biographical shaping *in toto*, i.e., the life historical sequence of experience-dominant processual structures in the individual life periods up to the presently dominant processual structure' (1983, p. 286).

Only after this reconstruction of patterns of process do you integrate the other, non-narrative parts of the interview into the analysis. Finally, the case analyses produced in this way are compared and contrasted with each other. The aim is less to reconstruct the narrators' subjective interpretations of their lives than to reconstruct the 'interrelation of factual process courses' (1983, p. 284).

Thus Rosenthal and Fischer-Rosenthal (2004) accordingly suggest analyzing narrative interviews in five steps, as follows:

1. analysis of biographical data (data of events)
2. text and thematic field analysis (sequential analysis of textual segments from the self-presentation in the interview)
3. reconstruction of the case history (life as lived)
4. detailed analysis of individual textual locations
5. contrasting the life story as narrated with life as lived
6. formation of types.

Lucius-Hoene and Deppermann (2002) have proposed an alternative procedure. They describe the following steps, in which they move from a structural (rough) analysis to a fine analysis of the material. First, structural analysis identifies presentational segments in the text (transitions, sections, life-historical ruptures, thematic changes) in order to derive an internal structure of the text. Furthermore, some interview passages are selected for the fine analysis at this stage. Ideally, you should select a passage from the beginning of the interview, which is not too long and represents a clear episode completely in narrative form. Excerpts should be small enough and distinct in their topic and determined in their logic of action and their narrative structure.

The fine analysis should proceed with a selected excerpt in a strictly sequential fine segmentation (one that proceeds word by word, sentence by sentence, without jumping back and forth in the text). In addition, structural aspects of the text that go beyond the single sentences (which function has the passage as part of a longer narrative?) should be considered at the same time.

As a heuristic of analyzing a text, the authors suggest a number of questions (2002, p. 321):

- What is presented?
- How is it presented?
- For which purpose is this presented – and not something else?
- For which purpose is this presented now – and not at a different moment?
- For which purpose is this presented in this way – and not in a different way?

Finally, you will elaborate a case structure by collecting, bundling and comparing recurrent findings, core concepts and more abstract structural features in different passages of the sequential analysis. For example, you may develop a typology based on analyzing several narratives. Or you may identify turning points in several narratives about illness experiences, which show some kind of regularity. Or you may identify that several narrators turn to very abstract language when they address the aspect of terminality in their illness narrative.

What do the methods for analyzing narrative data discussed above have in common? They take the overall form of the narrative as a starting point for the interpretation of statements, which are seen in the context of the process of the narrative. Furthermore, they include a formal analysis of the material: which passages of the text are narrative passages, which other forms of text can be found?

In these methods, the narrative has a varying importance for analyzing the issues under study. If something is presented in the interview in the form of a narrative, Schütze sees this as an indicator that it has happened in the way it is told. Other authors, however, see narratives as a specifically instructive form of presentation of events and experiences and analyze them as such. Sometimes the assumption is made that narratives as a form of constructing events can be met in everyday life and knowledge as well. Thus, this mode of construction can be used for research purposes in a particularly fruitful way. Combining a formal analysis with a sequential procedure in the interpretation of presentations and experiences is typical for narrative analyses in general.

However, particular approaches deriving from Schütze exaggerate the quality of reality in narratives. The influence of the presentation on what is recounted is underestimated; the possible inference from narrative to factual events in life histories is overestimated. Only in very rare examples are narrative analyses combined with other methodological approaches in order to overcome their limitations. A second problem is how closely analyses stick to individual cases. The time and effort spent analyzing individual cases restricts studies from going beyond the reconstruction and comparison of a few cases.

Objective hermeneutics

Objective hermeneutics was originally formulated for analyzing natural interactions (e.g. family conversations). Subsequently the approach has been used to analyze all sorts of other documents, including even works of art and photographs. This approach makes a basic distinction between (a) the subjective meaning that a statement or activity has for one or more participants and (b) its objective meaning. The latter is understood by using the concept of a 'latent structure of meaning'. This structure can be examined only by using the framework of a multi-step scientific procedure of interpretation. Owing to its orientation to such structures, the label 'structural hermeneutics' has also been used.

Analyses in objective hermeneutics must be 'strictly sequential': that is, you should follow the temporal course of the events or the text in conducting the interpretation. You should work as one of a group of analysts working on the same text. First, the members define the case to be analyzed and on which level it is to be located. It could for example be defined as a statement or activity of a specific person, or of someone who performs a certain role in an institutional context, or of a member of the human species.

This definition is followed by a sequential *rough analysis* aimed at analyzing the external contexts in which a statement is embedded in order to take the influence of such contexts into account. The focus of this rough analysis is mainly on considerations about the nature of the concrete action problem for which the studied action or interaction offers a solution. First, you will develop case structure hypotheses, which you may falsify in later steps, and the rough structure of the text and of the case. The specification of the external context or the interactional embedding of the case serves to answer questions about how the data came about.

In the following sequential *fine analysis*, the interpretation of interactions proceeds on nine levels (Oevermann et al. 1979, pp. 394–402):

1. explication of the context, which immediately precedes an interaction

2. paraphrasing the meaning of an interaction according to the verbatim text of the accompanying verbalization

3. explication of the interacting subject's intention

4. explication of the objective motives of the interaction and of its objective consequences

5. explication of the function of the interaction for the distribution of interaction roles

6. characterization of the linguistic features of the interaction

7. exploration of the interpreted interaction for constant communicative figures

8. explication of general relations

9. independent test of the general hypotheses that were formulated at the preceding level on the basis of interaction sequences from further cases.

The procedure at levels 4 and 5 focuses on reconstructing the objective context of a statement by constructing possible contexts in thought experiments and then excluding them again one after the other. Here, the analysis of the subjective meanings of statements and actions plays a minor role. The interpreters reflect about the consequences that the statement they have just analyzed might have for the next turn in the interaction. They ask, what could the protagonist say or do next? This produces a variety of possible alternatives of how the interaction *might* proceed. Then the next *actual* statement is analyzed. It is compared with those possible alternatives which might have occurred (but which did not in fact do so). By increasingly excluding such alternatives and by reflecting why the protagonists did not choose them, the analysts elaborate the structure of the case. This structure is finally generalized to the case as a whole. For this purpose, it is tested against further material from the case – which means subsequent actions and interactions in the text.

Here, the analysis of the subjective meanings of statements and actions plays a minor role. The procedure at level 4 is oriented towards interpretations using the framework of conversation analysis (see below), whereas at level 5 the focus is on the formal linguistic (syntactic, semantic or pragmatic) features of the text. At level 6 the focus is on the formal linguistic (syntactic, semantic or pragmatic) features of the text.

Levels 7 to 9 strive for an increasing generalization of the structures that have been found (e.g. an examination is made of whether the forms of communication found in the text can be repeatedly found as general forms – i.e. communicative figures – and also in other situations). These figures and structures are treated as hypotheses and are tested step by step against further material.

According to Wernet (2006), interpretative practices are oriented on five principles:

1. *Freedom of context.* According to this, a statement is analyzed independent of the specific context in which it was made. Therefore, thought experimental contexts that are compatible with the text (p. 23) are formulated. This clarifies which meanings the statement could have, after which an interpretation referring to the concrete context follows.

2. *Literality.* According to this, the statement has to be interpreted in the way it was actually made and not how the speaker possibly meant it – in particular when a mistake is made. 'The principle of literality makes a direct interpretative approach to the difference between manifest meanings and latent meaning structures of a text' (p. 25).

3. *Sequential analysis.* Here you do not search for content in the text, but interpret its process step by step. 'For the sequential analysis, it is absolutely important *not* to consider the text that follows a sequence that is currently being interpreted' (p. 28).

4. *Extensiveness.* This means to include a multitude of interpretations (meanings the text might have).

5. *Parsimony.* 'The principle of parsimony … defines that only those interpretations may be formulated which are forced by the text that is interpreted without any additional assumption about the case' (p. 35).

Following these principles should guarantee that your text is analyzed in a comprehensive way – without either drawing on additional assumptions outside the material, or reading something into the text that is not documented in it.

Objective hermeneutics was developed for analyzing *everyday language* interactions, which are available in recorded and transcribed form as material for interpretation. The sequential analysis seeks to reconstruct the layering of social meanings from the process of the actions. When the empirical material is available as a tape or video recording and as transcript, you can analyze them step by step from the beginning to the end. Therefore, always begin the analysis with the opening sequence of the interaction. When one is analyzing interviews using this approach, the problem arises that interviewees do not always report events and processes in their chronological order. For example, the interviewees may recount certain phases in their lives and then refer to them during their narrative of events, which have to be located earlier. In the narrative interview too, and particularly in the semi-structured interview, events and experiences are not recounted in chronological order. When using a sequence analytic method for analyzing interviews, you first have to reconstruct the sequential order of the story – or of the action system under study – from the interviewee's statements. Therefore, rearrange the events reported in the interview in the temporal order in which they occurred. Then orient the sequential analysis to this order of occurrence, rather than the temporal course in the interview: 'The beginning of a sequential analysis is not the analysis of the opening of the conversation in the first interview but the analysis of those actions and events reported by the interviewee which are the earliest "documents" of the case history' (Schneider 1988, p. 234).

A consequence of this approach is that the sequential analytical procedure has developed into a program with clearly demarcated methodological steps. A further consequence of this is that it is made clear that subjective views provide only *one* form of access to social phenomena: what an individual sees as the meaning of his or her illness is one level, and this maybe is mainly linked to issues of how to cope with it. There are also social meanings, of that same illness, which are perhaps more linked to stigmatizing it than to coping with it. (On this in a different context see Silverman 2001.) Another aspect is the call for conducting group interpretations in order to increase the variety of the versions and perspectives brought to the text and to use the group to validate interpretations that have been made.

A problem with this approach is that, because of the great effort involved in the method, it is often limited to single case studies. The leap to general statements is often made without any intermediate steps. Furthermore, the understanding of the method as art, which can hardly be transformed into didactic elaboration and mediation, makes it more difficult to apply generally (for general skepticism see Denzin 1988).

BOX 8.3

Example: counselor–client interactions

Sahle (1987) has used this procedure to study the interactions of social workers with their clients. Additionally, she interviewed the social workers. She presents four case studies. In each case, the author has extensively interpreted the opening sequence of the interactions in order to elaborate the 'structure formula' for the interaction, which is then tested against a passage randomly sampled from the further text. From the analyses she derives hypotheses about the professional self-concept of the social workers and then tests them in the interviews. In a very short comparison, Sahle relates the case studies to each other and finally discusses her results with the social workers who were involved.

Conversation analysis

When applying this method, you will be less interested in interpreting the content of texts than in analyzing the formal procedures with which people communicate and with which specific situations are produced. Classic studies have analyzed the organization of turn-taking in conversations or explained how closings in conversations were initiated by the participants. Basic assumptions of conversation analysis are that (a) interaction proceeds in an orderly way and (b) nothing in it should be regarded as random. The context of interaction influences this interaction; the participants of therapy interaction act according to that framework, and the therapist talks like a therapist should do. At the same time, this sort of talking also produces and reproduces this context: by talking like a therapist should do, the therapist contributes to making this situation a therapy and to preventing it turning into a different format of talk – like gossip for example. The decision about what is relevant in social interaction and thus for the interpretation can only be made through the interpretation and not by *ex ante* settings. Drew (1995, pp. 70–2) has formulated a series of methodological precepts for conversation analysis (CA). He suggests focusing on how talk is organized and in particular on how the speakers organize turn-taking in the conversation. Another focus is on errors and how they are repaired by the speakers. CA looks for patterns of talk and of its organization by comparing several examples of conversations. In presenting the analysis of a conversation, it is important that you give enough examples in verbatim quotes that readers can assess your analysis. For example, if you analyze counseling, you could look at the opening interactions and at how the two participants arrive at defining the issue which the consultation will be about. By comparing several examples, you could show patterns of organizing an issue for the conversation and thus a consultation with a focus.

The procedure of conversation analysis of the material itself involves the following steps. First, you identify a certain statement or series of statements in transcripts as a potential element of order in the respective genre of conversation. The second step is that you assemble a collection of cases in which this element of order can be found. You will then specify how this element is used as a means for producing order in interactions and for which problem in the organization of interactions it is the answer (see Bergmann 2004). This is followed by an analysis of the methods with which those organizational problems are dealt with more generally. Thus, a frequent starting point for conversation analyses is to enquire into how certain conversations are opened and which linguistic practices are applied for ending those conversations in an ordered way.

Research in conversation analysis originally concentrated on everyday conversations (e.g. telephone calls, gossip or family conversations in which there is no specific distribution of roles). Increasingly, however, it has become occupied with specific role distributions and asymmetries as found in, for example, counseling conversation, doctor–patient interactions, and trials (i.e. conversations occurring in specific institutional contexts). The approach has also been extended to include analysis of written texts, mass media or reports, i.e. text in a broader sense (Bergmann 2004).

Discourse analysis

Discourse analysis has been developed from different backgrounds, one of which was conversation analysis. There are various versions of discourse analysis now available. Discursive psychology, as developed by Edwards and Potter (1992), Harré (1998) and Potter and Wetherell (1998), is interested in showing how, in conversations, 'participants' conversational versions of events (memories, descriptions, formulations) are constructed to do communicative interactive work' (Edwards and Potter 1992, p. 16). There is a special emphasis on the construction of versions of the events in reports and presentations. The 'interpretative repertoires', which are used in such constructions, are analyzed. Interpretative repertoires are ways of talking about a specific issue. They are called repertoires as it is assumed that these ways are not completely spontaneous, but that people apply certain ways of talking about an issue. At the same time, for example, the way an issue is treated in the press sets up such repertoires (for example, if a specific ethnic minority is always talked about by referring to violence and crime).

Willig (2003) has described research process in discourse analysis in several steps. After selecting texts and talk occurring in natural contexts, which have to be described first, you will carefully read the transcripts. Coding and then analyzing the material follows from guide questions like: why am I reading this passage in this way? What features of the text produce this reading? The analysis focuses on context, variability and constructions in the text and, finally, on the interpretative repertoires used in the texts. The last step, according to Willig, is writing up a discourse analytic research. Writing should be part of the analysis and return the researcher back to the empirical material.

Features of interpretative methods

Common to the hermeneutical methods discussed above is that they focus on the temporal-logical structure of the text and take this as a starting point of the interpretation. Thus, they stick more closely to the text than the methods based on categories, which we discussed before. The relation of content and formal aspects is shaped here in different ways. In narrative analyses, the formal difference between narrative and argumentative passages in interviews informs decisions over which passages receive how much interpretative attention and how credible the contents are. In objective hermeneutic analyses, in contrast, the formal analysis of the texts is a rather subordinate level of interpretation. Conversation analysis mainly focuses on formal aspects, which are used to design conversations – e.g. counseling conversations – and how this is employed for negotiating the specific contents of a topic. Discourse analysis again makes a turn in analyzing text and talk for contents and formal aspects.

Case Studies and Typologies

In Chapter 5, case studies were discussed as one of the basic designs in non-standardized research. The methods of data interpretation discussed so far work with case studies in various phases of treating the material. Hermeneutic methods mostly produce a case study in the first stage, consisting of a single interaction, document or interview. Comparing the cases is a later step.

In the approach of Glaser and Strauss, however, the single case (the interview, a document or an interaction) is given less attention. When they talk of 'case', they mean instead the field or issue of the study as a whole. This approach starts immediately by comparing interviewees or specific situations.

Producing and Reading Case Studies

Sometimes, for example in the evaluation of an institution, a case study may be the *result* of the research. In other approaches, case studies form the beginning, before comparison becomes more central. A third possibility is to use case studies for illustrating a basically comparative study, in order to highlight links between the different issues studied in the research. In this sense, we included a number of case studies in addition to a thematically structured comparative presentation in our study on health and illness concepts of homeless adolescents (see Flick and Röhnsch 2008).

An essential point in the production and assessment of case studies is the localization of the case and its analysis. What does the case represent and what do you intend to show by analyzing it? Is the presentation about the single person (or institution etc.) *per se*? Does it represent the person as typical for a specific subgroup in the study, or does it represent a specific professional perspective (e.g. the physicians in this field)? What were the criteria for selecting this specific case – for the data collection, for the analysis and for the presentation?

Constructing Typologies

Typologies are constructed in quantitative research, too. However, this step of condensing and presenting results is more often part of qualitative research. Kelle and Kluge (2010) have made some suggestions for how to apply this, which can be used for developing the following procedure.

The first step is either to construct case studies for the cases that are included in the research or, alternatively, to begin with analyses referring to certain issues. This is followed by systematic comparisons (of cases or referring to issues).

The next step is to define relevant dimensions of comparison. Consider what is the focus of the intended comparison – for example, the contents of the concepts of health that had been mentioned on the one hand and age and gender on the other. This may reveal here which substantial dimension characterized the ranges of health concepts that were mentioned and how the various dimensions can be allocated in the differentiation of the age of the cases or what can be found more for male or more for female interviewees.

The next step is to group the cases (according to the substantial dimension and/or age) and to analyze empirical regularities (e.g. certain concepts can mainly be found for younger girls, other concepts more for older boys).

As far as possible, the range of statements should be documented and delimited in order to develop a contrastive framework for single statements. This can be the result of compiling all relevant statements and ordering them along a dimension. In the example of Gerhardt (1988) on family rehabilitation after the husband has fallen chronically ill, this feature space consists of the range of activities found for the husband (professional work; at home) and for the wives (professional work; at home) and the combinations that result from the four possibilities in the concrete cases. In Gerhardt's study, four types result from this: dual career (both professionally working), traditional (husband working, wife at home), rational (reversed when the husband can no longer work professionally) and unemployment (when no one is working). Gerhardt has compared these four types to see in which circumstance rehabilitation of the chronically ill husband was most successful.

The next step in the construction of a typology is to analyze substantive meanings. Therefore, you will again analyze the cases in the different types for which meanings for one's own practices can be identified in the interviews and which regularities become visible for this.

Finally you will characterize the constructed types, exploring which features or combinations of features characterize the cases that have been allocated to the various types: what do they have in common, what distinguishes the cases in the different types? It may be necessary to remove cases strongly deviating from the single type, to further combine groups in order to reduce the variety, or to differentiate into more groups in the case of strong differences within the types constructed so far.

This procedure involves analyzing cases systematically, comparing them, and defining a typology. The typology may refer to the cases as a whole, which means to allocate for example interviewees to the different types. It may also refer to specific topics, which leads to a typology of how the interviewed adolescents manage sexual risks in their street lives and to a typology referring to their utilization of medical support in the case of health problems. The allocation of the interviewees to these two typologies will not necessarily be identical.

Checklist for Analyzing Data

If you conduct an empirical project, it will help to consider the questions in Box 8.4 for the analysis of your data. These questions can be used for doing your own study or for assessing the research of other researchers.

BOX 8.4

Checklist for data analysis

1. Is the method of analysis you chose appropriate to the data you collected?
2. Does it meet the complexity of the data?
3. Does the nature of the data permit you to apply the analytic structure that you chose?
4. Does the kind of analysis allow reducing the complexity of the data in a way that the results become easily understandable?
5. Can you answer your research question with the form of analysis you chose?
6. What is the research question or the aspect of it that is intended to be the focus of the analysis?
7. Can your analysis assess whether your result came up by chance or if it is a singular result?
8. Are your quantitative results statistically significant?
9. Do any regularities (e.g. a typology) become visible in the qualitative results?
10. How does your analysis consider deviant cases or data?

| **Key Points** |

- **Content analysis works with texts – in a quantitative way in analyzing newspapers, for example, and in a qualitative way also in analyzing interviews and other data.**
- **Quantitative analysis starts with elaborating, evaluating and cleaning data.**

- The next step is the descriptive analysis of frequencies, distributions, central tendencies and dispersions in the data.

- Quantitative analyses can focus on one, two or more variables and their relationships.

- Relationships found in this way are tested for their statistical significance with different tests.

- Qualitative analyses can aim at developing a theory by applying various methods of coding the data.

- They also can focus on analyzing narratives for the processes and life histories represented in them.

- The analysis of interactions is an option in analyzing qualitative data.

- Qualitative analysis moves between case-oriented and comparative analysis with the aim of developing typologies.

Further Reading

The following texts provide more detailed discussion of the issues covered in this chapter.

Bryman, A. (2008) *Social Research Methods*, 3rd edn. Oxford: Oxford University Press.

Flick, U. (ed.) (2007) *The Sage Qualitative Research Kit*, 8 vols. London: Sage.

Flick, U. (2009) *An Introduction to Qualitative Research*, 4th edn. London: Sage.

Flick, U., Kardorff, E. v. and Steinke, I. (eds) (2004) *A Companion to Qualitative Research*. London: Sage.

CHAPTER 9
E-RESEARCH: DOING SOCIAL RESEARCH ONLINE

Chapter Overview

Chapter Objectives

This chapter is designed to help you:

- understand the use of the Internet in social research
- appreciate the advantages of using the Internet as a support for your study
- understand how traditional approaches to social research can be transferred to Internet-based research
- recognize the limits of doing social research online.

Table 9.1   Navigator for Chapter 9

Orientation	• What is social research? • Research question • Literature review
Planning and design	• Planning research • Designing research • Deciding methods
Working with data	• Gathering data • Analyzing data • E-research • Integrated research
Reflection and writing	• Evaluating research • Ethics • Writing and using research

You are here in your project →

What Is E-Research and Why Do It?

The Internet has become a part of many people's lives in one way or another. It can be interesting, therefore, to study (a) who is using the Internet and (b) for what purposes, and (c) who is not using the Internet. If you were to pursue such questions, you would be making the Internet an *issue* of your research.

In such studies you could of course apply the methods we discussed in the preceding chapters in a traditional way. You could, for example, distribute a questionnaire or do face-to-face interviews in your student community or a sample of the general population. This would be helpful, especially for pursuing the third of the questions itemized above – i.e. who is *not* using the Internet.

Besides becoming an issue of your research in this way, the Internet has become an important instrument for doing research – sometimes on issues not directly linked to the Internet itself. Research that uses the Internet as an instrument for doing social research is sometimes called 'e-research' and it is on this that we focus in this chapter. Here we find traditional methods of social research transferred, and sometimes adapted, to e-research. Examples include online surveys, online and e-mail interviews, online focus groups, virtual ethnography and the like.

There are two sets of preliminary questions to ask yourself before embarking on e-research. (1) Do you like working with computers and using the Internet and its various forms of communication? Do you feel comfortable working in this context? (2) Do you have the technical skills to create and use online tools (e.g. a survey or an interview)? If not, do you have the necessary support for doing so? If your answer to such questions is 'no', you might prefer a different method for your research project.

Sampling and Access

As in general research, so in e-research: the concept of sampling involves a wider population from which you draw a sample, and so your sample of actual participants represents some larger group of potential participants. In e-research, however, you may have the problem of a double reality. To take a simple example: if you wish to study trends in book purchasing and you use an online shop like Amazon to find your participants, you will be using a very selective approach: you cannot necessarily equate the clients of this shop with those of (a) offline bookshops or even (b) other shops on the Internet. Thus in this example it will be difficult to draw conclusions from a sample (of Internet bookshop users) to a population of book buyers in general. This example entails questions not only of how representative online samples are for real-world populations, but also of access – where you will find participants, how you will contact them, and so on.

Here we may consider a number of forms of access for an online survey (see below) aiming at a random sample (see Baur and Florian 2009). They are:

- web surveys without scientific claims
- open web surveys with no limitations on who is expected to take part; everyone is invited (through, say, a banner on a website) and may even be able to participate several times over
- self-recruited volunteer panels that address potential participants drawn to a certain issue
- intercept surveys that draw a random sample of all people who visit a certain webpage and then invite the members of that sample to participate in a survey
- list-based surveys that use institutions with a complete e-mail list of its members (e.g. a university with all its students and employees), all of whom are invited to participate (or from which a random sample is drawn)
- mixed mode surveys that use a random sample of the population; members of the sample may then choose between paper and online questionnaires for their participation
- a panel of the population recruited beforehand, drawn from a random sample of the population and where, if members of this sample do not have access to the Internet, the researchers will provide them with access.

These alternatives differ with regard to where you find your population to draw a sample from and also how far you can realize the idea of random sampling in this context. The population can consist either of the users of a website or Internet portal or of the general population of a country. In the latter case, you have to take into account that Internet users constitute a selection from the general population: by no means everyone uses the Internet. For example,

Internet users tend to be younger than the average population and are more likely to have received a higher education. This may lead to problems of *under-coverage* in your Internet sample compared to the general population: that is, certain groups of the population (e.g. older people or those without children) will be systematically under-represented in your Internet-based sample. At the same time, you may face *over-coverage* as a problem: people who are not in your target group or sample may respond to your questionnaire, sometimes without revealing their identity, which then makes it difficult to exclude them from your dataset. Or some people fill in your questionnaire several times. Other problems include non-response to certain items/questions or respondents who drop out, for example after answering the first group (or page) of questions and then losing interest or because of a breakdown in the Internet connection.

Another problem of access is what and how much you will really know about your participants if you use people's e-mail address or the nickname they use in discussion groups or chatrooms for identifying them. In some cases, you will know no more about them or have to rely on the information they give you about their gender, age, location and so on. This may raise questions about the reliability of such demographic information and lead to problems of contextualizing the statements in the later interview. As Markham asks: 'What does it mean to interview someone for almost two hours before realizing (s)he is not the gender the researcher thought (s)he was?' (2004, p. 360).

In addition, using e-mail address as the identifier for participants in your study may raise other issues. Many people use more than one e-mail address or several Internet providers at the same time. In contrast, several people within the same household may use the same computer (see Bryman 2008, p. 647).

Several responses to these problems of sampling have been suggested. One is that not every study needs a sample as closely representative of the 'population at large' as possible: this applies to online research as well as offline (Hewson et al. 2003). Qualitative studies follow a different logic of sampling, and maybe it does make sense to study the shopping trends of amazon.com clients (in our example above) for some purpose. So such a sample may be adequate as long as you refrain from generalizing your results to inadequate populations (e.g. book buyers in general). You need to be careful in generalizing your results to other populations and to reflect on what is adequate and what is not. Finally, for some studies and research questions, it may not be a problem that participants respond repeatedly or use unclear identities as this may represent typical user practices on the Internet. The questions and issues mentioned by Gaiser and Schreiner in this context may be helpful:

> **Consider who you want in the study and where you are going to find them. Who is likely to frequent your type of online environment? How can you get participants to participate in your site? How might a researcher best engage a particular population? What technologies do sample participants use or are more likely to use? (2009, p. 15)**

In general, as in other forms of survey, you should consider two steps for increasing the response rate. Before you send a questionnaire to potential participants, you should contact them and ask for their permission to include them in your study. You should follow up non-respondents at least once (Bryman 2008, p. 648).

Online Surveys, Interviews and Focus Groups

The three basic methods for gathering participants' statements – namely drawing on opinions, stories and other forms of verbal data – have been transferred to e-research.

Online Surveys

There are several assessments of online surveys. Most research using the Internet is quantitative and consists of online surveys, web-based questionnaires, or Internet experiments (see Hewson et al. 2003). It has been estimated that at least a third of all surveys worldwide are online surveys (Evans and Mathur 2005, p. 196) and the trend is upwards. Bryman (2008) discusses e-mail surveys and web surveys. The first, as the name suggests, is sent by e-mail to recipients selected in advance. The questionnaire is attached to an e-mail with the expectation that the recipients answer the questions and send the questionnaire back as an attachment to their reply e-mail. An alternative is to send the questionnaire embedded in the e-mail itself, and the answers are given by adding an 'x' to the questions or by writing text into the e-mail and send it back by touching the reply button. Although the latter version may be easier to handle for the respondent, some e-mail programs may produce problems with the formatting. Web surveys are more flexible in formatting the whole questionnaire and the answer options. Questionnaires can be designed appealingly and it is easier to include filter questions or skip questions (the answer directs the participant to different questions to refer to next, or questions are left out after a specific answer). Participants may be addressed by placing a banner similar to an advertisement on a webpage and respondents can click on the questionnaire and fill it in. There are also software tools and services available on the Internet which can facilitate doing your online survey; many companies offer these services professionally (which means you have to pay for them). If you search 'Google survey' you will end up at a long list of such services like Survey Monkey or Bristol Online Surveys (http://www.survey.bris.ac.uk).

Compared to postal questionnaire surveys, online surveys have a number of advantages. These include:

- *Low cost.* As you will not have to print your questionnaire, you can save money on envelopes and stamps. The questionnaires you receive back are already 'in' the computer and more easily transferred into the statistics software.

- *Time.* Online questionnaires come back more quickly than postal questionnaires.

- *Ease of use.* Online questionnaires are easier to format and easier to navigate for the participant (see above).

- *Lack of spatial restrictions.* You can reach people over long distances without waiting for the questionnaire to travel back and forth.

- *Response rate.* The number of unanswered questions in most cases is lower with online surveys, while open questions tend to be answered in a more detailed way and the answers are already given in a digital format.

However, there are also a number of disadvantages of online questionnaires compared to traditional surveys. The response rates can be lower in some cases; you will only reach populations that are already online (see above). There is skepticism about anonymity, especially on the part of potential participants; this may reduce the motivation to respond. Alternatively, people sometimes reply more than once (see Bryman 2008, p. 648; Hewson et al. 2003, p. 43).

BOX 9.1

Case study: longitudinal monitoring of students' quality assessments

At the university of Potsdam, an online panel was established to monitor student biographies, course evaluations, and assessments of the study program quality, in a longitudinal perspective. Students were invited to join the online panel through online and offline contacts. Students were contacted before they started their studies and before enrolling for the programs and were motivated by a lottery for participants. Nevertheless, of the 18,000 students of the university, only 700 were in the panel after a year. The research team took careful precautions to guarantee the anonymity of the participants and to be able to link data from the several waves of survey (see Pohlenz et al. 2009 for details).

Sue (2007, pp. 20–1) has outlined a research timeline for online surveys to be completed in 13 weeks. The first three weeks are devoted to writing the study objectives, reviewing the literature, and revising the objectives. The next three weeks are devoted to selecting survey software and developing, pre-testing and revising the questionnaire. In week 7, the actual data collection is run and incoming responses are monitored. Weeks 8 and 9 focus on reminding non-respondents and analyzing the data. In the remaining four weeks you will write first and second drafts of research reports and present them. This timeline looks very tight, in particular in the part where the research is run – but it at least gives an initial indication of how to progress.

Online Interviews

You can organize online interviewing in several ways. You may use a *synchronous* form. This means that you contact your participant while you are both online at the same time – for example in a chatroom where you can directly exchange questions and answers. This comes closest to the verbal exchange in a face-to-face interview. Alternatively, you can organize online interviews in an *asynchronous* form, which means you send your questions to the participants and they send their answers back later: here you are not necessarily online at the same time. The latter version is mostly done through e-mail exchanges and comes close to what you do in a questionnaire study. You can also use messaging services like Skype to establish an *immediate* dialogue in the format of question and answer. If the technical resources are available, you can even establish a video dialogue in which you see your respondent and vice versa.

Each of these alternatives needs technical resources (like a camera, a fast broadband connection and the like) on both sides. Mann and Stewart (2000, p. 129) following Baym (1995) see five questions as important to consider for computer-mediated interaction in interviews. They are:

1. What is the purpose of the interaction/interview? This will influence the interest of possible participants in whether or not to become involved in the study.

2. What is the temporal structure of the research? Are synchronous or asynchronous methods used, and will there be a series of interactions in the research or not?

3. What are the possibilities and limitations of the software which will influence the interaction?

4. What are the characteristics of the interviewer and the participants? What about their experience of and attitude to using technology? What about their knowledge of the topics, writing skills, insights etc.? Is one-to-one interaction or researcher–group interaction planned? Has there been any interaction between researcher and participant before? How is the structure of the group addressed by the research (by hierarchy, gender, age, ethnicity, social status etc.)?

5. What is the external context of the research – the inter/national culture and/or communities of meaning that are involved? How do their communicative practices outside the research influence the latter?

If you do your interviews in an asynchronous form, the delay between question and answer may influence the quality of your data and the thread of the interview may get lost. When running the interview itself, you can either send one question or a couple of questions, wait for the answers, and then probe (as in a face-to-face interview), or continue sending the next questions. If there is a longer delay before answers come, you can send a reminder (after a few days for example). Bampton and Cowton (2002) view a decline in the length and quality of responses, as well as a tendency for answers to come more slowly, as a sign of fading interest on the part of the participant and the signal for the interview to come to an end.

The advantages mentioned for interviewing online are the same as for online research in general. You may save time and costs and can reach people over big distances. An additional advantage is the greater anonymity for the participant, in particular in e-mail interviews. If you choose a video call, the anonymity for the participant is no longer given as it is in the e-mail interview, where only statements are exchanged as text. At the same time, you can more easily contextualize statements in paralinguistic contexts like facial expressions. The disadvantages are doubts about the 'real' identities (who am I talking to), the loss in direct rapport with the participants, and the problems in probing when answers remain unclear. The latter applies more to e-mail interviews, which come closer to the situation of filling in a questionnaire (see Salmons 2010 for more details of planning and doing online interviews in a synchronous way).

Online Focus Groups

There has been particular interest in online focus groups. Again, one can distinguish between synchronous (or real-time) and asynchronous (non-real-time) groups. The first type of online focus group requires that all participants are online at the same time. They may participate via a chatroom or by using specific conferencing software. The latter option requires all participants to have this software on their computers or to be provided with it. Besides the technical problems this may cause, many people may hesitate to receive and install software for the purpose of taking part in a study. Asynchronous focus groups do not require that all participants are online at the same time (and this prevents the problems of coordination).

For online focus groups to work, ready access for the participants is required. Mann and Stewart (2000, pp. 103–5) describe in some detail the software you can use for setting up synchronous focus groups ('conferencing software'). They also describe the alternatives of how to design websites, and how these can facilitate access for those who are intended to participate and exclude others not intended to have access. The authors also discuss how the concepts of naturalness and neutrality concerning the venue of a focus group also apply online. For example, it is important that the participants can take part in the discussions from their computers at home or at their workplace, rather than from a special research site. As a beginning, it is important to create a welcome message, which invites the participants, explains the procedures and what is expected from the participants, and describes what the rules of communication

among the participants should be (e.g. 'please be polite to everyone') and so on (see 2000, p. 108 for an example). The researcher should – as with any focus group – create a permissive environment.

The advantages of doing focus groups online are that you may save time and costs, as you will not have to set up your group at the same time and place and you will save transcription costs as data already come in digital form. Other advantages are that there is greater anonymity for the participants and that group dynamics play a smaller role compared to real-world focus groups: it is less likely here that participants will dominate the group or suppress other participants' contribution.

At the same time, there are disadvantages. An asynchronous group may take a long time to respond. Also contributions may 'come late': discussion may already have moved on, when respondents after some time refer to an earlier state of discussion. The tendency for non-response may be higher than in face-to-face interviews. Technical requirements and problems (for example, connection difficulties) may influence the data quality as well the process of an asynchronous discussion.

Virtual Ethnography

If you transfer methods of surveying or individual or group interviews to e-research, you turn to the Internet as a *tool* to study people you could not otherwise reach. But you can also see the Internet as a *place* or as a *way of being* (for these three perspectives see Markham 2004). In these cases, you can study the Internet as a form of milieu or culture in which people develop specific forms of communication or, sometimes, specific identities. This requires a transfer of ethnographic methods to Internet research and to studying the ways of communication and self-presentation on the Internet: 'Reaching understandings of participants' sense of self and of the meanings they give to their online participation requires spending time with participants to observe what they do online as well as what they say they do' (Kendall 1999, p. 62). Box 9.2 provides a case study of ethnography online.

BOX 9.2

Case study: virtual ethnography

In her study, Hine (2000) took a widely discussed trial (the Louise Woodward case – a British au pair who was tried for the death of a child she was responsible for in Boston) as a starting point. She wanted to find out how this case was constructed on the Internet by analyzing webpages concerned with this issue. She also interviewed web authors by e-mail about their

---

intentions and experiences and analyzed the discussions in newsgroups in which 10 or more interventions referring to the case had been posted. She used www.dejanews.com for finding newsgroups. At this site, all newsgroup postings are stored and can be searched by using keywords. Her search was limited to one month in 1998.

Hine posted a message to several of the newsgroups which had dealt with the issue more intensively. However, the response was rather limited, as other researchers had obviously found repeatedly (2000, p. 79). Hine also set up her own homepage and mentioned it while contacting prospective participants or in posting messages about her research. She did this to make herself and her research transparent for potential participants.

In summarizing her results, she stated that:

> The ethnography constituted by my experiences, my materials and the writings I produce on the topic is definitely incomplete … In particular, the ethnography is partial in relation to its choice of particular applications of the Internet to study. I set out to study 'the Internet', without having made a specific decision as to which applications I intended to look at in detail. (2000, p. 80)

Nevertheless, Hine produced interesting results of how people dealt with the issue of the trial on the Internet. Her thoughts and discussions on virtual ethnography are very instructive beyond her own study. However, they also show the limitations of transferring ethnography – or, more generally, qualitative research – to online research, as Bryman's critical comment illustrates: 'Studies like these are clearly inviting us to consider the nature of the Internet as a domain for investigation, but they also invite us to consider the nature and the adaptiveness of our research methods' (2008, p. 636).

In general, interest in doing ethnographies of the Internet – also called 'netnographies' (Kozinets 2010) – is increasing. Often forms of interviewing are used, as opposed to ethnographic methods in the strict sense of the term.

Analyzing Internet Documents and Interactions

Bergmann and Meier (2004) go one step further. Starting from a conversation analytic background, they suggest analyzing the formal parts of interaction on the web. Conversation analysis is interested in the linguistic and interactive tools (like taking turns, repairing, opening up closings: see Chapter 8) that people use when they communicate about an issue. In a similar way, the authors suggest that you identify the traces online communication leaves for understanding how communication is practically produced on the web. Thus they use electronic process data, that is 'all data that are generated in the course of computer-assisted communication processes and work activities – either automatically or on the basis of adjustments by the user' (2004, p. 244). These data are not simply ready to hand: rather they must be reconstructed on the basis of a detailed and ongoing documentation of what is happening on the

screen (and, if possible, in front of it) when someone sends an e-mail, for example. This includes the comments of the sender while typing an e-mail, and paralinguistic aspects like laughing and so on. It is important to document the temporal structure of computer-mediated communication. Here you can use special software (like Lotus ScreenCam) that allows filming of what is happening on the computer screen together with recording the interaction in front of the screen with video, for example.

Similarly, you may take webpages as a medium of online interaction and analyze them for their content and for the means that are used for communicating these contents. You can use qualitative methods for such a study – like a hermeneutic approach or qualitative content analysis – or approach these objects with quantitative methods like content analysis, or by analyzing the frequencies with which they are addressed or used.

A specific feature of webpages is the intertextuality of documents on the web, organized and symbolized by (electronic) links from one text (or one page) to other texts. This kind of cross-referencing goes beyond the traditional definition and boundaries of a text and links a large number of single pages (or texts) to one big (sometimes endless) text. Many webpages constantly update, change, disappear and reappear on the web. It is necessary therefore to always mention the date you accessed a page when referring to it as a source. As with other forms of analyzing documents as means of interaction, you should ask: who produced this webpages, for whom, and with what intentions? Which means are used to reach these goals?

E-Research Today: Using Web 2.0

The approaches mentioned so far have been made possible by the development of the Internet, or web, over the last couple of decades. More recently, from around 2005 onwards, a set of new developments has changed forms of communication on the web again. Together they are usually referred to as 'Web 2.0'. New forms of communicating (blogs for example) and of social networking sites (like Facebook, YouTube, or Twitter) have become public and widely used.

Again, these developments can be an issue for research (who uses them and for what purposes?). They can also be used as instruments for doing research as well, together with other Web 2.0 developments. A recent study (RIN 2010) has focused on the use of Web 2.0 tools in particular for research purposes and on who is already using them and what developments this will lead to.

What is Web 2.0?

The following definition highlights what is characteristic for Web 2.0 and what makes it relevant for research purposes:

> Web 2.0 encompasses a variety of different meanings that include an increased emphasis on user-generated content, data and content sharing and collaborative effort, together with the use of various kinds of social software, new ways of interacting with web-based applications, and the use of the web as a platform for generating, re-purposing and consuming content. (Anderson 2007, quoted in RIN 2010, p. 14)

A central feature is the way communication and the production of knowledge are organized:

> Web 2.0 services emphasize decentralized and collective generation, assessment and organization of information, often with new forms of technological intermediation. (2010, p. 14)

How Can You Make Use of Web 2.0 for Your Own Research?

For using this approach in the context of social research, the sharing of information is a central issue. This involves (a) retrieving information (publications for example), (b) making information accessible (sharing of data, public datasets etc.) and (c) publishing research (results, reports etc.). Thus the main issue is how these new media are used to organize and facilitate scholarly communication. You can use these media for collaborative research by sharing your data and experiences with other researchers. So you could work on the same datasets with other people, use blogs for this purpose, and make your results public in this context.

The variety of developments is evident in what was studied in the research mentioned above:

> We include common forms such as blogs and wikis, widely adopted generic services such as video-sharing, bookmarking or reference-sharing, and social networking systems offered by commercial providers. In addition, we investigated services provided by actors such as publishers and libraries, and some individual open access publishers and aggregators, along with some more specialised tools adapted for specific workflows or research communities. (2010, p. 14)

Examples of applying these forms of communication are to use and contribute to public wikis (the best known may be Wikipedia, but there are other examples) or private wikis set up for a specific purpose. Other forms are to write blogs or comment on blogs, to post presentations, slides, images or videos publicly. These forms can be used for working in collaborative teams in one institution or across several institutions (see also http://www.oii.ox.ac.uk/microsites/oess/ for more information in this area in general).

A major issue in this context is the use of open access software, and even more the use of open access online journals for one's own publications, for seeking existing publications and for commenting on other people's publications. There are also commercial services like SlideShare (www.slideshare.net), where slide presentations can be made public as a more informal way of communicating about research and findings. And finally, there is a strong trend towards open access repositories making literature available online and for free (e.g. the Social Science Open Access Repository at http://www.ssoar.info/).

These developments will change social research in the near future by making new forms of collaboration, of retrieving information and of publishing results and reports easier.

Checklist for Designing Social Research Online

When you do your research project on the Internet, you should consider the questions listed in Box 9.3. These questions can be helpful for doing your own study online, but also for assessing other researchers' online studies.

BOX 9.3

Checklist for designing social research online

1. Why do you wish to do your research online as opposed to on-site?
2. Is your target group a population specifically linked to the Internet, which thus makes an online study necessary?
3. Is your target population likely to have the Internet access required for participating in your study?
4. Do the advantages of applying your methods online outweigh the disadvantages?
5. Do you have the necessary computer skills for designing your instruments and administering the project online?
6. What is the potential of Web 2.0 communication for doing your research?

Key Points

- Survey, interviews, observation and documentary research are the major methods in social research that have been transferred to online research.
- Online research requires computer and Internet literacy on the part of researchers, but also on the part of the potential participants.

- Sampling issues are doubled here: what inferences can you make from your online sample to (a) populations in the virtual world and (b) real-world populations?

- It may be difficult to preserve the specific characteristics of a method when using it online – for example, to prevent an e-mail interview from becoming an e-mail questionnaire.

- For analyzing online communication as a research topic, methods need to be further developed.

- New forms of online communication support and change the way of doing and publishing research.

▨ ▨ Further Reading ▨

The four texts listed below provide a helpful overview of e-research.

Flick, U. (2009) *An Introduction to Qualitative Research*, 4th edn. London: Sage. Chapter 20.

Gaiser, T.J. and Schreiner, A.E. (2009) *A Guide to Conducting Online Research*. London: Sage.

Hewson, C., Yule, P., Laurent, D. and Vogel, C. (2003) *Internet Research Methods: A Practical Guide for the Social and Behavioral Sciences*. London: Sage.

RIN (2010) 'If You Build It, Will They Come? How Researchers Perceive and Use Web 2.0', http://www.rin.ac.uk/our-work/communicating-and-disseminating-research/use-and-relevance-web-20-researchers (accessed 21 August 2010).

Salmons, J. (2010) *Online Interviews in Real Time*. London: Sage.

CHAPTER 10
INTEGRATED SOCIAL RESEARCH: COMBINING DIFFERENT RESEARCH APPROACHES

Chapter Overview

Chapter Objectives

This chapter is designed to help you:

- understand the limits of social research
- appreciate the arguments for combining various procedures in a research project
- understand the concept of triangulation
- understand the idea of integrated social research
- see that combining methods can be productive, if you use them to collect or analyze data on different levels.

Table 10.1   Navigator for Chapter 10

Orientation	• What is social research? • Research question • Literature review
Planning and design	• Planning research • Designing research • Deciding methods
Working with data	• Gathering data • Analyzing data • E-research • Integrated research
Reflection and writing	• Evaluating research • Ethics • Writing and using research

You are here in your project →

For all the value of social research, it should be recognized that it has its limits. One cannot study everything – for ethical (see Chapter 12), for methodological and sometimes for practical reasons. Research projects limited to single methods are particularly limited. This chapter is designed both to make those limitations clearer and to show how using a combination of methods can expand the range of what is possible in research.

Limits of Quantitative Research

Let us first consider the main limitations of standardized research.

Limits of Representativeness

To ensure that studies are representative, researchers need to draw appropriate samples. Yet this is easier said than done. In many cases, you will find that biases in the sample arise. For example, you may find that you cannot reach some of the potential participants: they may have moved away or died, for example, or they may refuse to take part in your study. In particular, the increasing number of telephone surveys in the context of market research may result in resistance from potential participants. Sometimes an increase in funding for a particular area of research results in participants being approached too often and so refusing. As a result, obtaining a representative sample may require considerable effort.

Limits of Standardized Surveys

Standardized surveys are intended to collect views on the issues under study, independently of both the situation in which data are collected and the person of the interviewer. That is the aim, whether you are using questionnaires to be completed by the participant or standardized interviews with a catalogue of questions to be asked by an interviewer. Yet there are difficulties with these methods. Interviewees' characteristics – for example, their age or gender – can influence the way they approach questions in an interview situation (e.g. Bryman 2008, pp. 210–11). Responses may be influenced by ideas about their social desirability: interviewees may ask themselves, which answer is expected from me? Which opinion would I rather not express? Another problem is that respondents might answer all questions with consistently positive (or consistently negative) answers.

In addition, there is the problem that respondents may interpret questions differently from each other. Can you, for example, assume that everybody who ticks 'agree completely' for a question has understood it in the same way as all the others giving the same answer, and that this answer represents the same attitude in every case? Do interviewee and interviewer share the same meaning of the words in the question? Both would be a precondition for summarizing identical answers under the same category.

Limits of Structured Observation

For structured observation that uses an observation scheme or guidelines with predefined categories, there are also limitations. Such instruments may force an inappropriate or irrelevant framework upon the setting that you observe. Structured observation documents behaviors rather than underlying intentions, and in general pays too little attention to their context (2008, p. 269).

Limits of Quantitative Content Analysis

Content analyses are only as good as the documents that you study with them. Moreover, it is difficult to develop a category system that does not to some extent depend on the interpretation of the coder. Underlying or latent meanings are very difficult to capture through content analysis: such analysis usually remains at a surface level. Also, it is difficult to identify the reasons behind certain statements. Finally, this method has been criticized for its lack of theoretical reference (see Bryman 2008, p. 291 for these points).

Limits in Analyzing Secondary Data

The main limitation of secondary (statistical or routine) data is that researchers may be only partly familiar with the data. You may be over-challenged by the complexity of the data (their volume, their internal structure etc.). In addition, you will have little control over the quality of the data (how exact was the documentation in the statistics, who conducted the error control or data cleaning and how?). Moreover, sometimes entries or values that are important for your research question may be missing (2008, p. 300). In many cases, it will be impossible for you to go back to the raw data, as the data are accessible only in aggregated form (summaries, calculations, distributions). If you use official statistics as data, you will need to ensure that category labels are not misleading and that your definitions are the same as those used in data collection.

Limits of Standardized Research

Standardized research has the advantage that it works with a large number of cases and a clearly structured data basis. Thus it often provides representative results. The price for this, however, is that data collection and analysis have to be strongly structured and focused in advance. The scope for new aspects, for the specific experiences of individual participants and for taking concrete contexts into account in data collection remains very limited. The data available for the analysis then are significantly reduced in richness due to the way they were collected (e.g. participants may be limited to five alternative responses). Subjective views that fall outside the range anticipated when you designed your instruments will be difficult to handle. This may limit what you are able to study through standardized methods.

Limits of Qualitative Research

Qualitative research also has its limitations, as described below.

Limits of Theoretical Sampling

If you use theoretical sampling, you will adapt the selection of material as much as possible to the existing gaps in knowledge. Additional cases are then selected according to which aspects of the research question the analysis has not answered so far. The problem here is that neither the beginning nor the end of selecting material can be defined and planned in advance. Unless you can apply this strategy with much sensitivity, experience and flexibility, the scope of the material that you then analyze, and the generalizability of your results, may remain rather limited.

Limits of Interviewing

When you use prepared questions as the core of your interviews, there is a danger that they might omit points that are in fact essential for the interviewees. However, compared to questionnaire studies, you can make this an issue more easily and can repair it more easily. Despite the use of an interview schedule, you will be able to predict what happens in your interviews in a relatively limited way. This also refers to how comparable the situations in your interviews will be. The flexibility in doing the interview permits more sensitivity for the interviewee, but reduces the comparability of the collected data at the same time. Narratives are even more oriented to the single case when you collect your data. Therefore the path from the single interviewee to (theoretically) generalized statements is even longer. The quality of your data will depend very much on your 'success' in the interview situation: do you manage to mediate between what the interviewee mentions and your questions, or to initiate narratives which include the aspects that are relevant for your study? In any case, the data will be limited to reports about an event or an activity and will not give you direct access to them.

Limits of Participant Observation

The strength of participant observation is that you as observer are really involved in the events. Because of your participation, you will have insights into the internal perspective of the setting. As in other forms of observation, participant observation has access only to what happens during the time the researchers participate and observe. What happened before or beyond the setting or concrete situations remains closed to observation and can be covered only through more or less formal conversations. The proximity to what is studied is both the strength and the weakness of the method at the same time. In many reports (e.g. Sprenger 1989), it is evident that the research situation may overwhelm the researchers; their distance from the situation or people that are observed is then endangered. At the same time, there is the question of how situations, and access to them, are selected. We may ask: how far do the periods in which you make your observations enable you to gain the insights you seek? Do your observations actually elucidate the issue you are researching and show its relevance to the field?

Limits of Qualitative Content Analysis

Compared to quantitative content analysis, there will in qualitative research be a stronger consideration of context and the meaning of texts. Compared to other interpretative or hermeneutic approaches, an analysis will be achieved which is much more based on rules and pragmatism. Often the rules that are formulated for a content analysis are as demanding in their application as other methods. The need to interpret text when classifying may make it difficult to maintain procedural clarity. It puts the promised procedural clarity of the method and its rules in perspective again. Categorization of the material employing categories derived externally or from theories, rather than from the material itself, may direct the researchers' focus more to the content than to exploration of the meanings and depth of the text. Interpretation of text through analytic methods, such as objective hermeneutics or grounded theory analysis, plays a role in qualitative content analysis only in a rather schematic way – in explicative content analysis (as outlined in Chapter 8). Another problem is that in qualitative content analysis one often works with paraphrases: these may be useful for explaining the original material, but cause problems if used in place of original material for content analysis.

Limits of Qualitative Analyses of Documents

The advantage of documents is that they are often already available, as they have been produced for purposes other than the research. Institutions produce records, notes, statements and other documents that you can use for your research. Again, however, you face the problem that you cannot influence the quality of the data (production). Documents may have other points of focus and different contents than required for answering your research questions. Sometimes documents have not been produced systematically enough to permit their comparison across institutions. Finally, problems of access to specific documents may arise.

Limits of Non-standardized Research

Qualitative research also has important limitations. The very openness, flexibility and richness of qualitative research may make it difficult to make comparisons between data or to see the big picture – 'the wood for the trees'.

Qualitative research may also intrude into the lives and the private spheres of the participants more than standardized research does. For example, if a disease has led to a stressful situation in one's life, it may be easier to answer some questions in a questionnaire than to recount in a narrative interview the whole process of becoming ill.

Overall, we can see from the above summary of the typical limitations associated with single research methods that both qualitative and standardized research have their limits. We can now consider whether these limits can be overcome by combining different methods.

Combining Different Approaches

At the end of Chapter 6, the importance of deciding between qualitative and quantitative research was highlighted. For many research problems, however, a decision may lead to narrowing the perspective on the issue under study. The number of research problems that require a *combination* of qualitative and quantitative approaches, and thus of several perspectives on what is studied, is growing. Therefore, we will consider approaches for (a) combining methods within either qualitative or quantitative research and also for (b) combining qualitative and quantitative research within the same study. Bryman (1988; 1992) has identified 11 ways of integrating quantitative and qualitative research as follows:

1. The logic of triangulation means checking qualitative findings against quantitative results.

2. Qualitative research can support quantitative research.

3. Quantitative research can support qualitative research.

4. Integration may provide a more general picture of the issue under study.

5. Structural features are analyzed with quantitative methods and processual aspects with qualitative approaches.

6. The perspective of the researchers drives quantitative approaches, while qualitative research emphasizes the viewpoints of the participants.

7. The problem of generality can be solved for qualitative research by adding quantitative findings.

8. Qualitative findings may facilitate the interpretation of relationships between variables in quantitative datasets.

9. The relationship between micro and macro levels in an area under study can be clarified by combining qualitative and quantitative research.

10. Using qualitative or quantitative research can be appropriate at different stages of the research process.

11. Hybrid forms may use qualitative research in quasi-experimental designs (see Bryman 1992, pp. 59–61).

Overall, this classification includes a broad range of variants. Items 5, 6 and 7 rest on the idea that qualitative research captures different aspects than quantitative research. Theoretical considerations are not very prominent in the list of 11 variants Bryman identifies, as the focus is more on the pragmatics of research.

Triangulation

In the social sciences, triangulation means to view a research issue from at least two vantage points. Mostly, the analysis from two or more points is realized by using several methodological approaches. As a strategy for grounding empirical research and its results (see Chapter 11), triangulation has attracted a lot of attention in the context of qualitative research. In particular, the conceptualization provided by Denzin has proved popular (1970/1989). Denzin initially understood triangulation as a strategy of validation (see Chapter 11), but then developed a broader concept. As a result, Denzin has distinguished four forms of triangulation:

- *Triangulation of data* combines data drawn from different sources and at different times, in different places or from different people.

- *Investigator triangulation* is characterized by the use of different observers or interviewers to balance out the subjective influences of individuals.

- *Triangulation of theories* means 'approaching data with multiple perspectives and hypotheses in mind … Various theoretical points of view could be placed side by side to assess their utility and power' (1970, p. 297).

- Denzin's central concept is *methodological triangulation* 'within method' (e.g. through using different subscales within a questionnaire) and 'between method'. 'To summarize, methodological triangulation involves a complex process of playing each method off against the other so as to maximize the validity of field efforts' (1970, p. 304).

From these forms, we can develop the definition of triangulation provided in Box 10.1.

BOX 10.1

Definition of triangulation

Triangulation means that you take different perspectives on an issue you study or in answering your research questions. These perspectives can be substantiated through using several methods or several theoretical approaches. Furthermore, triangulation may refer to combining different sorts of data against the background of the theoretical perspectives which you apply to the data. As far as possible, you should treat these perspectives on an equal footing. At the same time, triangulation (of different methods or of data sorts) should provide additional knowledge. For example, triangulation should produce knowledge on different levels, which means it goes beyond the knowledge made possible by one approach and thus contributes to promoting quality in research.

Triangulation within Qualitative Research

Triangulation can involve combining different qualitative approaches. The case in Box 10.2 illustrates the definition of triangulation provided in Box 10.1.

BOX 10.2

Triangulation within qualitative research: case study

In Chapter 2, I mentioned our study on the situation of homeless adolescents with chronic illness (Flick and Röhnsch 2007; 2008). In this study we combined three methodological approaches: (a) participant observations in the everyday lives of the adolescents; (b) episodic interviews with the adolescents about their concepts of health and illness and their experiences with the health system; and (c) expert interviews with social workers and physicians about the health care situation of adolescents living under these circumstances. Thus, we achieved triangulation between methods and between different kinds of data (statements and observations). We also achieved within-method triangulation, since the episodic interviews combined two approaches ('questions' and 'narrative stimuli') leading to two sorts of data ('answers' and 'narratives') (see Chapter 7). At the same time, different theoretical approaches were brought together: (a) an approach oriented towards interactions and practices in the group under observation; (b) an approach more based on narrative theories in the interviews with the adolescents; and (c) an approach focused on expert knowledge as a specific form of knowledge in the expert interviews.

Triangulation within Quantitative Research

Similarly, you can use triangulation for combining several quantitative approaches. For example, you can use several subscales in a questionnaire, or combine several questionnaires, or complement questionnaires with standardized observations.

Triangulation of Qualitative and Quantitative Research

Finally, triangulation may involve the combination of qualitative and quantitative research. Triangulation of qualitative and quantitative research often becomes concrete at the level of the results produced. It is on that level that Kelle and Erzberger (2004) focus in their discussion of combining the two approaches. They discuss three alternatives:

1. Results may *converge*. That is, the results confirm each other. They may also partly confirm each other and support the same conclusions. For example, statements

from a representative survey with standardized questionnaires may align with statements from semi-structured interviews with a part of the sample in the survey.

2. Results may focus on different aspects of an issue (e.g. the subjective meanings of a specific illness and its social distribution in the population), but be *complementary* to each other and lead to a fuller picture. For example, interviews may provide results that complement (through, say, deepening, detailing, explaining or extending) findings obtained from questionnaire data.

3. Results may be *divergent* or *contradictory*. For example, in interviews, you receive different views from those provided by questionnaires. You could then take this as the starting point for further theoretical or empirical clarification of the divergence and the reasons behind it.

In all three alternatives, similar questions arise. For example: how far did you take into account the specific theoretical background of the two methods that you used in collecting and analyzing your data? Are any differences simply the result of the differing understanding of realities and issues in qualitative and quantitative approaches? Should convergences that go too far make you skeptical, rather than seeing them as a simple confirmation of the one by the other result? And finally: how far are the two approaches and their results seen as equally relevant and independent findings, so that using the concept of triangulation is justified? How far is one of the approaches reduced to a subordinate role, such as merely making plausible the results of the other, more dominant, approach?

Mixed Methods

When bridges are built in the other direction – i.e. when coming *from* quantitative research – the term 'mixed methods' tends to be preferred to 'triangulation'. Supporters of mixed methodologies are interested in combining qualitative and quantitative research pragmatically, seeking to end the 'paradigm wars' between the two approaches. Tashakkori and Teddlie (2003b, p. ix) declare this approach to be a 'third methodological movement'. They see quantitative research as the first movement. For them, qualitative research is the second movement, and mixed methods research is the third movement – one that resolves all of the conflicts and differences between the first and the second movements.

Mixed Methods Designs

When using mixed methods in your own project, the issue of how to design a mixed methods study will be most interesting on a practical level. Creswell (2003) has distinguished three forms of mixed methods design, namely:

1. Phase designs, in which qualitative and quantitative methods are applied separately one after the other (no matter in what order). Such designs can include two or more phases.

2. Dominant/less-dominant design, which is mainly committed to one of the approaches and uses the other only marginally.

3. Mixed methodology designs, which link the two approaches in all phases of the research process.

For the mixed methodologies approach, Tashakkori and Teddlie (2003a), Creswell (2003) and Creswell et al. (2003) have suggested a more elaborate version of designs that combine qualitative and quantitative research. Creswell et al. (2003, p. 211) see mixed methods as designs in their own right in the social sciences, and use the following definition:

> A *mixed methods study* involves the collection or analysis of both quantitative and/or qualitative data in a single study in which the data are collected concurrently or sequentially, are given a priority, and involve the integration of the data at one or more stages in the process of research. (2003, p. 212)

Overall, mixed methods have been used increasingly since the end of the 1990s for overcoming the tensions between qualitative and quantitative research. Here, a rather pragmatic methodological approach is chosen.

Integrated Social Research

As we shall see, the concept of *integrated* research goes a step further than the concepts that have been discussed so far. This concept draws on the range of methodological alternatives and approaches outlined in this book.

Relevance of Integrated Social Research

An argument for integrated research was advanced in the mid twentieth century by Barton and Lazarsfeld (1955). The authors refer to the ability of qualitative research with small numbers of cases to make visible the relations, causes, effects and dynamics of social processes that cannot be found through statistical analyses of larger samples. According to their view, qualitative and quantitative research will be used at different stages of a research project. Qualitative research would mainly be used at the beginning, though it can also be employed subsequently for the interpretation and clarification of statistical analyses.

The debate about qualitative or quantitative research, which was originally informed by epistemological and philosophical standpoints (see Becker 1996 or Bryman 1988 for overviews), has shifted towards issues of research practice

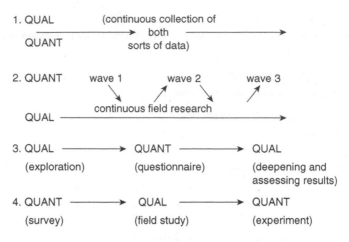

Figure 10.1   Research designs for the integration of qualitative and quantitative research (adapted from Miles and Huberman 1994, p. 41)

concerning the appropriateness of each approach. Wilson states that for the relation of the two methodological traditions, 'qualitative and quantitative approaches are complementary rather than competitive methods [and the] use of a particular method ... rather must be based on the nature of the actual research problem at hand' (1982, p. 501).

Procedures of Integrated Social Research

1. In a first step, you should consider how developed is the state of knowledge about the issue of your research and which empirical approaches are required, perhaps in combination.

2. Following the approach of integrated social research, you will take the different theoretical positions and distinctions of the approaches into account when you plan your concrete methodological procedures.

3. In planning a study in integrated social research, you can take the different designs suggested by Miles and Huberman (1994, p. 41) as an orientation, as illustrated in Figure 10.1. In the first design, you pursue both strategies in parallel. In the second design, one strategy (for example, continuous observation of the field) will provide a basis. You can use this basis for planning the waves of a survey. The several waves are related to the observation from which these waves are derived and shaped. In the third combination, you will begin with a qualitative method, e.g. a semi-structured interview. These interviews are followed by a questionnaire study as an intermediate step, before you deepen and assess the results from both steps in a second qualitative phase. In the fourth design, you will do a complementary field study in order to add more depth to the results of a survey in the first step. The last step is an experimental intervention in the field for testing the results of the first two steps.

4. The methodological approaches of collecting and analyzing data are based on the concepts of methodological and data triangulation formulated by Denzin.

5. Finally, the presentation of results (see Chapter 13) reflects the combination of research approaches – by combining case studies with overviews in tables or charts, for example.

It is useful here to consider an example of integrated research. Box 10.3 outlines one such case.

BOX 10.3

Integrated social research: an example

In a running study about the issues of sleep and sleep disorders in institutional everyday life in nursing homes (see Flick et al. 2010; Garms-Homolová et al. 2010), we take different perspectives towards this problem in analyzing its relevance for the routines of care and for the development of diseases. In a number of nursing facilities, we analyze routine data in a longitudinal perspective. Repeated assessments of around 4000 nursing home residents are analyzed three times after one-year periods. We look for interrelations between sleep problems documented in them and the numbers and intensities of diseases in this period. Parallel to such secondary analyses, we do interviews with nurses and physicians in the same facilities and complement them with interviews of relatives of residents in this context. These interviews focus on the perception of the problem in the caring routines and how these problems are dealt with. The design is oriented on the second suggestion by Miles and Huberman (1994; see Figure 10.1). This study allows analysis of the issue on two levels: (a) the reality of caring and (b) the professional perception of the problem. For this purpose, it combines two methodological perspectives: a quantitative secondary analysis of routine data, and a qualitative primary collection and analysis of interviews. On the methodological level, a triangulation of several approaches is realized. This research project is an example of integrated social research not only because the results of qualitative and quantitative analyses are referred to each other, but also because the two approaches are integrated within a comprehensive design.

Overall, the approach of integrated social research can take us beyond some of the limitations of one-sided research. It uses for this goal the theoretical and methodological triangulation of several approaches in a complex design for making possible a more comprehensive understanding of the issue under study.

E-Research as Complementary Strategy

Often the Internet is used as a context for social research because of the limitations of traditional forms of social research. Some of these limitations are practical ones concerning costs and time. However, there are also more general limitations. For example, you can reach people over greater distances when you use a web survey instead of a paper survey. You will reach some people only via the Internet, e.g. as members of a specific online community (see Chapter 9). At the same time, limitations of e-research have been identified. They include limited response rates, unclear sampling frames, restriction of samples to people who use the Internet, and so on.

To overcome these limitations, several authors suggest combining paper and web surveys (see Bryman 2008, pp. 651–2). This can be done in two ways. Either you run your study in two phases, sending out a questionnaire by mail to a sample and sending a second electronically to another sample via the Internet. Or you offer your respondents in a postal questionnaire survey the option to complete the questionnaire either on paper or online. In both cases, you combine the advantages of the two forms of research. Similarly you could complement face-to-face interviews with online interviews (or focus groups). All in all, e-research extends the options for which methods to mix or which perspectives to triangulate or integrate in your study.

Pragmatism and the Issue as Points of Reference

The preceding parts of this chapter have demonstrated that a rhetoric of strict separation (or incompatibility) between single research approaches has its limits. The point of reference for choosing and combining research approaches should be the requirements of the issue under study, rather than single-sided methodological certainties and claims. Combinations can mean that you link qualitative and quantitative research as well as triangulating different qualitative or different quantitative approaches. At the same time, you should see the combination of research approaches pragmatically. That is, you can ask yourself: what is necessary for a sufficiently comprehensive understanding of the issues you study? What is possible under the given circumstances of your own resources and in the field you study? When is it worth making the extra effort of combining methods? For making such a decision, consider whether the different methods will really focus on different aspects or levels or whether they will merely capture the same in very similar ways.

It is helpful here to differentiate between various possible levels of research, such as the four that follow, each of which are explained through examples.

Subjective Meaning and Social Structure

For understanding the subjective meaning of a phenomenon – for example of a disease – patients are interviewed. This is complemented by analyzing the frequency and distribution of the disease in the population or in subpopulations with different social backgrounds (see Flick 1998b).

State and Process

The situation and the current practices of adolescents living on the street are analyzed for issues of health and illness by using participant observation as an approach. This description of a state is combined with interviews revealing which processes in the single adolescents' biographies have led them into their current situation (see Flick and Röhnsch 2007).

Knowledge and Practices

Counselors' subjective theories of trust held in relations to clients are reconstructed in interviews. These are juxtaposed with conversation analyses of consultations done by these counselors with clients in order to find out how trust is built up or impeded (see Flick 1992).

Knowledge and Routines

Nurses' knowledge about the effects of sleep problems on the health of nursing home residents is analyzed in interviews. In addition, routine data are analyzed which are based on diagnoses of certain diseases and documentations of sleep disorders (see Flick et al. 2010).

Integrated Social Research and Its Limits

At the beginning of this chapter we discussed the limitations of social research, beginning with the limitations of single methods. This sought to show that no single method by itself can provide comprehensive access to a phenomenon under study or always be relied upon to provide the appropriate approach. It should also have become clear that quantitative and qualitative approaches in general each have their limitations.

One step towards overcoming the specific limitations of particular methods or approaches is the combination or integrated use of a number of methods. This does not altogether solve the problem of the limitation of research, since each of the methods used remains selective in what it can capture. However, combination or integration can make a research project less restrictive in what it can achieve.

Beyond these limitations, there remain fundamental limits to social research. In addition to the ethical questions discussed in Chapter 12, there are issues that cannot be 'translated' into empirical concepts or approaches. For example, it is not very realistic to try to study the meaning of life empirically! (You can, of course, ask participants in a study what for them personally would be the meaning of their lives – but the phenomenon 'meaning of life' in a comprehensive sense will escape an empirical study.) Furthermore, social research reaches its limits when *immediate* solutions are expected. That this is less a methodological than a fundamental problem should have become evident in Chapter 1.

Checklist for Designing Combinations of Methods

When deciding on using and combining several methods, you should consider the questions listed in Box 10.4. These questions can be used to inform the planning of your own study and also for assessing the studies of other researchers.

BOX 10.4

Checklist for designing combinations of methods

1. What are the limits of the single method which can be overcome by combining several methods?
2. What is the extra gain in knowledge that you can expect from combining the methods?
3. Do the methods really address different levels or qualities in the data, so as to justify their combination?
4. Can the extra effort required for combining methods be accommodated in your framework of research (resources, time etc.)?
5. Are these efforts proportionate for the gain in knowledge they make possible?
6. Are the combined methods compatible with each other?
7. How should you sequence the methods you will use? How will sequencing affect the study?
8. How far are the methods applied according to their characteristics, so that their specific strengths are taken into account?

Key Points

- Every method has its limitations in what it can grasp and how it can do so.
- Distinct limits can be identified for quantitative research and for qualitative research.
- Combinations of research strategies can help to overcome such limits.

- Triangulation, mixed methods and integrated social research provide ways of combining methods.
- Combinations should be grounded in the issue under study and in the additional gain of knowledge they make possible.

▨ ▨ Further Reading ▨

The first two books address the approach of triangulation, whereas the other works focus on mixed methods research.

Denzin, N.K. (1989) *The Research Act: A Theoretical Introduction to Sociological Methods*, 3rd edn. Englewood Cliffs, NJ: Prentice Hall.

Flick, U. (2008) *Managing Quality in Qualitative Research*. London: Sage.

Kelle, U. and Erzberger, C. (2004) 'Quantitative and Qualitative Methods: No Confrontation', in U. Flick, E. v. Kardorff and I. Steinke (eds), *A Companion to Qualitative Research*. London: Sage. pp. 172–7.

Tashakkori, A. and Teddlie, Ch. (eds) (2003) *Handbook of Mixed Methods in Social and Behavioral Research*. Thousand Oaks, CA: Sage.

PART IV
REFLECTION AND WRITING

Successful social research involves much more than merely applying research methods. It is also important to reflect on how methods have been applied – and to make your procedures transparent to others. This final part of the book, therefore, focuses on issues of reflection and writing.

First, we consider quality assessment in quantitative and qualitative research, and then focus on these questions in the context of e-research (Chapter 11).

Second, we discuss research ethics and what it means to make a research project ethically sound. In the process we consider codes of ethics and ethics committees, as well as specific problems of e-research in this context (Chapter 12).

The final chapter considers how to write up research and results in a transparent way, how to feed them back to participants, and how to use data and results in practical or political contexts (Chapter 13).

CHAPTER 11

WHAT IS GOOD RESEARCH? EVALUATING YOUR RESEARCH PROJECT

Chapter Overview

Chapter Objectives

This chapter is designed to help you:

- identify the most important criteria for evaluating empirical research
- recognize that these criteria were originally developed for standardized research
- recognize that for qualitative research, other criteria and approaches of evaluation are applicable
- recognize that generalization of results forms a major part in the assessment of social research
- distinguish between quantitative and qualitative research with regard to approaches to evaluation.

Table 11.1   Navigator for Chapter 11

Orientation	• What is social research? • Research question • Literature review
Planning and design	• Planning research • Designing research • Deciding methods
Working with data	• Gathering data • Analyzing data • E-research • Integrated research
Reflection and writing	• Evaluating research • Ethics • Writing and using research

You are here in your project ⟶ (Reflection and writing)

Evaluating Empirical Studies

As well as the question of the utility of empirical research, we also need to examine its quality. Here we need to assess whether the methods you applied are reliable, and also how far the results you have obtained can claim validity and objectivity. The last is essentially a question of how far the results could have been obtained by other researchers and are independent from the researcher who did the study. For assessing the quality of empirical research, criteria have been formulated to facilitate assessment of the methodological procedures that led to the results. Here we can ask whether one uniform set of criteria is adequate for every form of empirical research, or whether we should differentiate between criteria that are appropriate for qualitative or quantitative research. Accordingly, in this chapter we first will discuss the criteria of reliability, validity and objectivity, which are generally accepted in quantitative research, and then consider specific approaches in qualitative research.

A fundamental question here is how far results can be generalized. That is, how far may they be transferred to other situations beyond the research situation? Here again, we should ask whether procedures of or claims for generalization should be formulated in a unified way for all sorts of empirical research or whether we need differentiated approaches.

Quality and Evaluation of Quantitative Research

Reliability

The first generally accepted criterion for assessing studies originates from test theory: 'The reliability ... indicates the degree of exactness in measurement (precision) of an instrument. The reliability is the higher the smaller the part of error E linked to a measurement value X is' (Bortz and Döring 2006, p. 196). We can assess the reliability of a measurement in different ways.

Retest reliability

For assessing retest reliability, you will need to apply a measurement (for example, a test or a questionnaire) *twice* to the same sample and then calculate the correlation between the results of the two applications. In the ideal case, you will obtain identical results. This presupposes, however, that the attribute that was measured is stable in itself and has not changed between the two measurement times. When one is repeating performance tests, differences in the results can arise from a change in performance in the meantime (for example, because of additional knowledge that was obtained). Differences in the measurements can result because on the second occasion questions are recognized by participants and learning effects may occur.

Parallel test reliability

For assessing parallel test reliability, you will need to apply two different instruments, so that you operationalize the same construct in parallel. For example, if you wish to find out how reliable a specific intelligence test is, you can apply a second test in parallel. If the first one has measured the intelligence in a reliable way, the second test should produce the same result – i.e. the same intelligence quotient. 'The more alike the results of the two tests, the less error effects obviously are involved' (Bortz and Döring 2006, p. 197).

Split half

In a test or a questionnaire, you can calculate the resulting scores for each half of the items (questions) and then compare the two scores. But then the results will depend on the method of splitting the instruments in two halves (for example, the first and the second half of the questions, even and uneven numbers of the questions, random allocation of questions to one or the other half). For excluding effects of the position of the questions, the internal consistency is calculated. For doing this you will treat each question separately like independent tests and compute the correlation between the results, i.e. the answers given to the various questions.

Inter-coder reliability

When you use content analysis, you can calculate inter-coder reliability to assess the extent to which different analysts allocate the same statements to the same categories and hence the reliability of the category system and its application.

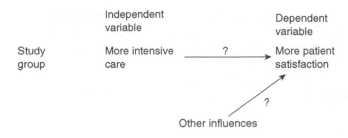

Figure 11.1   Internal validity

Validity

Validity is assessed both for research designs and for measurement instruments.

Validity of research designs

In the case of research designs, the focus will be on the evaluation of results. You will need to check the *internal* validity of a research design. Internal validity characterizes how far the results of a study can be analyzed unambiguously. If you want to study the effects of an intervention, you should check whether changes in the dependent variables can be traced to changes in the independent variable or whether they may result from changes in some other variable (see Figure 11.1).

Consider, for example, the case of a research project on intensive care, in which the introduction of more intensive care constitutes the independent variable, the satisfaction of the patients the dependent variable. If you wish to study the hypothesis 'more intensive care leads to more satisfaction of the patients', you should clarify how the relation between intensive care and satisfaction can be measured unambiguously. For assessing the internal validity, you will try to exclude other influences: how far other conditions have changed in parallel to increasing the intensity of care, and how far the increase in the patients' satisfaction comes from these conditions.

For assuring internal validity, conditions need to be isolated and controlled. A way to assess the effect of an intervention is to apply a control group design (see Chapter 5). In our example, in a second group, as comparable as possible to the first, the intervention would not be introduced – that is, the intensity of care would not be increased. Then one could check whether the effect found in the study group – i.e. the increase in the patients' satisfaction – is evident.

Internal validity is achieved if the changes in the dependent variables can be unambiguously traced back to the influence of the independent variable, i.e. if there are no better alternative explanations beyond the study hypothesis. (Bortz and Döring 2006, p. 53)

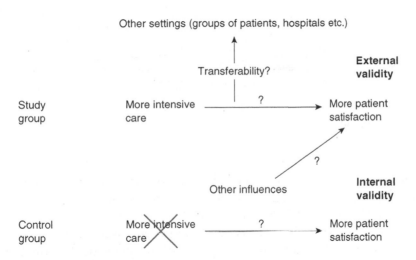

Figure 11.2   External validity

Internal validity is best achieved in the laboratory and in experimental research. However, this is at the expense of the second form of validity of a research design, namely *external* validity. Here, the general question is: how far can we transfer results beyond the situations and persons for which they were produced, to situations and persons outside the research? For example, can we transfer a relation between the intensity of care and the patients' satisfaction to other wards, hospitals or situations of care in general, or is it only valid under the concrete conditions under which it was studied and found (see Figure 11.2)?

There is a difficulty here. Although in the laboratory and under more or less controlled conditions, internal validity will be high, external validity will in contrast be rather limited. In research in the field and under natural conditions, external validity is higher and internal validity is lower, as here the control of conditions is possible only in a very limited way: 'External validity is achieved when the result found in studying a sample can be generalized to other people, situations or points in time' (Bortz and Döring 2006, p. 53). To meet both criteria in one research design at the same time and to the same extent is seen as difficult (Bortz and Döring 2006). Here we face a dilemma of empirical research, which is difficult to solve in a research design.

External and internal validity are assessed for research designs. Validity, however, is also assessed for measurement instruments.

Validity of measurement instruments

The issue of the validity of a research instrument can be summarized in the question: does the method measure what it is supposed to measure? To answer this question, you can apply various forms of validity checks, namely (a) content validity, (b) criterion validity and (c) construct validity.

Figure 11.3 Criterion validity

Content validity is achieved when the method or measurement instrument captures the issue under study in its essential aspects and in an exhaustive way. You can check this yourself based on your subjective judgment – by reflecting on how far your instrument covers all the important aspects of your issue and whether it does so in a way that is appropriate to this issue. Even better is to have the measurement instrument assessed by experts or laypeople. Errors should catch the eye in such assessments. Thus the term 'face validity' is used for this assessment. To continue our example: consider whether you would document the caring intensity in the relevant situations of the day routines in a hospital or only in a specific situation – for example at the admission of patients.

Criterion validity is achieved if the result of a measurement corresponds with an external criterion. This will be case, for example, if the results of vocational testing correspond with the professional success of the tested person (see Figure 11.3). Such external criteria can be defined in parallel, which allows you to check the concurrent validity. This means that you apply a second measurement at the same time. For example, you do the test and at the same time observe the candidate's behavior in a discussion group. Then you compare the results of the two measurements – how far the part of the vocational test on communicative skills corresponds to the communication in the group. Alternatively, you check the measurement later, in which case the predictive validity will be assessed – for example, do the results of a vocational test allow the prediction of professional success?

One problem here is that the external criterion has to be valid itself if it is going to be used as a means for checking measurements. Here, you have to take the differential validity into account: concordance between the test score and the external criterion can be different in different populations. If we again take our example, the communicative behavior in the discussion groups may be systematically different for male and female participants, whereas the original test mainly focused on general aspects of vocational qualification. Then the relation between the test score and the external criterion will be different for the two gender subgroups. Methods in general should be able to capture differences in various groups.

Finally, *construct validity* should be assessed. Here you will check whether the construct that is captured by your method is linked sufficiently closely to variables that can be theoretically justified. You will also check here how far

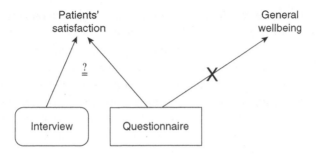

Figure 11.4   Construct validity

the construct allows hypotheses to be derived that can be tested empirically. One way to assess construct validity is to use various measurements: constructs are measured with several methods. When several methods measure the same construct with corresponding results, *convergent validity* is given. For example, you may study the patients' satisfaction with a questionnaire and an interview. When both methods produce results which confirm each other, this shows the convergent validity of your construct. This would indicate your theoretical concept of 'patients' satisfaction' is valid and your study meets this criterion of validity. *Discriminant validity* refers to the question of how far your measurements are able to distinguish the construct you study from other constructs. In our example, you would assess how far your theoretical concept and your measurements really capture the patients' satisfaction with the care. Or do they just capture a general state of wellbeing instead of specific satisfaction with aspects of the care situation? In that case, your concept of 'patients' satisfaction' is not valid and your study misses this criterion of validity (see Figure 11.4).

Validity of indices

An index will need to be constructed when something cannot be directly observed or measured (see Chapter 7), because several aspects of a theoretical construct are integrated in it. For example, patients' general satisfaction with their stay in a hospital cannot be measured directly. Such satisfaction includes satisfaction with the treatment, with the staff's friendliness, with the food, with the atmosphere and so on. For measuring the construct 'general satisfaction' you would have to select one or more indicators. In order to reduce the biases in the measurement of complex constructs as far as possible, several indicators should be used in order to increase the quality of measurement. (For example, grading a school essay combines evaluations of orthography, of style, of content and of form – either in equal shares or with different weights because the style is seen as more important than the number of spelling mistakes.)

In a similar way, one would try to derive patients' satisfaction from various indicators. For example, you could use an instrument for assessing quality of life, a questionnaire for measuring satisfaction with the service by the hospital staff, and another questionnaire addressing satisfaction with the infrastructure of the hospital. Then the question is how to weight the single variables. For example, in constructing a patient satisfaction index, how much weight should be given to the questionnaire results about the staff service compared to, say, the results concerning the quality of life in the hospital?

A further problem here is that if you want to assess the validity of the index, the included variables – e.g. quality of life, satisfaction with staff – themselves have to be measured in a valid way so that the index as a whole can be valid. Thus validity assessments become relevant on two levels here: on the level of the single indicator, and on the level of the index constructed with these indicators. 'The quality of an index essentially depends on how far all the relevant dimensions have been selected and weighed appropriately' (Bortz and Döring 2006, p. 144). For indices, overall validity is composed of the validity of (a) single items or questions, (b) the scales constructed with these items and (c) the weighting of the components.

The construction of an index is based on the use of several indicators for measuring a value which cannot be directly observed or measured. This raises specific problems concerning the validity of indices. Thus you should check whether

- the relevant dimensions have been selected and weighted appropriately

- the instruments for measuring the selected indicators are valid

- the items in the indicators are valid.

Validity addresses different aspects for checking the quality of study results. If you consider external validity, this already includes aspects of the transferability and generalization of results.

Objectivity

The objectivity of instruments, such as tests or questionnaires, depends on the extent to which the application of the instrument is independent of the person applying it. If several researchers apply the same method to the same persons, the results have to be identical. Three forms may be distinguished:

- Objectivity in the data *collection* concerns how far the answers or test results of the participant are independent of the interviewer or person of the researcher. This will be obtained by standardization of the data collection (standardized instructions for applying the instrument and standardized conditions in the situation of the data collection).

- Objectivity of the *analysis* concerns how far the classification of answers in a questionnaire or test are independent of the person who does the classification in the concrete case (for example, by allocating an answer to a specific score).

- Objectivity of the *interpretation* means that any interpretation of statements or scores in a test should be independent of the persons of the researchers and their subjective views or values. Thus norm values (for example, age, gender or education) may be identified with representative samples, which can be used for classifying the achievement or values of the participant in the concrete study.

Achieving objectivity of an instrument or a study principally requires standardization of the ways in which data are collected, analyzed and interpreted. This will exclude the subjective or individual influences of the researcher or the concrete situation in which data were collected.

Quality and Evaluation of Qualitative Research

The criteria discussed so far are well established for quantitative research. They are based more or less on the standardization of the research situation. Sometimes it has been suggested that the classical criteria of empirical social research – reliability, validity and objectivity – may also be applied to qualitative research (see Kirk and Miller 1986). This raises the question of how far these criteria, with their strong emphasis on standardization of procedures and the exclusion of communicative influences by the research, can do justice to qualitative research and its procedures, which are mainly based on communication, interaction and the researcher's subjective interpretations. Often these bases are seen not as biases but as strengths or even preconditions of the research. Accordingly, Glaser and Strauss

> **raise doubts as to the applicability of the canons of quantitative research as criteria for judging the credibility of substantive theory based on qualitative research. They suggest rather that criteria of judgement be based on generic elements of qualitative methods for collecting, analyzing and presenting data and for the way in which people read qualitative analyses. (1965, p. 5)**

In the light of such skepticism, a series of attempts has been made over time to initiate a debate about criteria in qualitative research (see Flick 2009, Chapter 28). One also finds a number of attempts to develop 'method-appropriate criteria' (see Flick 2008a) in order to replace criteria like validity and reliability.

Reformulation of Traditional Criteria

Suggestions for reformulating the concept of reliability with a more procedural emphasis have focused on the question of how data are produced. A requirement is that (a) statements by participants and (b) interpretation by the researcher should be clearly distinguishable. Finally, a way to increase the reliability of the whole process is to document it in a detailed and reflexive way. This refers mainly to documenting and reflecting on the decisions taken in the research process – showing which ones were taken and why (see Chapter 6 for decision-making in the research process).

The concept of validity also requires reformulation. One suggestion is that researchers should scrutinize interview situations for any signs of strategic communication. That means that the interviewee did not openly respond to the questions but was selective or reluctant to give the answers. That leads to a question of how far you can trust the statements of the interviewee. You should also check whether a form of communication occurred in the interview which is not adequate for the interview situation. For example, if the interview produced a therapy-like conversation, this should raise doubts about the validity of the interviewee's statements (Legewie 1987).

A second suggestion is to check the validity by integrating the participants as individuals or groups in the further research process. One way is to include communicative validation at a second meeting, after an interview has been conducted and transcribed (for concrete suggestions see Flick 2009, p. 159). Sometimes communicative validation has been discussed for validating the interpretations of texts. Because of the ethical problems in confronting participants with interpretations of their statements, this form of communicative validation is only seldom applied. For a more general application of communicative validation, two questions remain to be answered, namely:

- How can one design the methodological procedure in communicative validation (or member checks) in a way that does justice to the issues under study and to the viewpoints of the participants?

- How can one answer the question of validity beyond the participants' agreement to the data and interpretations?

Mishler (1990) goes one step further in reformulating the concept of validity. He starts from the *process* of validating (rather than the *state* of validity). He defines 'validation as the social construction of knowledge' (1990, p. 417) by which we 'evaluate the "trustworthiness" of reported observations, interpretations, and generalisations' (1990, p. 419).

Method-Appropriate Criteria

The criteria used for assessing objectivity need to be appropriate to the methods of qualitative research. Beyond the already mentioned communicative validation and triangulation (see Chapter 10), we find a number of suggestions for new criteria in American discussion (see Flick 2009, Chapter 29; 2008a).

For example Lincoln and Guba (1985) have proposed (a) trustworthiness, (b) credibility, (c) dependability, (d) transferability and (e) confirmability as appropriate criteria for qualitative research. Of these, trustworthiness is considered most important. Lincoln and Guba have outlined five strategies for increasing the credibility of qualitative research:

- activities for increasing the likelihood that credible results will be produced by a 'prolonged engagement' and 'persistent observation' in the field and the triangulation of different methods, researchers and data

- 'peer debriefing': regular meetings with other people who are not involved in the research in order to disclose one's own blind spots and to discuss working hypotheses and results with them

- the analysis of negative cases in the sense of analytic induction

- appropriateness of the terms of reference of interpretations and their assessment

- 'member checks' in the sense of communicative validation of data and interpretations with members of the fields under study.

For assessing dependability a process of auditing is suggested, based on the procedure of audits in the domain of accounting. The aim is to produce an auditing trail (Guba and Lincoln 1989) covering:

- the raw data, their collection and recording

- data reduction and results of syntheses by summarizing, theoretical notes, memos and so on, summaries, short descriptions of cases etc.

- reconstruction of data and results of syntheses according to the structure of categories (themes, definitions, relationships), findings (interpretations and inferences), and the reports produced with their integration of concepts and links to the existing literature

- process notes, i.e. methodological notes and decisions concerning the production of trustworthiness and credibility of findings

- materials concerning intentions and dispositions like the concepts of research, personal notes, and the expectations of the participants

- information about the development of the instruments including the pilot version and preliminary plans.

The question of transferability of results has been discussed already in the context of external validity. We will address it again below in relation to evaluation.

Generalization

In quantitative research, the extent to which results can be generalized may be checked in two ways: by assessing external validity, one would (a) assure that the results found for the sample are valid for the population and also (b) test how far they can be transferred to other, comparable populations. Bortz and Döring hold that 'generalizability in quantitative research is achieved by the inference from a random sample (or sample parameters) to populations (or population parameters), which is founded in probability theory' (2006, p. 335).

Various sampling procedures (see Chapter 5) may be used to ensure this. One procedure is to use a random sample, in which every element in the population has the same chance to be an element in the sample. This procedure enables the exclusion of any biases resulting from the disproportionally weighted distribution of features in the sample compared to the population. Thus the sample is representative for the population. An inference from the sample to the population concerning the validity of the results is therefore justified. Other procedures aim at representing the distribution in the population in a more focused way, as, for example, when you draw a stratified sample. Then you will take into account that your population consists of several subgroups, which are unevenly distributed. You will try to cover that distribution in your sample. This allows you to generalize your findings from the sample to the population.

Generalization can be checked by assessing the external validity of a study (see above). This generalization is based on the degree of similarity between the participants in the study and the populations for which the study and its results are supposed to be valid. Accordingly, Campbell (1986) uses the term 'proximal similarity' rather than external validity: in the dimensions that are relevant for the study and its results, the sample should be as similar as possible to the population to which the results are to be transferred.

Generalization in Qualitative Research

In quantitative research, generalization is primarily a numerical problem, to be solved by statistical means. In qualitative research, this question is more difficult. At root there is the familiar issue of generalization: a limited number of cases which have been selected according to specific criteria, or sometimes a single case, have been studied and the results are claimed to be valid beyond the material in the study. The case or the cases are taken as representative of more general situations, conditions or relations. Yet the question of generalizability in qualitative research often arises in a fundamentally different way. In some qualitative research the aim is to develop theory from empirical material (according to Glaser and Strauss 1967) – in which case the question is raised as to how far the resulting theory may be applied to other contexts.

Accordingly, one approach for evaluating qualitative research is to ask what measures have been taken to define or extend the area of validity of empirical results (and indeed of any theories developed from them). Starting points are the analysis of cases and the inferences from them to more general statements. The problem here is that the starting point is often an analysis focused on a specific context or a concrete case, addressing the specific conditions, relations, processes etc. It is often precisely the reference to a specific context that gives qualitative research its value. Yet if one then proceeds to generalize, the specific context is lost and one must consider how far the findings are valid independent of the original context.

In highlighting this dilemma, Lincoln and Guba (1985) have suggested that 'the only generalization is: there is no generalization'. Yet in terms of the 'transferability of findings from one context to another' and 'fittingness as to the degree of comparability of different contexts', they outline criteria for judging the generalization of findings beyond a given context. A first step is to clarify the degree of generalization the research is aiming at and which it is possible to attain. A second step involves the cautious integration of different cases and contexts in which the relations under study are empirically analyzed. The generalizability of the results is often closely linked to the way the sampling is done. Theoretical sampling, for example, offers a way of designing the variation of the conditions under which a phenomenon is studied as broadly as possible. The third step consists of the systematic comparison of the collected material.

The constant comparative method

In the process of developing theories, Glaser (1969) suggests the 'constant comparative method' as a procedure for interpreting texts. It consists of four stages: '(1) comparing incidents applicable to each category, (2) integrating categories and their properties, (3) delimiting the theory, and (4) writing the theory' (1969, p. 220). For Glaser, the systematic circularity of this process is an essential feature:

> **Although this method is a continuous growth process – each stage after a time transforms itself into the next – previous stages remain in operation throughout the analysis and provide continuous development to the following stage until the analysis is terminated. (1969, p. 220)**

This procedure becomes a method of *constant* comparison when interpreters take care that they compare coding over and over again with codes and classifications that have already been made. Material which has already been coded is not finished with after its classification: rather it is continually integrated into the further process of comparison.

Contrasting cases and ideal type analysis

The process of constant comparison may be systematized further through strategies of contrasting cases. Gerhardt (1988) has made the most consistent suggestions based on the construction of ideal types. This strategy involves several steps. After reconstructing and contrasting the cases with one another, types are constructed. Then 'pure' cases are tracked down. Compared with these ideal types of processes, the understanding of the individual case can be made more systematic. After constructing further types (see Chapter 8), this process culminates in a structural understanding (i.e. the understanding of relationships pointing beyond the individual case).

The main instruments here are (a) the *minimal* comparison of cases that are as similar as possible, and (b) the *maximal* comparison of cases that are as different as possible. They are compared for differences and correspondences.

Generalization in qualitative research involves the gradual transfer of findings from case studies and their context to more general and abstract relations – for example in the form of a typology. The expressiveness of such patterns can then be specified according to how far different theoretical and methodological perspectives on the issue – if possible by different researchers – have been triangulated and how negative cases were handled. The degree of generalization claimed for a study should also be taken into consideration. Then, the question of whether the intended level of generalization has been reached provides a further criterion for evaluating the qualitative research project in question.

Standards and Quality in E-Research

All that has been said in this chapter about the criteria and quality of quantitative and qualitative research in principle applies to e-research as well as to traditional research. However, some issues of quality can be raised here with a specific focus on e-research. For example, in e-research the question of generalization refers not only to how far you can infer from a sample of online users (that were part of a survey) to the population of Internet users in general, but also to how far that specific online sample relates to populations beyond the Internet. There are also specific issues of data protection to take into account. For this reason, extra 'standards for quality assurance for online surveys' have been formulated (see ADM 2001) which are helpful for assessing (your) research with this specific approach (see also Chapter 9 for some of these issues).

Checklist for Evaluating a Research Project

For the evaluation of an empirical project in social research, the questions in Box 11.1 are designed to inform your practice. These aspects are relevant for evaluating your own research as well as for assessing other researchers' studies.

BOX 11.1

Checklist for evaluating a research project

1. In a quantitative study, have the criteria of (a) reliability, (b) validity and (c) objectivity been checked?
2. In a qualitative study, which criteria or approaches for assessment of quality have been applied?
3. How far have you made the study and the assessment of its quality transparent and explicit in the presentation of the results and of the procedures?
4. What did you do with deviant results or negative cases?
5. How have you examined the generalizability of your results? What were the aims in this, and how were they reached?

Key Points

- For evaluating quantitative research, the established criteria are reliability, validity and objectivity.

- In qualitative research, these criteria in most cases cannot be applied immediately. Rather they have first to be reformulated. A number of suggestions have been made for how to reformulate these criteria for qualitative research.

- In addition, method-appropriate criteria have been developed for qualitative research.

- Generalization in quantitative research is based on (statistical) inference from the sample to the population.

- In qualitative research, in contrast, theoretical generalization may be the aim.

- In qualitative research, the building of typologies and the contrasting of cases play a major role.

▨ ▨ Further Reading ▨ ▨

The first and third references below discuss quality issues in quantitative research; the second and fourth cover quality in qualitative research.

Campbell, D.T. and Russo, M.J. (2001) *Social Measurement*. London: Sage.

Flick, U. (2008) *Managing Quality in Qualitative Research*. London: Sage.

May, T. (2001) *Social Research: Issues, Methods and Process*. Maidenhead: Open University Press. Chapter 1.

Seale, C. (1999) *The Quality of Qualitative Research*. London: Sage.

CHAPTER 12
ETHICAL ISSUES IN SOCIAL RESEARCH

Chapter Overview

Chapter Objectives

This chapter is designed to help you:

- see how ethical issues are involved in social research projects
- develop your sensitivity to ethical questions in social research
- appreciate the complexity of ethical considerations
- plan and conduct your research project within an ethical framework.

Table 12.1   Navigator for Chapter 12

Orientation	• What is social research? • Research question • Literature review
Planning and design	• Planning research • Designing research • Deciding methods
Working with data	• Gathering data • Analyzing data • E-research • Integrated research
Reflection and writing	• Evaluating research • Ethics • Writing and using research

You are here in your project ⟶

In Chapter 10, we considered the limitations of social research. There the main focus was on methodological or technical limitations. We considered such questions as: what can we grasp with one method, what is missed by it, how can we overcome this by using several methods? We also considered a more fundamental limitation, asking: when should you rather refrain from doing your research?

This chapter also focuses on limitations to social research, though of a different sort. We explore such questions as: which ethical problems should be taken into account in research? Which ethical boundaries are touched and how can you approach ethical issues in doing your social research project? As we shall see, these questions involve us in some very general rules and problems.

Principles of Ethically Acceptable Research

Definitions of Research Ethics

Ethical issues are relevant to research in general. They are especially relevant in medical and nursing research. Here we find the following definition of research ethics, which can be applicable to other research areas too:

> **Research ethics addresses the question of which ethically relevant issues caused by the intervention of researchers can be expected to impact on the people with or about whom they research. It is concerned in addition with the steps taken to protect those who participate in the research, if this is necessary. (Schnell and Heinritz 2006, p. 17)**

Principles

In the context of the social sciences, Murphy and Dingwall (2001, p. 339) have developed an 'ethical theory' that provides a useful framework for this chapter. Their theory is based on four principles:

- *Non-maleficence* – researchers should avoid harming participants.
- *Beneficence* – research on human subjects should produce some positive and identifiable benefit rather than simply be carried out for its own sake.
- *Autonomy or self-determination* – research participants' values and decisions should be respected.
- *Justice* – all people should be treated equally.

We shall examine in more detail below how these principles apply in social research.

In addition, Schnell and Heinritz (2006, pp. 21–4), working in the context of health sciences, have developed a set of principles specifically concerning the ethics of research. Their eight principles are listed in Box 12.1.

BOX 12.1

Principles of research ethics (Schnell and Heinritz 2006, pp. 21–4)

1. Researchers have to be able to justify why research about their issue is necessary at all.
2. Researchers must be able to explain what the aim of their research is and under what circumstances subjects participate in it.
3. Researchers must be able to explicate the methodological procedures in their projects.
4. Researchers must be able to estimate whether their research acts will have ethically relevant positive or negative consequences for the participants.
5. Researchers must assess the possible violations and damages arising from doing their project – and be able to do so *before* they begin the project.
6. Researchers have to take steps to prevent violations and damages identified according to principle 5.
7. Researchers must not make false statements about the usefulness of their research.
8. Researchers have to respect the current regulations of data protection.

Overall, such principles aim to ensure that researchers are able to make their procedures transparent (necessity, aims, methods of the study), that they can avoid or eliminate any harm or deception for the participants, and that they take care of data protection.

Informed Consent

Informed Consent as a General Principle

It should be self-evident that studies should generally involve only people who (a) have been informed about being studied and (b) are participating voluntarily. Principles of informed consent and of voluntary participation for social research are to be found in the code of ethics of the German Sociological Association. For example:

> A general rule for participation in sociological investigations is that it is voluntary and that it takes place on the basis of the fullest possible information about the goals and methods of the particular piece of research. The principle of informed consent cannot always be applied in practice, for instance if comprehensive pre-information would distort the results of the research in an unjustifiable way. In such cases an attempt must be made to use other possible modes of informed consent. (Ethik-Kodex 1993: I B2)

There are of course some difficulties here. As mentioned in the quote, informing participants beforehand may contradict the aims of a study. Also there are research settings in which it is not possible to inform all people who might become part of the research in advance. For example, in observations in open spaces (marketplaces, train stations etc.) many people just passing by might become part of the observation for very short moments. For these people, it will be very difficult to obtain their consent. If, however, this is not the case, and consent *can* practically be obtained, you should never refrain from doing so. Accordingly it is generally assumed that informed consent is a precondition for participating in research. For applying this principle in concrete terms, you can find some criteria in the literature:

- The consent should be given by someone competent to do so.

- The person giving the consent should be adequately informed.

- The consent is given voluntarily (Allmark 2002, p. 13).

Informed Consent in Researching Vulnerable Groups

Research with people who are, for special reasons, unable to give their consent raises specific ethical problems. These people are termed vulnerable groups:

> Vulnerable ... subjects are people who, because of their age or their limited cognitive abilities, cannot give their informed consent or who, because of their specific situation, would be particularly stressed or even endangered by their participation in a research project. (Schnell and Heinritz 2006, p. 43)

How then to proceed, if you want to do research with people not able or not seen as able to understand your concrete procedures or to assess them and to decide independently? Examples include small children, or people who are very old or who suffer from dementia or mental problems (for research with vulnerable people see Liamputtong 2007). In such cases, you could ask other people to give the consent as substitutes – the children's parents, family members or responsible medical or nursing staff in the case of the aged or ill persons. But do you then still meet the criteria of informed consent? Can you always assume that these other persons will take the same perspective as the participants you want to study? If you apply the principle of informed consent in a very strict sense in such cases, research is not permitted with these groups of participants, and thus research about relevant issues from the viewpoint of those concerned would be forgone. If you are conducting research involving vulnerable people, you should certainly not ignore the principle of informed consent. You should establish a way in which informed consent can be obtained either from or for the participants: consider carefully who is able to give this consent either together with or for them. However, these are tradeoffs that can only be made for a specific study and not generally. There is no general rule on how to manage this problem: you will have to think for your particular study and your particular target group about how to solve this dilemma between doing necessary research and avoiding any mistreatment of your participants.

Confidentiality, Anonymity and Data Protection

Box 12.2 provides an example of a form developed for the author's own research projects. It is helpful to consider it here as a way to focus both on the issues of informed consent (discussed above) and on anonymity and data protection for the participants.

The form should be completed and signed by both the researcher and the participant. Sometimes an oral agreement can be used as a substitute for the written contract if the participant does not want to sign it. Note that the form specifies a certain period after which the participants can withdraw their consent. Furthermore, the form specifies who will have access to the data and whether the data can be used for teaching after anonymization.

BOX 12.2

Agreement about data protection for scientific interviews

- Participation in the interview is voluntary. It has the following purpose:
  [issue of the study]

- Responsible for doing the interview and analyzing it are:

  Interviewer:
  [name]
  [name of institution]
  Supervisor of the project:
  [name]
  [name and address of institution]
  The responsible persons will ensure that all data will be treated confidentially and only for the purpose agreed herewith.

- The interviewee agrees that the interview will be recorded and scientifically analyzed. After finishing the recording he or she can ask for erasure of particular parts of the interview from the recording.

- For assuring data protection, the following agreements are made (please delete what is not accepted):

  The material will be processed according to the following agreement about data protection:

  Recording

  1. The recording of the interview will be stored in a locked cabinet and in password protected storage media by the interviewers or supervisors and erased after the end of the study or after two years at the latest.
  2. Only the interviewer and the members of the project team will have access to the recording for analyzing the data.
  3. In addition the recording can be used for teaching purposes. (All participants in the seminar will be obliged to maintain the data protection.)

  Analysis and archiving

  1. For the analysis, the recording will be transcribed. Names and locations mentioned by the interviewee will be anonymized in the transcript – as far as necessary.
  2. In publications, it is guaranteed that an identification of the interviewee will not possible.

- The interviewer or the supervisor of the project holds the copyright for the interviews.
- The interviewee may revoke his or her declaration of consent completely or partially within 14 days.

Location, date:
Interviewer:
Interviewee:

In case of an oral agreement:
I confirm that I informed the interviewee about the purpose of the data collection, explained the details of this agreement about data protection, and obtained his or her agreement.

Location, date:
Interviewer:

Confidentiality and anonymity may be particularly relevant if the research involves several participants in a specific, very small, setting. If you interview employees in the same enterprise or family members independently of each other it will be necessary to ensure confidentiality not only with respect to the public beyond that setting, but also within it. Readers of a publication should not be able to identify the individuals who participated as an interviewee, for example. Therefore, you should change personal data such as names, addresses, workplaces etc. so that inferences to persons etc. become impossible or, at the very least, are hampered. Accordingly the researcher has to ensure that the other participants cannot identify their colleagues in the presentation of their common workplace or in what the researcher reveals about their study. For this purpose, a consistent anonymization of the data and a parsimonious use of context information are necessary.

If children are interviewed, parents often want to know what their children said in the interviews – which may be problematic for interviews referring to relations of parents to children or to conflicts among them. To avoid this problem, it may be necessary to inform the parents beforehand when such information cannot be given to them.

It is particularly important to store the data (questionnaires, recordings, transcripts, field notes, interpretations etc.) physically in a safe and locked way (data safes, cupboards that can be locked for example), so that nobody gains access to the data who is not supposed to have this access (see Lüders 2004b). The same precautions have to be taken if the data are stored electronically – which means that they are password protected at least, and that the number of persons having access to the site is strictly limited.

How to Avoid Harm for Participants

The risk of harm for participants is a major ethical issue in social research. If, for example, you ask in an interview or a questionnaire how people live with their chronic illness and cope with it, you will confront your respondents with the severity of their illness and maybe with the limits to or lack of their life expectancy, again or additionally. This might cause a crisis or lead to extra stress for the interviewees. Is it ethically correct to produce such a risk for the participants in the research?

A specific problem arises in testing the effects of medications (or other forms of intervention) in randomized control studies (see Chapters 5 and 11). Here people with a diagnosis are randomly allocated to an intervention group (receiving treatment with the medication) and to a control group (receiving instead a placebo without effect, which means no treatment). Is it ethically justified to deprive this second group of a treatment, or to give it to them only after the end of the study? Should you do randomized studies in such cases – in particular, if it is about a serious or life threatening disease? (See Thomson et al. 2004 for this issue.)

The examples just given are drawn from medical research. However, the need to avoid harm applies to *all* research, not just medical studies. According to the code of ethics of the German Sociological Association:

> **Persons who are observed, questioned or involved in some other way in investigations, for example in connection with the analysis of personal documents, shall not be subject to any disadvantages or dangers as a result of the research. All risks that exceed what is normal in everyday life must be explained to the parties concerned. The anonymity of interviewees or informants must be protected. (Ethik-Kodex 1993: I B 5)**

Demands on the Participants Resulting from the Research

Research projects always make demands on participants (see Wolff 2004). For example, participants may be required to sacrifice time to complete a questionnaire or to answer the interviewers' questions. In addition, they may be expected to deal with embarrassing questions and issues and to give the researchers access to their privacy.

From an ethical point of view, you should reflect on whether the demands your research would make on participants are reasonable – especially in the light of their specific situations. For example, you should consider whether a confrontation with their own life history and illness in an interview or survey might even intensify your participants' illness.

Rule of Economy of Demands and Stress

If you are requesting personal information, you should always consider whether you really need the whole life history (in a narrative interview for example) for answering your research question, or whether responses to more focused questions might be sufficient. However, we can observe a trend in standardized research to add this questionnaire to the data collection or to include that question in the survey. This leads, on the one hand, to an extension of the datasets in the single study. On the other hand, I see this as a demonstration that questions of economy are not only an issue for qualitative research. In both contexts, you should check what are justifiable demands on the participants, what is already stressful and no longer justified as a demand, and when harming the participants begins.

Codes of Ethics

Many scientific associations have published codes of ethics. They are formulated for regulating the relations between researchers and the people and fields they study. Sometimes they also regulate how therapists or caregivers should work with their clients or patients, as in psychology and nursing. Some of them refer to specific questions of the research in the area, as in research with children in education. Examples of codes of scientific associations, available on the Internet, include:

- The British Psychological Society (BPS) has published a Code of Conduct, Ethical Principles, and Guidelines (www.bps.org.uk/the-society/ethics-rules-charter-code-of-conduct/ethics-rules-charter-code-of-conduct_home.cfm).

- The British Sociological Association (BSA) has formulated a Statement of Ethical Practice (www.britsoc.co.uk).

- The American Sociological Association (ASA) refers to its Code of Ethics (www.asanet.org/members/ecoderev.html).

- The Social Research Association (SRA) has formulated Ethical Guidelines (www.the-sra.org.uk/Ethicals.htm).

- The German Sociological Association (GSA) has developed a Code of Ethics (www.soziologie.de/index_english.htm).

Such codes of ethics demand that research be pursued only under the condition of informed consent and without harming the participants. This includes a requirement that the research does not intrude on the participants' privacy in inappropriate ways and that the participants are not deceived about the research aims.

Ethics Committees

Professional associations, hospitals and universities typically have ethics committees to ensure that ethical standards are met.

> Ethics committees are in charge of assessing whether researchers have made enough ethical considerations before beginning the research they plan. For this purpose, ethics committees have two instruments. They can decide about projects by accepting or rejecting them. Secondly they can become active in consulting researchers and discuss with them suggestions for the ethical planning of a project. (Schnell and Heinritz 2006, p. 18)

For this purpose, the committees assess proposed research designs and methods before they are applied to human beings. Such assessments normally consider three aspects (see Allmark 2002, p. 9): (a) scientific quality; (b) the welfare of participants; and (c) respect for the dignity and rights of participants.

A relevant question for ethics committees is whether a research project will provide new insights to add to existing knowledge. A project that merely duplicates earlier results can be seen as unethical – in particular, research that repeatedly does the same studies again (see for example Department of Health 2001). Here, the question is raised of how the stress for the participants is justified by the benefits to science and the novelty of results. Exceptions are studies with the explicit aim to test whether it is possible to replicate findings from earlier studies.

In considering the quality of research, we can see a source of conflict. To be able to judge the quality of research, the members of the ethics committee should have the necessary knowledge to assess a research proposal on a methodological level. In effect, this may mean that the members of the committee or at least some of the members should be researchers themselves. Yet if you talk for a while with researchers about their experiences with ethics committees and with proposals submitted to them, you will come across many stories about how a research proposal was rejected because the members did not understand its premise, or lacked the methodological background of the applicant, or simply disliked the style of research. Thus ethics committees may in practice end up rejecting research proposals for non-ethical reasons. Such a reservation can be particularly strong when a qualitative research proposal is confronted by committees or members who think only in natural science categories, or where experimental research is confronted by committees mainly thinking in interpretative categories.

In assessments by ethics committees, questions of welfare often involve weighing the risks (for the participants) against the benefits (of new knowledge and insights about a problem or of finding a new solution to an existing problem). For example if you want to find out the effects of a medication in a control group study (see Chapter 5), this means that you will give the participants in the control group a placebo rather than the medicine under study. If the control group is to be comparable to the study group, you will need people for it who are also in need of a treatment with the medication. Thus the dilemma arises between depriving the control group members of a possible treatment (at least for the moment) and otherwise being unable to study the effects of this medication adequately (see Thomson et al. 2004). Again, we find a potential conflict here: weighing the risks and benefits is often relative rather than absolute and clear.

The dignity and rights of the participants pertain to issues of (a) consent given by the participant, (b) sufficient information provided as a basis for giving consent, and (c) the need for consent to be voluntary (Allmark 2002, p. 13). Beyond this, researchers need to guarantee participants' confidentiality. This requires that the information about them will be used only in ways that make it impossible for other persons to identify the participants or for any institution to use it against the interests of the participants.

Ethics committees review and canonize the principles discussed here. For a detailed discussion of such principles, see Hopf (2004) and Murphy and Dingwall (2001).

Rules of Good Scientific Practice

Unfortunately, researchers have sometimes been guilty of concealing their results (for examples see Black 2006). Because of this, the German Research Council has developed proposals for safeguarding good scientific practice. These are outlined in Box 12.3 and are available (in English) at http://www.dfg.de/antragstellung/gwp/index.html. These rules define standards concerning honesty in using data, scientific fraud, and the documentation of original data (completed questionnaires, recordings and transcripts of interviews etc.).

BOX 12.3

Rules for good scientific practice (excerpt) (Deutsche Forschungsgemeinschaft 1998)

Recommendation 1
Rules of good scientific practice shall include principles for the following matters (in general, and specified for individual disciplines as necessary):

- fundamentals of scientific work, such as

  o observing professional standards
  o documenting results
  o consistently questioning one's own findings
  o practising strict honesty with regard to the contributions of partners, competitors, and predecessors

- cooperation and leadership responsibility in working groups …
- mentorship for young scientists and scholars (recommendation 4)
- securing and storing primary data (recommendation 7)
- scientific publications (recommendation 11).

Recommendation 7
Primary data as the basis for publications shall be securely stored for ten years in a durable form in the institution of their origin.

Recommendation 8
Universities and research institutes shall establish procedures for dealing with allegations of scientific misconduct. They must be approved by the responsible corporate body. Taking account of relevant legal regulations including the law on disciplinary actions, they should include the following elements:

- a definition of categories of action which seriously deviate from good scientific practice [recommendation 1] and are held to be scientific misconduct, for instance the fabrication and falsification of data, plagiarism, or breach of confidence as a reviewer or superior
- jurisdiction, rules of procedure (including rules for the burden of proof), and time limits for inquiries and investigations conducted to ascertain the facts

- the rights of the involved parties to be heard, and to discretion, and rules for the exclusion of conflicts of interest
- sanctions depending on the seriousness of proven misconduct
- the jurisdiction for determining sanctions.

Recommendation 11
Authors of scientific publications are always jointly responsible for their content. A so-called 'honorary authorship' is inadmissible.

Research Ethics: Cases and Mass Research

Ethical principles in social research apply to qualitative as well as quantitative research – even though the concrete questions and details involved may be very different. Data protection and anonymization may be more easily guaranteed for a single participant in the random sampling and statistical analysis of data than for a participant in a qualitative study with purposive sampling and (a few) expert interviews. Note, in particular, that if you plan a survey with repeated data collection from the same people in the first instance, you will need to store the real contact data of the participants so that you can return to them. There is a risk here of inadvertently infringing participants' rights to anonymity and data protection. Contact data and questionnaire responses will need to be separated.

Research Ethics in Online Research

Gaiser and Schreiner (2009, p. 14) have listed a number of questions to consider from an ethical point of view if you are planning an online study. They are:

- Can participant security be guaranteed? Anonymity? Protection of the data?
- Can someone ever really be anonymous online? And if not, how might this impact on the overall study design?
- Can someone 'see' a participant's information, when s/he participates?
- Can someone unassociated with the study access data on a hard drive?
- Should there be informed consent to participate? If so, how might online security issues impact on the informed consent?
- If a study design calls for participant observations, is it okay to 'lurk'? Is it always okay? If not then when? What are the determining factors?
- Is it ever okay to deceive online? What constitutes online deception?

This list shows how general issues of research ethics are relevant for online as well as traditional research.

Conclusion

We may finish with two general points concerning the ethical principles in research. First, we should remember that research entails questions of integrity and objectivity. As the German Sociological Association states:

> Sociologists strive for scientific integrity and objectivity in pursuing their profession. They are committed to the best standards that are possible in research, teaching and other professional practices. If they make discipline specific judgments, they will represent their field of work, the state of knowledge, their disciplinary expertise, their methods and their experience unambiguously and appropriately. In presenting or publishing sociological insights, the results are presented without any biasing omission of important results. Details of the theories, methods and research designs that are important for assessing the results of the research and of the limits of their validity are reported to the best of the researchers' knowledge. Sociologists should mention all their funding sources in their publications. They guarantee that their findings are not biased by the specific interests of their sponsors. (Ethik-Kodex 1993: I A 1–3)

This quotation refers specifically to 'sociologists'. It may be applied, however, to social researchers in general.

Second, questions of research ethics are raised in *any* kind of social research and with *all* sorts of methods. No methodological approach is free of ethical problems, even though these differ between methods:

> Research methods are not ethically neutral. That applies to qualitative, quantitative and triangulated methods in the same way. Criteria for assessing the quality of research at least implicitly ask for ethical issues as well. (Schnell and Heinritz 2006, p. 16)

Checklist for Taking Ethical Issues into Account

In pursuing an empirical project in social research, you should consider the ethical questions in Box 12.4. These questions can be applied to the planning of your own study and in a similar way to the evaluation of other researchers' existing studies.

BOX 12.4

Checklist for taking ethical issues into account in social research

1. How will you put the principle of informed consent into practice?
2. Have you informed all participants that they are taking part in a study or are involved in it?

---

3. How will you ensure that the participants do not suffer any disadvantages or damages from the study or from taking part in it?
4. How will you make sure that the participants in a control group do not suffer any disadvantage from the intervention they did not receive?
5. How will you guarantee the voluntariness of the participation?
6. How will you ensure that children or cognitively impaired people have agreed to being interviewed (for example) – i.e. that not merely the consent of parents or caregivers was obtained?
7. How will you organize the anonymization of the data and how will you deal with the issues of data protection in the study?
8. How will you take these issues into account for the storage of the data and in presenting the results?
9. Have you checked your method of proceeding against the relevant ethical code(s)?
10. If so, which problems became evident here?
11. Is a statement from an ethics committee necessary for your study and if so have you obtained it?
12. How will the project conform to requirements formulated in this process?
13. What is the novelty in the expected results, which justifies doing your project?
14. Can you specify the expected results?

Key Points

- Every research project should be planned and assessed according to ethical principles.

- Voluntariness of participation, anonymity, data protection, and avoidance of harm for the participants are preconditions.

- Informed consent should be obtained for every research project. Exceptions from this have to be justified rigorously.

- Codes of ethics provide an orientation for taking ethical principles into account and applying them.

- Ethics committees seek to ensure that ethical principles are upheld.

- For qualitative and quantitative research, ethical questions may be raised in different ways.

Further Reading

The following resources provide further discussion on the ethics of social research.

Bryman, A. (2008) *Social Research Methods,* 3rd edn. Oxford: Oxford University Press.

Flick, U. (2009) *An Introduction to Qualitative Research*, 4th edn. London: Sage. Chapter 4.

Hopf, C. (2004) 'Research Ethics and Qualitative Research: An Overview', in U. Flick, E. v. Kardorff and I. Steinke (eds), *A Companion to Qualitative Research*. London: Sage. pp. 334–9.

Mertens, D. and Ginsberg, P.E. (eds) (2009) *Handbook of Research Ethics*. London: Sage.

CHAPTER 13
WRITING RESEARCH AND USING RESULTS

Chapter Overview

Chapter Objectives

This chapter is designed to help you:

- recognize that presentation of results and methods is an integral part of social research projects
- know which forms of presentation are appropriate to (a) qualitative and (b) quantitative projects
- know which factors to consider when presenting results to (a) participants and (b) interested institutions and other audiences.

Table 13.1   Navigator for Chapter 13

Orientation	• What is social research? • Research question • Literature review
Planning and design	• Planning research • Designing research • Deciding methods
Working with data	• Gathering data • Analyzing data • E-research • Integrated research
Reflection and writing	• Evaluating research • Ethics • Writing and using research

You are here in your project →

Essentially, social research consists of three steps: (1) planning a study; (2) working with data; and (3) communicating the results. According to Wolff, communication (in the form of a 'text') is integral to social science:

> **To do social science means mainly to produce texts ... Research experiences have to be transformed into texts and to be understood on the basis of texts. A research process has findings only when and as far as these can be found in a report, no matter whether and which experiences were made by those who were involved in the research. The observability and practical objectivity of social science phenomena is constituted in texts and nowhere else. (1987, p. 333)**

When you communicate your research findings, you should aim to make the process that led you to them transparent to the reader. In the process, you should aim to demonstrate that your findings are not arbitrary, singular or question-able – but rather that they are based on evidence. This chapter considers the relevance of research, the utilization of its results, and their elaboration and presentation.

Goals of Writing Social Research

When you report your research, you may have various aims. For example:

1. to document your results

2. to show how you proceeded during your research – how you arrived at your results

3. to present results in such a way that you can achieve specific objectives – for example, to obtain a qualification, to influence a process (such as through

evidence-based policy-making) or to show something fundamentally new in your scientific field

3. to legitimize the research in some way – by showing that the results are not arbitrary, but rigorously based on data.

Writing Quantitative Research

In quantitative research, a research report will normally include the following elements:

1. the research problem
2. the conceptual framework
3. the research question
4. the method of data collection
5. analysis of the data
6. conclusions
7. discussion of the results.

When presenting your research, you should include statements referring to each of these points. They should permit an assessment of your methodology, the robustness of your results and their relationship to previous literature and research.

The Empirical Procedure

When writing about your empirical procedure, you should answer the following questions for your readers (see Neuman 2000, p. 472):

1. What type of study (e.g. experiment, survey) have you conducted?
2. Exactly how did you collect data (e.g. study design, type of survey, time and location of data collection, experimental design used)?
3. How were variables measured? Are the measures reliable and valid?
4. What is your sample? How many subjects or respondents are involved in your study? How did you select them?
5. How did you deal with ethical issues and specific concerns of the design?

The essential point is to allow the reader to evaluate your study. This will make it possible to assess the relevance and reliability of your results.

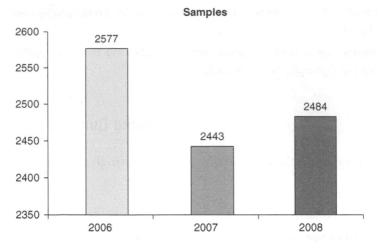

Figure 13.1   Bar chart

Elaboration of Results

Often researchers face the problem that a study may produce a multitude of findings. Here the first step is to provide a number of detailed findings. You can then distill, extrapolate or construct the fundamental results that emerge from the detailed findings. For example, you may do more to sort the data into classes.

Maybe even the researchers themselves feel confused by the multitude of findings produced in their study. In this case, they need to develop a framework for the continuing analysis. For example, they may focus on the distribution of data or they may adopt a comparative perspective (focusing, for example, on the differences between two subgroups in the sample). Above all, the researchers will need to be selective. As Neuman explains:

> **Researchers make choices in how to present the data. When analyzing the data, they look at dozens of univariate, bivariate, and multivariate tables and statistics to get a feel for the data. This does not mean that every statistic or table is in a final report. Rather, the researcher selects the minimum number of charts or tables that fully inform the reader and rarely presents the raw data himself. Data analysis techniques should summarize the data and test hypotheses (e.g. frequency distributions, tables with means and standard deviations, correlations and other statistics). (2000, p. 472)**

Presenting Results

Frequencies and numbers can often be presented more clearly in charts than in words. Consider, for example, Figure 13.1, which presents the

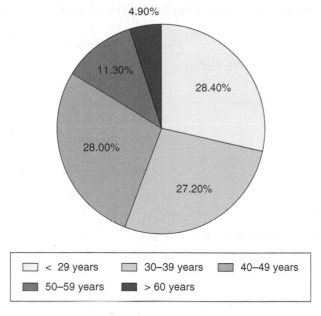

Figure 13.2   Pie chart

sample sizes in a longitudinal study at three times of measurement (2006, 2007, 2008).

An alternative is to use pie charts. Figure 13.2 provides an example in which the age distribution of homeless people in Germany is summarized in age groups (e.g. 30–39 years).

A third means of presentation is to use tables. Table 13.2 provides an example. Here, the frequencies of responses to the question of how to prevent diseases are summarized according to the age of children, who could give more than one answer.

These examples demonstrate how you can present findings visually so that they become apparent for readers 'at first sight'. The three methods above are not, of course, the only methods available; they are included here merely to illustrate the usefulness of visual presentation.

Evidence

In many areas of research, the notion of evidence-based practice has become very important. This emphasizes the need to distinguish reliable from less reliable scientific results. Here we can consider the example of medical practice. In evidence-based medicine, a medication is tested in a specific form of research before it is introduced in regular medical routines. Greenhalgh gives as a definition:

Categories	5-year-old	8-year-old	12-year-old	16-year-old
Healthy eating, fruit, vegetables, tea, juice	28	56	83	88
Vitamins, minerals	–	8	29	16
Take care of clothing, dress warmly	24	24	33	8
Moving, sports	20	32	38	76
Outdoor, fresh air	12	20	17	16
Not smoking	–	–	25	32
No alcohol	–	–	13	12
Little or no stress	–	–	–	4
Relax, sleep	–	4	4	8
Not getting infected, avoid contact with ill people	–	4	4	12

Source: Schmidt and Fröhling 1998, p. 39

> **Evidence-based medicine is the use of mathematical estimates of the risk of benefit and harm, derived from high-quality research on population samples, to inform clinical decision making in the diagnosis, investigation or management of individual patients. The defining feature of evidence-based medicine, then, is the use of figures derived from research on *populations* to inform decisions about *individuals*. (2006, p. 1)**

Here, double blind tests (see Chapter 5) are applied, which are also labeled randomized controlled studies (RCTs). Participants in a medication study are allocated randomly to the treatment group (with the medication) and a control group (with a placebo) for testing the effect of the medication by comparing the two groups. For the existence of evidence in the area of the epidemiology of diseases (e.g. lung cancer) in relation to certain risk factors (e.g. smoking), Stark and Guggenmoos-Holzmann hold:

> **If certain criteria of scientific evidence are fulfilled, a causal relation between the influential variable (risk factor) and the target variable (disease) is generally accepted. As major criteria we find:**
>
> - **A strong correlation between influential and target variable exists.**
> - **The results could be confirmed in several studies (reproducibility).**
> - **A dose–effect relation between influential and target variable exists.**
> - **The temporal course of cause and effect is logical.**
> - **The results are biologically plausible.**
> - **If the risk factor is eliminated, the illness risk is reduced. (2003, p. 417)**

Thus, a very specific understanding of what evidence is and, moreover, what kind of research can produce such evidence, has been developed. More generally, evidence-based practice means that professional practice and decision-making in the single case should be based on research and results, i.e. on evidence. This scientific foundation of professional practice should replace decision-making based on anecdote ('I knew a similar case …'), or what is just fashionable in the press.

Here we may note two implications of the development just mentioned. First, this understanding of evidence and of research threatens to push back other approaches of research and to challenge their relevance. Consequently we find several suggestions for classifying types of evidence. Such classification ranges from meta-analyses, based on randomized studies, as the most accepted form, to case studies and expert evaluations, which are the forms with the least acceptance (see Chapter 3).

Second, other disciplines – like social work, education, nursing and others – have also been developing evidence-based practice in their field. The trend towards evidence basing threatens to question other forms of research. There is a problem here: what makes a lot of sense in assessing the effect of medications is not necessarily justified for social research in general. Other forms to be replaced by evidence are concepts of cost minimizing etc. (Greenhalgh 2006, pp. 9–11). The challenge is to develop a broader understanding of what evidence is. Thus analyzing life histories of cancer patients, for example, will not meet the criteria of evidence basing in the sense outlined above – but will produce helpful evidence when it comes to understanding how people live with cancer and how they try to cope with it.

Writing Qualitative Research

For qualitative research, many commentators have expressed doubts that we can use the same approach as for quantitative research. Lofland (1976) and Neuman (2000, p. 474) have proposed an alternative structure for reporting qualitative research:

1. introduction

    (a) most general aspects of the situation
    (b) main contours of the general situation
    (c) how materials were collected
    (d) details about the setting
    (e) how the report is organized

2. the situation

    (a) analytical categories
    (b) contrast between situation and other situations
    (c) development of situation over time

3. strategies of interaction

4. summary and implications.

This structure provides a possible framework for your report. The advantage is that you then will go from more general aspects of your issue of research to the more concrete procedures and finally to the findings you obtained. Thus, this structure contributes to leading your readers through your report and directing them to the central points you want to make about your findings.

The Empirical Procedure

For qualitative projects, the presentation of the empirical procedures is often chronological, providing in the process insights into the field or situation under study. Van Maanen (1988) distinguishes three forms of presentation, namely (a) 'realist', (b) 'confessional' and (c) 'impressionist' tales.

In *realist tales*, one reports observations as facts, or documents them by using quotations from statements or interviews. Emphasis is laid on the *typical* forms of what is studied (see Flick et al. 2010 as an example). Therefore, you will analyze and present many details. Viewpoints of the members of a field or of interviewees are emphasized in the presentation: how did they experience their own life in its course? What is health for the interviewees? The interpretation does not stop at subjective viewpoints but goes beyond them by various and far-reaching interpretations.

Confessional tales are characterized by the personalized authorship and authority of the researcher as an expert. Here, the authors express the role that they played in what was observed, in their interpretations, and also in the formulations that are used. The authors' viewpoints are treated as an issue in the presentation, alongside the problems, breakdowns, mistakes, etc. (1988, p. 79) in the field. Nevertheless, authors will attempt here to present their findings as *grounded* in the issue that they studied. Such reports combine descriptions of the studied object and of the experiences of studying it. An example of this kind of report is Frank's book *The Wounded Storyteller* (1997).

Impressionist tales take the form of dramatic recall. The aim is to place the audience imaginatively in the research situation, including the specific characteristics of the field and of the data collection. A good example for this kind of report is Geertz's (1973) analysis of the Balinese cockfight.

Results

Qualitative studies can produce various forms of results. They may range from detailed case studies to typologies (e.g. several types of health concepts) or to the frequency and distribution of statements in a category system. In qualitative research one may again be able to condense information in the form of

Table 13.3 Sample I: Street youth by age and gender

Age (years)	Gender		
	Male $N = 12$	**Female** $N = 12$	**Total** $N = 24$
14	–	3	3
15	1	3	4
16	2	2	4
17	2	1	3
18	4	2	6
19	3	–	3
20	–	1	1
Mean	17.5	16.0	16.75

Source: Flick and Röhnsch 2008

Table 13.4 Sample II: Chronically ill street youth by age groups and gender

Age (years)	Gender		
	Male $N = 6$	**Female** $N = 6$	**Total** $N = 12$
14–17	1	3	4
18–25	5	3	8
Mean	21.5	16.8	19.2

Source: Flick and Röhnsch 2008

Table 13.5 Health concepts of the street youth interviewees

Health concept	Street youth				
	Total	Male	Female	General	Chronically ill
Health as physical and mental wellbeing	14	9	5	9	5
Health as absence of illness and of complaints	11	4	7	4	7
Health as result of certain practices	7	2	5	7	–
Health as functionality	4	3	1	4	–
N	36	18	18	24	12

Source: Flick and Röhnsch 2008

tables – for example about the composition of a sample regarding gender and age in years (see Table 13.3) or age groups and gender (see Table 13.4).

In qualitative research, this has mostly the aim of contextualizing the single statements and their interpretations (see Table 13.5, which summarizes the health definitions given by the adolescents in both samples displayed in Tables 13.3 and 13.4 according to gender and subgroups).

One specific form of result (or outcome) of a qualitative study may be the development of a theory. The presentation of such a theory requires, according to Strauss and Corbin, four components:

1. **A clear analytic story.**
2. **Writing on a conceptual level, with description kept secondary.**
3. **The clear specification of relationships among categories, with levels of conceptualization also kept clear.**
4. **The specification of variations and their relevant conditions, consequences, and so forth, including the broader ones. (1990, p. 229)**

Here, presentation of research will highlight the core concepts and lines of the theory that has been developed. Visualization in the form of conceptual networks, trajectories and so on is a means to give the presentation more pregnancy. The suggestions of Lofland (1974) for presenting findings in the form of theories lead us in a similar direction. He mentions as criteria for writing the same criteria as for evaluating such reports, namely ensuring that:

(1) The report was organized by means of a *generic* conceptual framework; (2) the generic framework employed was *novel*; (3) the framework was *elaborated* or developed in and through the report; (4) the framework was *eventful* in the sense of being abundantly documented with qualitative data; (5) the framework was interpenetrated with the empirical materials. (1974, p. 102)

In qualitative research one again faces the problem of selecting essentials from a multitude of data and relationships that the study has identified. Here you have to find a balance in your report between providing insight into, on the one hand, the occurrences and conditions in the field and, on the other, the data and the more general issues you can derive from such insights and details. This is necessary for making your results accessible and transparent for the readers. One way is to combine topic-related summaries and structures with case studies, which go beyond those topics and show commonalities between the topics.

Evidence in Qualitative Research

The concept of evidence according to the evidence-based approaches outlined above cannot be transferred to qualitative research without problems. However, the question has to be asked of how to define evidence in the use of qualitative methods, and what role qualitative research can play in this development (see Denzin and Lincoln 2005; Morse et al. 2001). The discussion includes the suggestion of linking several studies – in the sense of meta-analyses – and also extending and transferring results to practical contexts as a from of 'test' (Morse 2001). For example, we found in one of our studies (Flick et al. 2010) three types of knowledge about the link between residents' sleeping problems at night and the lack of daytime activities in the nursing home for nurses. One of them was rather limited; one of them was much more developed. We can use these results for training nurses and then assess whether this intervention changes their practices and reduces the intensities of sleeping problems. In this way, practice provides a kind of 'test' concerning the evidence of our findings.

Issues of Writing

There are some general issues concerning the writing of research, regardless of the type of research project. In producing a text, researchers need to consider their potential readers or audience:

> **Making your work clearer involves considerations of audience: who is it supposed to be clearer to? Who will read what you write? What do they have to know so that they will not misread or find what you say obscure or unintelligible? You will write one way for the people you work with closely on a joint project, another way for professional colleagues in other specialities and disciplines, and differently yet for the 'intelligent layman'. (Becker 1986, p. 10)**

The choice of audience will have implications for the style of presentation. One needs to ask, what can you assume as already existing knowledge and available terminologies on the part of the readers? How complex and detailed should the account be? Which forms of simplification are specifically necessary for my audience?

Feeding Back Results to Participants

In practice-oriented research, feedback of preliminary or final results to the participants is often expected – particularly if the results are likely to be used for evaluation or decision-making. In this case you will need to consider how to present your research transparently in a form that the participants will find accessible. Furthermore you should take into account the dynamics in the field – what the results may initiate or change in this context. When describing how she fed back the results and evaluations in her studies in the context of police research, Mensching (2006) used the term 'mediating work': her research had to be presented very sensitively in order to avoid being either too challenging or too simplistic. You must also ensure that you protect the single participants from being identified from the results – even by their colleagues. See Box 13.1.

Feedback of results to participants

In our study on health professionals' social representations about health and aging (Flick et al. 2004), we organized the feedback of our results to our participants as follows. After episodic interviews with the single participants about their health concepts and ideas and experiences with prevention and health promotion, and after analyzing the data, we did focus groups with general practitioners and home care nurses. The results of the study were reported back to the participants for collecting their comments to the findings. Then we discussed practical implications with them concerning any improvement in the routines and practices in home care nursing and medicine.

In order to avoid discussion in groups becoming too general or heterogeneous, we selected a concrete part of the data as a stimulus for opening up the more comprehensive discussions. For this purpose we selected the results concerning the barriers to a stronger orientation of one's own practice towards prevention. The results about the readiness for and resistance to more prevention on the part of the professionals and of the patients were presented. First, we gave an overview of the barriers that had been mentioned. Then the participants were asked to rank these barriers for their relevance, before discussing this relevance for their own professional practice and for the role about health in it. When this discussion abated, we asked the participants to make suggestions about how to overcome the barriers discussed before, and again to discuss these suggestions. At the end, we had not only the evaluations of the results of the initial interviews but also a list of comments and suggestions from every group. These lists could be analyzed and integrated in the final results of the study.

Using Data in Debate

The specific problems of using data in debates has been highlighted by Lüders (2006). There are questions concerning how far the data and the conclusions drawn from them are credible and can be trusted:

> From the viewpoint of the political administration ... the question simply is: can we also rely on the data and the results in the classical understanding of reliability and at least internal validity? ... The questions of credibility and of trust refer not merely to the problem of whether the data are reliable and valid for the units that were studied, but mainly to the problem of the transferability to similar contexts. (2006, p. 456)

This issue is heightened when the data come from a qualitative study with very few cases and where political initiatives may be based on the results. Here, the issue is the robustness of the results in the process of argumentation and the implications that follow.

When in a small qualitative study with seven cases in two areas of a country the result is that juvenile intensive offenders – and in these seven cases the concept is adequate – keep the responsible organizations (police, legal services, child and youth services, mental services for children and adolescents, schools etc.) so busy that no one has an overview anymore, then this result is first valid for these seven cases without doubt. The *politically* relevant question, however, is: are the results robust enough that a process is inaugurated using them to redefine the institutional responsibilities in the country for such a constellation – and how is this defined? – with all the necessary effort, extending even to changing the laws? This also refers to the risks linked to those changes, for example of conflict between interest groups that are concerned and the possible advantage handed to the political opposition in parliament. (2006, pp. 458–9)

Lillis (2002, p. 36) has argued in a different context (i.e. market research) that the movement from the data to practical suggestions or implications entails three steps:

- The first step focuses on what the participants (in qualitative studies) think and mean. By analogy, you can see what the numbers in a quantitative study say (what correlates with what for example). That refers to the report about the research and the immediate results.

- The second step in both cases relates to what patterns emerge and what they mean. That is mainly based on the interpretation of the data and results by the researchers.

- The third step asks for the implications for the commissioner of the study and thus for the applicability of the results for them.

For research-based consultation, we should distinguish between those suggestions which (1) are grounded in the research alone, (2) involve knowledge about the relevant market beyond the results and (3) additionally take the commissioners' specific product or service into account (2002, p. 38). Suggestions will only rarely be based on the empirical results alone: if they are to have any effect, they will have to take into account the current political situation and the specific mandate of the institution.

Utilization of Results

It should be recognized that the results of a research project will not necessarily be taken up one-to-one in the different contexts in which they are read. Rather they will be the subject of further interpretation. Studies about the utilization of social science research results (e.g. Beck and Bonß 1989) have shown that various processes of using, reinterpreting, evaluating and selecting occur in utilization:

> Since the results of the social science utilization research, we know that the utilization of scientific knowledge more or less occurs according to the logic of the respective field of practice – in our case the logic of political administration in a way that is often rather confusing for the scientists. (Lüders 2006, p. 453)

As we have seen in Chapter 11, the evaluation of the research is no longer conducted using only the internal criteria of sciences alone. Rather it becomes evident that the 'quality criteria and checks of the research ... are no longer exclusively defined out of the disciplines and with "peer reviews", but that additional or even competing social, political and economic criteria emerge from the contexts of application (of the results)' (Weingart 2001, p. 15).

If social science and its results are intended to have practical, political or other forms of impact, such processes must be taken into account. The results and the scientific quality of research alone will not prove decisive. Rather, results have to be elaborated and presented in such a way that they become relevant and understandable for the specific context of discussion and application.

> One is made aware that scientific knowledge is always presented scientific knowledge. And the consequence is that a 'logic of presentation' has to be considered as well as a 'logic of research'. How researchers' constitution of experiences is linked to the way those experiences are saved in presentations has only begun to become an issue for reflection and research. (Bude 1989, p. 527)

Checklist for Presenting Empirical Procedures

When presenting an empirical project in social research you should take the aspects listed in Box 13.2 into account. These questions again are relevant not only for writing your own report but also for assessing how other researchers presented their research.

BOX 13.2

Checklist for presenting empirical procedures

1. Have the aims of the project been made clear?
2. Has the research question been explicitly formulated and grounded?
3. Is it evident why particular persons or situations have been involved in the study and what the methodological approach of the sampling is?
4. Is it evident how the data were collected, for example by presenting example questions?
5. Is it transparent how data collection proceeded and which special occurrences played a role – perhaps for the quality of the data?

---

6. Will the readers be able to understand how the data were analyzed?
7. Have questions (criteria and strategies) of quality assurance in the research been addressed?
8. Have the results been condensed so that their essentials become evident for the readers?
9. Have consequences been drawn from the study and the results and discussed?
10. Is the report easy to read and understand and has the text been complemented by illustrations?
11. Did you provide enough evidence (e.g. quotations or extracts from the calculations) to enable the readers to evaluate your results?

Key Points

- Social research and its results become accessible only through the form of writing that you choose.

- The aim is to make transparent to readers both how the researchers proceeded and what results they have obtained.

- There is a need to select and weigh what you found in order to direct your readers' attention to what is essential in the results.

- Quantitative and qualitative research differ in the ways they present their findings and the processes that have led to them. However, the two types of research also have some aims in common.

- Particular needs of elaborating data and results pertain to political or administrative consultations and the feedback presented to participants.

- The utilization of results often follows logics other than those of research and researchers.

Further Reading

The works listed below provide further discussion of the issues of writing and presenting social research and evidence. The final two books in the list focus on how to display quantitative research.

Becker, H.S. (1986) *Writing for Social Scientists*. Chicago: University of Chicago Press.

Flick, U. (2009) *An Introduction to Qualitative Research*, 4th edn. London: Sage. Chapter 30.

Greenhalgh, T. (2006) *How to Read a Paper: The Basics of Evidence-Based Medicine*. Oxford: Blackwell-Wiley.

Matt, E. (2004) 'The Presentation of Qualitative Research', in U. Flick, E. v. Kardorff and I. Steinke (eds), *A Companion to Qualitative Research*. London: Sage. pp. 326–30.

Neuman, W.L. (2000) *Social Research Methods: Qualitative and Quantitative Approaches*, 4th edn. Boston: Allyn and Bacon.

Tufte, E.R. (1990) *Envisioning Information*. Cheshire: Graphics.

Tufte, E.R. (2001) *Visual Display of Quantitative Information*. Cheshire: Graphics.

Glossary

Applied research   Different from basic research, studies are done in specific practical fields and theories are tested for contexts of use in practice (e.g. the hospital).

Assessment   (In medical or psychological contexts) measurement of the (cognitive) performance or the health and illness status of patients, for example.

Audit   Strategy to assess a process (in accounting or in research) in all its steps and components.

Background theories   Theories that inform social research approaches through their conceptualization of reality or research.

Basic research   Research that starts from a specific theory in order to test its validity without restriction to a specific field of application or topic.

Bivariate analysis   Calculations showing the relation between two variables.

Burnout   A syndrome of exhaustion by one's own profession, often caused by high stress and a lack of positive feedback.

Categorization   Allocation of certain events to a category. Summarizing several identical or similar events under a concept.

Central tendency   Average in a distribution (e.g. mean, median).

Closed question   A finite range of answers are presented, often in the form of a scale of answer possibilities.

Code of ethics   A set of rules of good practice in research (or interventions) established by professional associations or by institutions as an orientation for their members.

Coding Development of concepts in the context of grounded theory. For example, to label pieces of data and allocate other pieces of data to them (and the label). In quantitative research, coding means to allocate a number to an answer.

Coding paradigm A set of basic relations for linking categories and phenomena among each other in grounded theory research.

Communicative validation Criterion for validity for which the consent of the study participants is obtained for data that were collected, for interpretations or for results.

Complete collection Form of sampling that includes all elements of a population defined in advance.

Constant comparative method Part of grounded theory methodology focusing on comparing all elements in the data with each other. For example, statements from an interview about a specific issue are compared with all the statements about this issue in other interviews and also with what was said about other issues in the same and other interviews.

Constructionism/constructivism A variety of epistemologies in which the social reality is seen as the result of constructive processes (activities or the members or processes in their minds). For example, living with an illness can be influenced by the way the individuals see their illness, what meaning they ascribe to it, and how this illness is seen by other members of their social world. On each of these levels, illness and living with it are socially constructed.

Context sensitivity Methods that take the context of a statement or observation into account.

Contingency analysis Analysis of how often certain concepts appear together with other concepts in the study period in the press.

Control group design A design that includes two groups, of which one (the control group) will not receive the treatment that is studied in order to control whether the effects that were observed in the treatment group also occur without treatment or whether they can be really referred to the treatment.

Conversation analysis Study of language (use) for formal aspects (for example, how a conversation is started or ended, how turns from one to the other speaker are organized).

Correlation General concept for describing relations between variables – e.g. number of divorces and amount of income.

Covert observation A form of observation in which the observers do not inform the field and its members about the fact they are doing observations for research purposes. This can be criticized from an ethical point of view.

Data protection Conduct or means that guarantees the anonymity of research participants. To make sure that data do not end up in or are passed on to the hands of unauthorized persons or institutions.

Deduction The logical reference from the general to the particular or, put in other words, from the theory to that which can be observed empirically.

Dependent variable Variable that belongs to the 'then' part of a (if–then) hypothesis and which shows the effects of the independent variable (cause, effects).

Description Studies provide (only) an exact representation of a relation or of the facts and circumstances.

Dispersion A measure for the variation in the measurements.

Double blind test Empirical study in which participants and researchers do not know the aim of the study. A 'blind' researcher does not know whether he or she is in contact with a member of the study group or the control group. This avoids the participants being unconsciously influenced.

Episode A shorter situation in which something specific happens, for example an illness episode.

Epistemology Theories of knowledge and perception in science.

Ethics committees Committees in universities, or sometimes also in professional associations, that assess research proposals (for dissertations or funding) for their ethical soundness. If necessary, these committees pursue violations of ethical standards.

Ethnography A research strategy combining different methods, but based on participation, observation and writing about a field under study. For example, for studying how homeless adolescents deal with health issues, a participant observation in their community may be combined with interviewing the adolescents. The overall image of details from this participation, observation and interviewing is unfolded in a written text about the field. The way of writing gives the representation of the field a specific form.

Ethnomethodology Theoretical approach interested in analyzing the methods people use in their everyday life to make communication and routines work.

Evaluation research   The use of research methods with a focus on assessing a treatment or intervention for demonstrating the success or the reasons for failure of a treatment or intervention.

Everyday theory   Theories that are developed and used in everyday practices for finding explanations and making predictions.

Evidence-based practices   Interventions (in medicine, social work, nursing etc.) that are based on results of research done according to specific standards.

Experiment   An empirical study in which certain conditions are produced deliberately and observed in their effects. Participants are distributed randomly to experimental and control groups.

Explanation   Identification of regularities and relations in the experience and behavior by assuming external causes and testing their effects.

External validity   A criterion of validity focusing on the transferability of results to other situations beyond the research situation.

External variables   Influences other than those to be studied.

Factor analysis   A form of statistical analysis, focusing on identifying a limited number of basic factors and summarizing them so that they can explain the relations in a field.

Falsification   Disproof of a hypothesis.

Field notes   Notes taken by the researcher about their thoughts and observations when they are in the field 'environment' they are researching.

Field research   Studies done not in a laboratory but in practical fields – like a hospital – in order to analyze the phenomena under study under real conditions.

Focus groups   Research method used in market and other forms of research, in which a group is invited to discuss the issue of a study for research purposes.

Generalizability   The degree to which the results derived from a sample can be transferred to the population.

Generalization   Transfer of research results to situations and populations that were not part of the research situation.

Grounded theory   Theories developed from analyzing empirical material or from studying a field or process.

Hermeneutics   The study of interpretations of texts in the humanities. Hermeneutical interpretation seeks to arrive at valid interpretations of the meaning of a text. There is an emphasis on the multiplicity of meanings in a text, and on the interpreter's foreknowledge of the subject matter of a text.

Heuristic   Something that is used for reaching a certain goal.

Homogeneous sample   A form of sampling in which all elements of the sample have the same features (e.g. age and profession).

Hypothesis   Assumption that is formulated for study purposes (mostly coming from the literature or an existing theory) in order to test it empirically in the course of the study. Often formulated as 'if–then' statements.

Ideal type   Pure cases that can represent the phenomenon under study in a specifically typical way.

Independent variable   Variable that belongs to the 'if' part of a (if–then) hypothesis.

Index construction   A combination of several single indicators, which are collected and analyzed together (e.g. the social states is composed from the states of education, profession and income).

Indication   Decision about when exactly (under what conditions) a specific method (or combination of methods) should be used.

Indicator   Something representing a specific phenomenon that is not directly accessible.

Induction   Reference from the specific to the general or, in other words, from empirical observation to theory.

Informed consent   The agreement by the participants in a study to be involved in it that is based on information about the research.

Internal validity   Form of validity that defines how unambiguously a relation that was measured can be captured (how far biases coming from external variables can be excluded).

Intervening variable   A third variable that influences the relation between independent and dependent variables.

Interview   Systematic form of asking people for research purposes – either in an open form with an interview schedule or in a standardized form similar to a questionnaire.

In vivo code   A form of coding based on concepts taken from an interviewee's statements.

Key person   A person that will make access to the field under study (or to certain persons in it) possible or easier for the researcher.

Likert scale   Five-step scale for measuring attitudes, for which certain statements are presented and agreement with those statements is collected.

Longitudinal study   A design in which the researchers return repeatedly, after some time, to the field and the participants to do interviews several times again in order to analyze development and changes.

Market research   Use of research methods in analyzing the market for specific products.

Measurement   Allocation of a number to a certain object or event in dependence of their degree according to defined rules.

Member check   Assessment of results (or of data) by asking the participants for their consensus.

Mixed methodologies   An approach combining qualitative and quantitative methods in a pragmatic manner.

Multivariate analysis   Calculation of the relations between more than two variables.

Narrative   A story told by a sequence of words, actions or images, and more generally the organization of the information within that story.

Narrative analysis   Study of narrative data which takes the context of the whole narrative into account.

Narrative interview   A specific form of interview based on one extensive narrative. Instead of asking questions, the interviewer asks participants to tell the story of their lives (or their illness for example) as a whole, without interrupting them with questions.

Objective hermeneutics   A way of doing research by analyzing texts for identifying latent structures of meaning underlying those texts and explaining the phenomena that are the issues of the text and the research. For example, analyzing the transcript of a family interaction can lead to identifying and elaborating an implicit conflict underlying the communication of the members in this interaction and other occasions. This conflict as a latent structure of meaning shapes the members' interaction without them being aware of it.

Objectivity   Criterion for assessing whether a research situation (the application of methods and their outcome) is independent of the single researcher.

Open question   A form of questions in a questionnaire for which no pre-formulated responses are provided and which can be answered using keywords or a little paragraph written by the respondent.

Operationalization   Means for empirically covering the degrees of a feature, for which you will define methods of data collection and measurement.

Parallel test reliability   A criterion of reliability of an instrument which is tested by applying a second measurement instrument in parallel.

Paraphrase   A reformulation of the core of the information included in a specific sentence or statement.

Participant observation   A specific form of research in which the researcher becomes a member of the field under study in order to make observations.

Participative research   A form of research in which the study participants are integrated in designing the study. The aim is change through research.

Participatory action research   Research that intends to produce changes in the field under study. This is to be achieved by planning the interviews in a specific way and by feeding back results to the participants. The members in the field are made active participants in designing the research process.

Patients' career   The stages of a series of treatments of a chronic illness in several institutions.

Peer debriefing   A criterion of validity for which colleagues' comments about the results of a study are obtained.

Peer review   Assessment (of papers before publication) by colleagues from the same discipline acting as reviewers.

Population   Aggregate of all possible study objects about which a statement is intended (e.g. nurses). Research studies mostly include selections (samples) from this population and results are generalized from samples to populations.

Pragmatic test of theories   A form of theory assessment in everyday life, when people test their implicit theories by looking at how far they can be used for explaining certain relations.

Pre-test Application of a methodological instrument (questionnaire or category system) with the aim of testing it before its use in the main study.

Principle of openness A principle in qualitative research, according to which researchers will mostly refrain from formulating hypotheses and formulate (interview) questions as openly as possible in order to come as close as possible to the views of the participants.

Protocol A detailed process documentation of an observation or of a group discussion. In the first case, it is based on the researchers' field notes; in the second case, interactions in the group are recorded and transcribed, often complemented by researchers' notes about the features of communication in the group.

Qualitative methods Research methods aiming at a detailed description of processes and views that are therefore used with small numbers of cases in the data collection.

Quantitative methods Research methods aiming at covering the phenomena under study in their frequencies and distribution and thus working with large numbers in the data collection.

Questionnaire A defined list of questions presented to every participant of a study in an identical way either written or orally. The participants are asked to respond to these questions mostly by giving them a limited number of alternative answers.

Random sample Sample drawn according to a random principle from a complete list of all elements in a population (e.g. every third entry in a page of the telephone directory), so that every element in the population has the same chance to be integrated in the study. The opposite of purposive or theoretical sampling.

Reactivity Influences on persons in a study due to their knowledge about being studied.

Reconstruction Identification of continuous topics or basic conflicts in, for example, a patient's life history.

Reliability A standard criterion in standardized/quantitative research, which is based on repeated application of a test for assessing whether the results are the same in both cases.

Representative sample A sample that corresponds to the major features of the population: for example, a representative sample of all Germans corresponds in its features (e.g. age structure) to the features of the German population.

Representativeness   A concept referring to the generalization of research and results. It is understood either in a statistical way (e.g. is the population represented in the sample in the distribution of features such as age, gender, employment?) or in a theoretical way (e.g. are the study and its results covering the theoretically relevant aspects of the issue?).

Research design   A systematic plan for a research project specifying whom to integrate in the research (sampling), whom or what to compare for which dimensions etc.

Research methods   Everyday techniques such as asking, observing, understanding etc., but used in a systematic way in order to collect and analyze data.

Response rate   The number or share of questionnaires that are filled in and returned in a study.

Sample   Selection of study participants from a population according to specific rules.

Sampling   Selection of cases or materials for the study from a larger population or variety of possibilities.

Scaling   The allocation of numerical values to an object or event.

Secondary data   Data that have not been produced for the current study, but are available from other studies or from (for example) the documentation of administrative routines.

Segmenting   Decomposition of a text into the smallest meaningful elements.

Semi-structured interview   A set of questions formulated in advance, which can be asked in a variable sequence and perhaps slightly reformulated in the interview in order to allow the interviewees to unfold their views on certain issues.

Sequential analysis   Analysis of a text that proceeds from the beginning to the end along the line of development in the text, rather than by categorizing it.

Significant relation   A relation that (statistically) is stronger than the estimation of its non-existence.

Standard deviation   Root drawn from the variance.

Standardization   Control of a research situation by defining and delimiting as many features of it as necessary or possible.

Study design The plan according to which a study will be conducted, specifying the selection of participants, the kind and aims of the planned comparisons and the quality criteria for evaluating the results.

Survey Representative poll.

Systematic review A way of reviewing the literature in a field that follows specific rules, is replicable and transparent in its approach, and provides a comprehensive overview of the research in the field.

Thematic coding An approach involving analysis of data in a comparative way for certain topics after case studies (of interviews for example) have been done.

Theoretical sampling The sampling procedure in grounded theory research, where cases, groups or materials are sampled according to their relevance for the theory that is developed, and against the background of what is already the state of knowledge after a certain number of cases have been collected and analyzed.

Theoretical saturation The point in grounded theory research at which more data about a theoretical category do not produce any further theoretical insights.

Theory development The use of empirical observations to derive a new theory.

Theory test The assessment of the validity of an existing theory on the basis of empirical observations.

Transcription Transformation of recorded materials (conversations, interviews, visual materials etc.) into text for analysis.

Triangulation The combination of different methods, theories, data and/or researchers in the study of one issue.

Typology A form of systematization of empirical observation by differentiating several types of a phenomenon, allowing the bundling of single observations.

Utilization research Studies analyzing how research results are adopted in practical contexts.

Validity A standard criterion in standardized/quantitative research, for which you will check for example whether confounding influences affected the relations under study (internal validity) or how far the results are transferable to situations beyond the current research situation (external validity).

Variance   Sum of the square deviation of the values from the mean.

Verstehen   German word for 'to understand'. It describes an approach to understanding a phenomenon more comprehensively than reducing it to one explanation (for example a cause–effect relation). For example, to understand how people live with their chronic illness, a detailed description of their everyday life may be necessary, rather than merely identifying a specific variable (e.g. social support) for explaining the degree of success in their coping behavior.

Virtual ethnography   Ethnography through the Internet – e.g. participation in a blog or discussion group.

Vulnerable population   People in a specific situation (for example, social discrimination, risks, illness) that require particular sensitiveness when they are being studied.

Working hypothesis   An assumption that is made for orienting the work in progress. Different from hypotheses in general, these are not tested in a standardized way.

References

ADM (2001) *Standards for Quality Assurance for Online Surveys*, http://www.adm-ev.de/index.php?id=2&L=1 (accessed 2 July 2010).

Allmark, P. (2002) 'The Ethics of Research with Children', *Nurse Researcher*, 10: 7–19.

Anderson, P. (2007) *What is Web 2.0? Ideas, technologies and implications for education*. JISC Technology and Standards Watch, February, 2007. Bristol: JISC. www.jisc.ac.uk/media/documents/techwatch/tsw0701b.pdf (accessed 29 October 2010)

Bampton, R. and Cowton, C.J. (2002) 'The E-Interview', *Forum Qualitative Social Research*, 3 (2), www.qualitative-research.net/fqs/fqs-eng.htm (accessed 22 February 2005).

Banks, M. (2008) *Using Visual Data in Qualitative Research*. London: Sage.

Barton, A.H. and Lazarsfeld, P.F. (1955) 'Some Functions of Qualitative Analysis in Social Research', *Frankfurter Beiträge zur Soziologie*. I. Frankfurt a. M.: Europäische Verlagsanstalt. pp. 321–61.

Baur, N. and Florian, M. (2009) 'Stichprobenprobleme bei Online-Umfragen', in N. Jackob, H. Schoen and T. Zerback (eds), *Sozialforschung im Internet: Methodologie und Praxis der Online-Befragung*. Wiesbaden: VS-Verlag. pp. 109–28.

Baym, N.K. (1995) 'The Emergence of Community in Computer-Mediated Communication', in S. Jones (ed.), *Cybersociety: Computer-Mediated Communication and Community*. London: Sage. pp. 138–63.

Beck, U. and Bonß, W. (eds) (1989) *Weder Sozialtechnologie noch Aufklärung? Analysen zur Verwendung sozialwissenschaftlichen Wissens*. Frankfurt: Suhrkamp.

Becker, H.S. (1986) *Writing for Social Scientists*. Chicago: University of Chicago Press.

Becker, H.S. (1996) 'The Epistemology of Qualitative Research', in R. Jessor, A. Colby and R.A. Shweder (eds), *Ethnography and Human Development*. Chicago: University of Chicago Press. pp. 53–72.

Bergmann, J. (2004) 'Conversation Analysis', in U. Flick, E. v. Kardorff and I. Steinke (eds), *A Companion to Qualitative Research*. London: Sage. pp. 296–302.

Bergmann, J. and Meier, C. (2004) 'Electronic Process Data and Their Analysis', in U. Flick, E. v. Kardorff and I. Steinke (eds), *A Companion to Qualitative Research*. London: Sage. pp. 243–7.

Birnbaum, D. and Goscillo, H. (2009) 'Avoiding Plagiarism', http://clover.slavic.pitt.edu/~tales/plagiarism.html.

Black, A. (2006) 'Fraud in Medical Research: A Frightening, All-Too-Common Trend on the Rise', *Natural News*, http://www.naturalnews.com/019353.html (accessed 1 September 2010).

Bogner, A., Littig, B. and Menz, W. (eds) (2009) *Interviewing Experts*. Basingstoke: Palgrave Macmillan.

Bortz, J. and Döring, N. (2006) *Forschungsmethoden und Evaluation für Sozialwissenschaftler*, 3rd edn. Berlin: Springer.

Bryman, A. (1988) *Quantity and Quality in Social Research*. London: Unwin Hyman.

Bryman, A. (1992) 'Quantitative and Qualitative Research: Further Reflections on Their Integration', in J. Brannen (ed.), *Mixing Methods: Quantitative and Qualitative Research*. Aldershot: Avebury. pp. 57–80.

Bryman, A. (2008) *Social Research Methods*, 3rd edn. Oxford: Oxford University Press.

Bude, H. (1989) 'Der Essay als Form der Darstellung sozialwissenschaftlicher Erkenntnisse', *Kölner Zeitschrift für Soziologie und Sozialpsychologie*, 41: 526–39.

Burra, T.A., Stergiopoulos, V. and Rourke, S.B. (2009) 'A Systematic Review of Cognitive Deficits in Homeless Adults: Implications for Service Delivery', *Canadian Journal of Psychiatry*, 54: 123–33.

Campbell, D. (1986) 'Relabeling Internal and External Validity for Applied Social Sciences', in W.M.K. Trochin (ed.), *Advances in Quasiexperimental Design Analysis*, pp. 67–77.

Campbell, D.T. and Jean Russo, M. (2001) *Social Measurement*. London: Sage.

Charmaz, K. (2006) *Constructing Grounded Theory: A Practical Guide through Qualitative Analysis*. London. Sage.

Coldwell, C.M. and Bender, W.S. (2007) 'The Effectiveness of Assertive Community Treatment for Homeless Populations with Severe Mental Illness: A Meta-Analysis', *American Journal of Psychiatry*, 164: 393–9.

Creswell, J.W. (1998) *Qualitative Inquiry and Research Design: Choosing among Five Traditions*. Thousand Oaks, CA: Sage.

Creswell, J.W. (2003) *Research Design: Qualitative, Quantitative, and Mixed Methods Approaches*. Thousand Oaks, CA: Sage.

Creswell, J.W., Plano Clark, Vicki, L., Gutman, Michelle, L. and Hanson, W.E. (2003) 'Advanced Mixed Methods Research Design', in A. Tashakkori and C. Teddlie (eds), *Handbook of Mixed Methods in Social and Behavioral Research*. Thousand Oaks, CA: Sage. pp. 209–40.

Denscombe, M. (2007) *The Good Research Guide: For Small-Scale Social Research Projects*, 3rd edn. Maidenhead: McGraw Hill.

Denzin, N.K. (1970/1989) *The Research Act*, 3rd edn. Englewood Cliffs, NJ: Prentice Hall.

Denzin, N.K. (1988) *Interpretive Biography*. London: Sage.

Denzin, N.K. (2004) 'Reading Film: Using Photos and Video as Social Science Material', in U. Flick, E. v. Kardorff and I. Steinke (eds), *A Companion to Qualitative Research*. London: Sage. pp. 234–47.

Denzin, N. and Lincoln, Y.S. (2005) 'Introduction: The Discipline and Practice of Qualitative Research', in N. Denzin and Y.S. Lincoln (eds), *Handbook of Qualitative Research*, 3rd edn. London: Sage. pp. 1–32.

Department of Health (2001) *Research Governance Framework for Health and Social Care*. London: Department of Health.

Deutsche Forschungsgemeinschaft (DFG) (1998) *Vorschläge zur Sicherung guter wissenschaftlicher Praxis: Empfehlungen der Kommission 'Selbstkontrolle in der Wissenschaft'*. Denkschrift. Weinheim: Wiley-VCH.

Diekmann, A. (2007) *Empirische Sozialforschung*. Reinbek: Rowohlt.

Drew, P. (1995) 'Conversation Analysis', in J.A. Smith, R. Harré and L. v. Langenhove (eds), *Rethinking Methods in Psychology*. London: Sage. pp. 64–79.

Edwards, D. and Potter, J. (1992) *Discursive Psychology*. London: Sage.

Ethik-Kodex (1993) 'Ethik-Kodex der Deutschen Gesellschaft für Soziologie und des Berufsverbandes Deutscher Soziologen', *DGS-Informationen*, 1/93: 13–19.

Evans, J.R. and Mathur, A. (2005) 'The Value of Online Surveys', *Internet Research*, 15: 195–219.

Fleck, C. (2004) 'Marie Jahoda', in U. Flick, E. v. Kardorff and I. Steinke (eds), *A Companion to Qualitative Research*. London: Sage. pp. 58–62.

Flick, U. (1992) 'Knowledge in the Definition of Social Situations: Actualization of Subjective Theories about Trust in Counseling', in M. v. Cranach, W. Doise and G. Mugny (eds), *Social Representations and the Social Bases of Knowledge*. Bern: Huber. pp. 64–8.

Flick, U. (ed.) (1998a) *Psychology of the Social: Representations in Knowledge and Language*. Cambridge: Cambridge University Press.

Flick, U. (1998b) 'The Social Construction of Individual and Public Health: Contributions of Social Representations Theory to a Social Science of Health', *Social Science Information*, 37: 639–62.

Flick, U. (2000a) 'Episodic Interviewing', in M. Bauer and G. Gaskell (eds), *Qualitative Researching with Text, Image and Sound: A Practical Handbook*. London: Sage. pp. 75–92.

Flick, U. (2000b) 'Qualitative Inquiries into Social Representations of Health', *Journal of Health Psychology*, 5: 309–18.

Flick, U. (2004) 'Design and Process in Qualitative Research', in U. Flick, E. v. Kardorff and I. Steinke (eds), *A Companion to Qualitative Research*. London: Sage. pp. 146–52.

Flick, U. (ed.) (2006) *Qualitative Evaluationsforschung: Konzepte, Methoden, Anwendungen*. Reinbek: Rowohlt.

Flick, U. (ed.) (2007) *The Sage Qualitative Research Kit*, 8 vols. London: Sage.

Flick, U. (2008a) *Managing Quality in Qualitative Research*. London: Sage.

Flick, U. (2008b) *Designing Qualitative Research*. London: Sage.

Flick, U. (2009) *An Introduction to Qualitative Research*, 4th edn. London: Sage.

Flick, U. and Röhnsch, G. (2007) 'Idealization and Neglect: Health Concepts of Homeless Adolescents', *Journal of Health Psychology*, 12: 737–50.

Flick, U. and Röhnsch, G. (2008) *Gesundheit und Krankheit auf der Straße: Vorstellungen und Erfahrungsweisen obdachloser Jugendlicher*. Weinheim: Juventa.

Flick, U., Kardorff, E. v. and Steinke, I. (eds) (2004) *A Companion to Qualitative Research*. London: Sage.

Flick, U., Garms-Homolová, V. and Röhnsch, G. (2010) '"When They Sleep, They Sleep": Daytime Activities and Sleep Disorders in Nursing Homes', *Journal of Health Psychology*, 15: 755–64.

Frank, A. (1997) *The Wounded Storyteller: Body, Illness, and Ethics*. Chicago: University of Chicago Press.

Früh, W. (1991) *Inhaltsanalyse: Theorie und Praxis*, 3rd edn. München: Ölschläger.

Gaiser, T.J. and Schreiner, A.E. (2009) *A Guide to Conducting Online Research*. London: Sage.

Garms-Homolová, V., Flick, U. and Röhnsch, G. (2010) 'Sleep Disorders and Activities in Long Term Care Facilities: A Vicious Cycle?', *Journal of Health Psychology*, 15: 744–54.

Geertz, C. (1973) *The Interpretation of Cultures: Selected Essays*. New York: Basic.

Gerhardt, U. (1988) 'Qualitative Sociology in the Federal Republic of Germany', *Qualitative Sociology*, 11: 29–43.

Glaser, B.G. (1969) 'The Constant Comparative Method of Qualitative Analysis', in G.J. McCall and J.L. Simmons (eds), *Issues in Participant Observation*. Reading, MA: Addison-Wesley.

Glaser, B.G. (1978) *Theoretical Sensitivity*. Mill Valley, CA: University of California.

Glaser, B.G. and Strauss, A.L. (1965) *Awareness of Dying*. Chicago: Aldine.

Glaser, B.G. and Strauss, A.L. (1967) *The Discovery of Grounded Theory: Strategies for Qualitative Research*. New York: Aldine.

Greenhalgh, T. (2006) *How to Read a Paper: The Basics of Evidence-Based Medicine*. Oxford: Blackwell-Wiley.

Guba, E.G. and Lincoln, Y.S. (1989) *Fourth Generation Evaluation*. Newbury Park, CA: Sage.

Guggenmoos-Holzmann, I., Bloomfield, K., Brenner, H. and Flick, U. (eds) (1995) *Quality of Life and Health: Concepts, Methods and Applications*. Berlin: Blackwell Science.

Hammersley, M. and Atkinson, P. (1995) *Ethnography: Principles in Practice*, 2nd edn. London: Routledge.

Harré, R. (1998) 'The Epistemology of Social Representations', in U. Flick (ed.), *Psychology of the Social: Representations in Knowledge and Language*. Cambridge: Cambridge University Press. pp. 129–37.

Hart, C. (1998) *Doing a Literature Review*. London: Sage.

Hart, C. (2001) *Doing a Literature Search*. London: Sage.

Hermanns, H. (1995) 'Narratives Interview', in U. Flick, E. v. Kardorff, H. Keupp, L. v. Rosenstiel and S. Wolff (eds), *Handbuch Qualitative Sozialforschung*, 2nd edn. Munich: Psychologie Verlags Union. pp. 182–5.

Hewson, C., Yule, P., Laurent, D. and Vogel, C. (2003) *Internet Research Methods: A Practical Guide for the Social and Behavioural Sciences*. London: Sage.

Hine, C. (2000) *Virtual Ethnography*. London: Sage.

Hochschild, A.R. (1983) *The Managed Heart*. Berkeley, CA: University of California Press.

Hoinville, G. et al. (1985) *Survey Research Practice*. Aldershot: Gower.

Hollingshead, A.B. and Redlich, F.C. (1958) *Social Class and Mental Illness: A Community Sample*. Wiley.

Hopf, C. (2004) 'Research Ethics and Qualitative Research: An Overview', in U. Flick, E. v. Kardorff and I. Steinke (eds), *A Companion to Qualitative Research*. London: Sage. pp. 334–9.

Hurrelmann, K., Klocke, A., Melzer, W. and Ravens-Sieberer, U. (2003*) Konzept und ausgewählte Ergebnisse der Studie*, http://www.hbsc-germany.de/pdf/artikel_hurrelmann_klocke_melzer_urs.pdf (accessed 30 June 2008).

Jahoda, M. (1995) 'Jahoda, M., Lazarsfeld, P. and Zeisel, H. (1933): Die Arbeitslosen von Marienthal', in U. Flick, E. v. Kardorff, H. Keupp, L. v. Rosenstiel and S. Wolff (eds), *Handbuch Qualitative Sozialforschung*, 2nd edn. München: Psychologie Verlags Union. pp. 119–22.

Jahoda, M., Lazarsfeld, P.F. and Zeisel, H. (1933/1971) *Marienthal: The Sociology of an Unemployed Community*. Chicago: Aldine-Atherton.

Jörgensen, D.L. (1989) *Participant Observation: A Methodology for Human Studies*. London: Sage.

Kelle, U. and Erzberger, C. (2004) 'Quantitative and Qualitative Methods: No Confrontation', in U. Flick, E. v. Kardorff and I. Steinke (eds), *A Companion to Qualitative Research*. London: Sage. pp. 172–7.

Kelle, U. and Kluge, S. (2010) *Vom Einzelfall zum Typus: Fallvergleich und Fallkontrastierung in der qualitativen Sozialforschung*. Wiesbaden: VS-Verlag.

Kelly, K. and Caputo, T. (2007) 'Health and Street/Homeless Youth', *Journal of Health Psychology*, 12: 726–36.

Kendall, L. (1999) 'Recontextualising Cyberspace: Methodological Considerations for On-Line Research', in S. Jones (ed.), *Doing Internet Research: Critical Issues and Methods for Examining the Net*. London: Sage. pp. 57–74.

Kirk, J.L. and Miller, M. (1986) *Reliability and Validity in Qualitative Research*. Beverly Hills, CA: Sage.

Knoblauch, H., Schnettler, B., Raab, J. and Soeffner, H.-G. (eds) (2006) *Video Analysis: Methodology and Methods*. Frankfurt: Lang.

Kozinets, R.V. (2010) *Netography: Doing Ethnographic Research Online*. London: Sage.

Kromrey, H. (2006) *Empirische Sozialforschung: Modelle und Methoden der standardisierten Datenerhebung und Datenauswertung.* Opladen: Leske and Budrich/UTB.

Laswell, H.D. (1938) 'A Provisional Classification of Symbol Data', *Psychiatry*, 1: 197–204.

Legewie, H. (1987) 'Interpretation und Validierung biographischer Interviews', in G. Jüttemann and H. Thomae (eds), *Biographie und Psychologie.* Berlin: Springer. pp. 138–50.

Liamputtong, P. (2007) *Researching the Vulnerable: A Guide to Sensitive Research Methods.* Thousand Oaks, CA: Sage.

Lillis, G. (2002) *Delivering Results in Qualitative Market Research*, vol. 7 of the *Qualitative Market Research Kit.* London: Sage.

Lincoln, Y.S. and Guba, E.G. (1985) *Naturalistic Inquiry.* London: Sage.

Lofland, J.H. (1974) 'Styles of Reporting Qualitative Field Research', *American Sociologist*, 9: 101–11.

Lofland, J. (1976) *Doing Social Life: The Qualitative Study of Human Interaction in Natural Settings.* New York: Wiley.

Lofland, J. and Lofland, L.H. (1984) *Analyzing Social Settings*, 2nd edn. Belmont, CA: Wadsworth.

Lucius-Hoene, G. and Deppermann, A. (2002) *Rekonstruktion narrativer Identität: Ein Arbeitsbuch zur Analyse narrativer Interviews.* Opladen: Leske and Budrich.

Lüders, C. (1995) 'Von der Teilnehmenden Beobachtung zur ethnographischen Beschreiibung: Ein Literaturbericht', in E. König and P. Zedler (eds), *Bilanz qualitativer Forschung*, vol. 1. Weinheim: Deutscher Studienverlag. pp. 311–42.

Lüders, C. (2004a) 'Field Observation and Ethnography', in U. Flick, E. v. Kardorff and I. Steinke (eds), *A Companion to Qualitative Research.* London: Sage. pp. 222–30.

Lüders, C. (2004b) 'The Challenges of Qualitative Research', in U. Flick, E. v. Kardorff and I. Steinke (eds), *A Companion to Qualitative Research.* London: Sage. pp. 359–64.

Lüders, C. (2006) 'Qualitative Daten als Grundlage der Politikberatung', in U. Flick (ed.), *Qualitative Evaluationsforschung: Konzepte, Methoden, Umsetzungen.* Reinbek: Rowohlt. pp. 444–62.

Mallinson, S. (2002) 'Listening to Respondents: A Qualitative Assessment of the Short-Form 36 Health Status Questionnaire', *Social Science and Medicine*, 54: 11–21.

Mann, C. and Stewart, F. (2000) *Internet Communication and Qualitative Research: A Handbook for Researching Online.* London: Sage.

Markham, A.M. (2004) 'The Internet as Research Context Research', in C. Seale, G. Gobo, J. Gubrium and D. Silverman (eds), *Qualitative Research Practice.* London: Sage. pp. 358–74.

Marshall, C. and Rossman, G.B. (2006) *Designing Qualitative Research*, 4th edn. Thousand Oaks, CA: Sage.

Maxwell, J.A. (2005) *Qualitative Research Design: An Interactive Approach*, 2nd edn. Thousand Oaks, CA: Sage.

May, T. (2001) *Social Research: Issues, Methods and Process.* Maidenhead: Open University Press.

Mayring, P. (1983) *Qualitative Inhaltsanalyse: Grundlagen und Techniken.* Weinheim: Deutscher Studien Verlag.

Mensching, A. (2006) 'Zwischen Überforderung und Banalisierung: zu den Schwierigkeiten der Vermittlungsarbeit im Rahmen qualitativer Evaluationsforschung', in U. Flick (ed.), *Qualitative Evaluationsforschung: Konzepte, Methoden, Umsetzungen.* Reinbek: Rowohlt. pp. 339–60.

Mertens, D. and Ginsberg, P.E. (eds) (2009) *Handbook of Research Ethics.* London. Sage.

Merton, R.K. and Kendall, P.L. (1946) 'The Focused Interview', *American Journal of Sociology*, 51: 541–57.

Miles, M.B. and Huberman, A.M. (1994) *Qualitative Data Analysis: A Sourcebook of New Methods*, 2nd edn. Newbury Park, CA: Sage.

Mishler, E.G. (1990) 'Validation in Inquiry-Guided Research: The Role of Exemplars in Narrative Studies', *Harvard Educational Review*, 60: 415–42.

Morse, J.M. (1998) 'Designing Funded Qualitative Research', in N. Denzin and Y.S. Lincoln (eds), *Strategies of Qualitative Research*. London: Sage. pp. 56–85.

Morse, J.M. (2001) 'Qualitative Verification: Strategies for Extending the Findings of a Research Project', in J.M. Morse, J. Swanson and A. Kuzel (eds), *The Nature of Evidence in Qualitative Inquiry*. Newbury Park, CA: Sage. pp. 203–21.

Morse, J.M., Swanson, J. and Kuzel, A.J. (eds) (2001) *The Nature of Qualitative Evidence*. Thousand Oaks, CA: Sage.

Murphy, E. and Dingwall, R. (2001) 'The Ethics of Ethnography', in P. Atkinson, A. Coffey, S. Delamont, J. Lofland and L. Lofland (eds), *Handbook of Ethnography*. London: Sage. pp. 339–51.

Neuman, W.L. (2000) *Social Research Methods: Qualitative and Quantitative Approaches*, 4th edn. Boston: Allyn and Bacon.

Neville, C. (2010) *Complete Guide to Referencing and Avoiding Plagiarism*. Maidenhead: Open University Press.

Oevermann, U., Allert, T., Konau, E. and Krambeck, J. (1979) 'Die Methodologie einer "objektiven Hermeneutik" und ihre allgemeine forschungslogische Bedeutung in den Sozialwissenschaften', in H.G. Soeffner (ed.), *Interpretative Verfahren in den Sozial- und Textwissenschaften*. Stuttgart: Metzler. pp. 352–433.

Patton, M.Q. (2002) *Qualitative Evaluation and Research Methods*, 3rd edn. London: Sage.

Pohlenz, P., Hagenmüller, J.-P. and Niedermeier, F. (2009) 'Ein Online-Panel zur Analyse von Studienbiographien: Qualitätssicherung von Lehre und Studium durch webbasierte Sozialforschung', in N. Jackob, H. Schoen and T. Zerback (eds), *Sozialforschung im Internet: Methodologie und Praxis der Online-Befragung*. Wiesbaden: VS-Verlag. pp. 233–44.

Porst, R. (2000) 'Question Wording: Zur Formulierung von Fragebogen-Fragen', *ZUMA How-to-Reihe*, no. 2, http://www.gesis.org/fileadmin/upload/forschung/publikationen/gesis_reihen/howto/how-to2rp.pdf (accessed 17 March 2009).

Potter, J. and Wetherell, M. (1998) 'Social Representations, Discourse Analysis, and Racism', in U. Flick (ed.), *Psychology of the Social: Representations in Knowledge and Language*. Cambridge: Cambridge University Press. pp. 177–200.

Punch, K. (1998) *Introduction to Social Research*. London: Sage.

Ragin, C.C. (1994) *Constructing Social Research*. Thousand Oaks, CA: Pine Forge.

Ragin, C.C. and Becker, H.S. (eds) (1992) *What Is a Case? Exploring the Foundations of Social Inquiry*. Cambridge: Cambridge University Press.

Rapley, T. (2008) *Doing Conversation, Discourse and Document Analysis*. London: Sage.

Richter, M. (2003) 'Anlage und Methode des Jugendgesundheitssurveys', in K. Hurrelmann, A. Klocke, W. Melzer and U. Ravens-Sieberer (eds), *Jugendgesundheitssurvey: Internationale Vergleichsstudie im Auftrag der Weltgesundheitsorganisation WHO*. Weinheim: Juventa. pp. 9–18.

Richter, M., Hurrelmann, K., Klocke, A., Melzer, W. and Ravens-Sieberer, U. (eds) (2008) *Gesundheit, Ungleichheit und jugendliche Lebenswelten: Ergebnisse der zweiten internationalen Vergleichsstudie im Auftrag der Weltgesundheitsorganisation WHO*. Weinheim: Juventa.

Riemann, G. and Schütze, F. (1987) 'Trajectory as a Basic Theoretical Concept for Analyzing Suffering and Disorderly Social Processes', in D. Maines (ed.), *Social Organization and Social Process: Essays in Honor of Anselm Strauss*. New York: Aldine de Gruyter. pp. 333–57.

RIN (2010) 'If You Build It, Will They Come? How Researchers Perceive and Use Web 2.0', http://www.rin.ac.uk/our-work/communicating-and-disseminating-research/use-and-relevance-web-20-researchers (accessed 21 August 2010).

Rosenberg, M. (1968) *The Logic of Survey Analysis*. New York: Basic.

Rosenthal, G. and Fischer-Rosenthal, W. (2004) 'The Analysis of Biographical-Narrative Interviews', in U. Flick, E. v. Kardorff and I. Steinke (eds), *A Companion to Qualitative Research*. London: Sage. pp. 259–65.

Sahle, R. (1987) *Gabe, Almosen, Hilfe*. Opladen: Westdeutscher Verlag.

Salmons, J. (2010) *Online Interviews in Real Time*. London: Sage.

Schmidt, L. and Fröhling, H. (1998) 'Gesundheits- und Krankheitsvorstellungen von Kindern und Jugendlichen', in U. Flick (ed.), *Wann fühlen wir uns gesund? Subjektive Vorstellungen von Gesundheit und Krankheit*. Weinheim: Juventa. pp. 33–44.

Schneider, G. (1988) 'Hermeneutische Strukturanalyse von qualitativen Interviews', *Kölner Zeitschrift für Soziologie und Sozialpsychologie*, 40: 223–44.

Schnell, M.W. and Heinritz, C. (2006) *Forschungsethik: Ein Grundlagen- und Arbeitsbuch mit Beispielen aus der Gesundheits- und Pflegewissenschaft*. Bern: Huber.

Schnell, R., Hill, P.B. and Esser, E. (2008) *Methoden der empirischen Sozialforschung*. München: Oldenbourg.

Schütze, F. (1983) 'Biographieforschung und Narratives Interview', *Neue Praxis*, 3: 283–93.

Schwandt, T.A. (2002) *Evaluation Practice Reconsidered*. New York: Lang.

Silverman, D. (2001) *Interpreting Qualitative Data: Methods for Analysing Talk, Text and Interaction*, 2nd edn. London: Sage.

Spradley, J.P. (1980) *Participant Observation*. New York: Rinehart and Winston.

Sprenger, A. (1989) 'Teilnehmende Beobachtung in prekären Handlungssituationen: Das Beispiel Intensivstation', in R. Aster, H. Merkens and M. Repp (eds), *Teilnehmende Beobachtung: Werkstattberichte und methodologische Reflexionen*. Frankfurt: Campus. pp. 35–56.

Stark, K. and Guggenmoos-Holzmann, I. (2003) 'Wissenschaftliche Ergebnisse deuten und nutzen', in F.W. Schwartz (ed.), *Das Public Health Buch*. Heidelberg: Elsevier, Urban and Fischer. pp. 393–418.

Strauss, A.L. (1987) *Qualitative Analysis for Social Scientists*. Cambridge: Cambridge University Press.

Strauss, A.L. and Corbin, J. (1990/1998/2008) *Basics of Qualitative Research*, 2nd edn 1998, 3rd edn 2008. London: Sage.

Sue, V.M. (2007) *Conducting Online Surveys*. London: Sage.

Tashakkori, A. and Teddlie, Ch. (eds) (2003a) *Handbook of Mixed Methods in Social and Behavioral Research*. Thousand Oaks, CA: Sage.

Tashakkori, A. and Teddlie, Ch. (2003b) 'Major Issues and Controversies in the Use of Mixed Methods in Social and Behavioral Research', in A. Tashakkori and Ch. Teddlie (eds), *Handbook of Mixed Methods in Social and Behavioral Research*. Thousand Oaks, CA: Sage. pp. 3–50.

Thomson, H., Hoskins, R., Petticrew, M., Ogilvie, D., Craig, N., Quinn, T. and Lindsay, G. (2004) 'Evaluating the Health Effects of Social Interventions', *BMJ*, 328: 282–5.

Tufte, E.R. (1990) *Envisioning Information*. Cheshire: Graphics.

Tufte, E.R. (2001) *Visual Display of Quantitative Information*. Cheshire: Graphics.

University Library (2009) 'Gray Literature', California State University, Long Beach, www.csulb.edu/library/subj/gray_literature (accessed 17 August 2010).

Van Maanen, J. (1988) *Tales of the Field: On Writing Ethnography*. Chicago: University of Chicago Press.

Walter, U., Flick, U., Fischer, C., Neuber, A. and Schwartz, F.W. (2006) *Alt und gesund? Altersbilder und Präventionskonzepte in der ärztlichen und pflegerischen Praxis*. Wiesbaden: VS-Verlag.

Weingart, P. (2001) *Die Stunde der Wahrheit? Zum Verhältnis der Wissenschaft zu Politik, Wirtschaft und Medien in der Wissensgesellschaft*. Weilerswist: Velbrück.

Weischer, C. (2007) *Sozialforschung: Theorie und Praxis.* Konstanz: UVK-UTB.

Wernet, A. (2006) *Einführung in die Interpretationspraxis der Objektiven Hermeneutik,* 2nd edn. Wiesbaden: VS-Verlag.

Wiedemann, P.M. (1995) 'Gegenstandsnahe Theoriebildung', in U. Flick, E. v. Kardorff, H. Keupp, L. v. Rosenstiel and S. Wolff (eds), *Handbuch Qualitative Sozialforschung,* 2nd edn. Munich: Psychologie Verlags Union. pp. 440–5.

Willig, C. (2003) *Introducing Qualitative Research in Psychology: Adventures in Theory and Method.* Buckinghamshire: Open University.

Wilson, T.P. (1982) 'Quantitative "oder" qualitative Methoden in der Sozialforschung', *Kölner Zeitschrift für Soziologie und Sozialpsychologie,* 34: 487–508.

Wolff, S. (1987) 'Rapport und Report: Über einige Probleme bei der Erstellung plausibler ethnographischer Texte', in W. v. d. Ohe (ed.), *Kulturanthropologie: Beiträge zum Neubeginn einer Disziplin.* Berlin. Reimer. pp. 333–64.

Wolff, S. (2004) 'Analysis of Documents and Records', in U. Flick, E. v. Kardorff and I. Steinke (eds), *A Companion to Qualitative Research.* London: Sage. pp. 284–90.

World Health Organization (1986) *Ottawa Charta for Health Promotion. First International Conference on Health Promotion, Ottawa.* www.who.int/hpr/docs/ottawa.html.

Name Index

Subject Index

Tables and Figures are indicated by page numbers in **bold**.

gray literature, 34
grounded theory, 55
groups, selection of, 85–6, 92

harm to participants, 220–1
HBSC study, 8
health: everyday/scientific knowledge, 4–5
hypotheses, 26–8
    characteristics of, 27–8
    from questions, 20, 26–8, 49
    operationalization, 49
    testing, 50

ideal type analysis, 211–12
identity protection [confidentiality], 51
in vivo codes, 149
independent and dependent variables, 67, 82, 83
indices, 128
    validity of, 205–6
informed consent, 217–18
    and vulnerable groups, 217–18
integrated research, 189–91, **190**
    limits, 193–4
    procedures, 190–1
inter-coder reliability, 201
Internet *see* online research
interval scales, 126, 127
interviews, 112–18
    and confidentiality, 220
    episodic, 115–17
    focus groups, 117–18, 172–3
    limits of, 181, 183
    narrative, 113–14
    online, 14, 171–2
    with online research, 192
    open questions, 113
    preparation, 91, 113, 115
    in qualitative research, 55
    semi-structured, 112–13
        four criteria, 112

Jahoda, M. et al: *Marienthal: The Sociology of an
    Unemployed Community*, 19
journal articles, finding, 35

knowledge
    description, understanding, explanation, 7
    everyday and scientific, 4–**6**
    and practices, 193
    and routines, 193

libraries, 34
likert scale, **10**
literature, 32–7
    areas of, 35–7
    documentation, 39
    empirical studies, 37–8

literature *cont.*
    finding literature, 34–5
    gray literature, 34
    online, 177
    original works and reviews, 33–4
    primary and secondary sources, 33
    referencing, 39–40
    review checklist, 42
    review contents, 38–9
    reviewing and listing, 38
    types of, 32–4
    see also under process of quantitative research
longitudinal studies, 68, 70
Lotus Screen-Cam, 175

magazines, 33
Mann-Whitney test, 147
mean, 143
measurement, 11, 126
    reliability, 200–1
    validity, 203–5
median, 143
MEDLINE, 35
meta-analysis, 34
methodological literature, 36–7
methods, selection of, 50, 86–7, 92–3, 97–8
    checklist for, 99–100
mixed methods, 188–9
mode, 143
multiple regression, 146
multivariate analyses, **145**–6
    testing relations, 146

narratives, 115, 183
    analysis, 153–5
    'realist', 'confessional', 'impressionist' tales
        (Van Maanen), 236
neutrality, **99**
newspapers, 33
    analysis, 133–4, **135**
nominal scales, 126, 127, 148

objective hermeneutics, 155–9
    example, 158–9
    five principles (Wernet), 157
    procedure, 155–6
objectivity, 206–7
observation, 92, 93, 119–22, 181
    ethnography, 121–2
    in experimental research, 120
    by participants, 120–1, 183
    role of researcher, 119
    standardized, 119–20
online research, 166–77
    analysis of webpages, 175
    checklist, 177
    conversation analysis, 174

SPSS, 87, 146
standard deviation, 144
standardization, 87, 93, 129–30
state and process, 193
statistical analysis, 52
statistical sampling, **76**
structural hermeneutics *see* objective
        hermeneutics
subjective meaning, 192–3
Survey Monkey, 169
systematic sampling, 72–3

t-test, 147
testing relations, 146–7
thematic coding, 152–3
theoretical frameworks, 23, 83–4, 90
theoretical literature, 35, 36
theoretical sampling, 75–**6**
theoretical saturation, 150
theories
    development of, 238
    'discovery of', 55
    in qualitative research, 55, 238
Thomson Reuters' social sciences
        citation index, 35
timescale, **63**–5
triangulation, 185–8
    definition, 186
types of variables, **148**
typologies, 162–3

univariate analyses, 142–4
    central tendency, 143
    dispersion, 143–4
    frequencies, 142–**3**

validity, 202–6
    external and internal, **203**
    of indices, 205–6
    measurement instruments, 203–5
    in qualitative research, 208
    of research designs, 202
variance, 144
video dialogues, 171
video recordings, 55
videos, 129
visual data, 124–5
visualization, 238
vulnerable groups, consent of, 217–18

Web 2.0, 14, 15, 175–7
World Health Organization (WHO):
        'Health Behavior in Social Context',
        21–2
writing research, 230–9
    audience, 239
    feedback to participants, 239–40
    goals of writing, 230–1
    qualitative research, 235–9
        development of theory, 238
        empirical procedure, 236
        evidence, 238–9
        results, 236–8
        tables, **237**
    quantitative research, 231–5
        charts and tables, 232, **233**
        elaboration, 232
        empirical procedure, 231
        evidence, 233–5
        presentation, 232–3
        samples, 231, **232**